Prison Privatization

Volume I
The Environment of Private Prisons

Volume II
Private Prisons and Private Profit

Volume III
The Political Climate of Prison Privatization

Prison Privatization

THE MANY FACETS OF A CONTROVERSIAL INDUSTRY

VOLUME III: THE POLITICAL CLIMATE OF PRISON PRIVATIZATION

Byron Eugene Price and John Charles Morris, Editors

 PRAEGER

AN IMPRINT OF ABC-CLIO, LLC
Santa Barbara, California • Denver, Colorado • Oxford, England

Library of Congress Cataloging-in-Publication Data

Prison privatization : the many facets of a controversial industry / Byron Eugene Price and John Charles Morris, editors.
    v. cm.
Contents: v. 1. The Environment of private prisons —
Includes bibliographical references and index.
ISBN 978-0-313-39571-0 (hbk. : alk. paper) — ISBN 978-0-313-39572-7 (ebook)
1. Prisons—United States. 2. Privatization—United States. 3. Corrections—
Contracting out—United States. I. Price, Byron Eugene. II. Morris, John Charles.
HV9469.P747 2012
338.4′7365–dc23

                          2012024729

ISBN: 978-0-313-39571-0
EISBN: 978-0-313-39572-7

16 15 14 13 12   1 2 3 4 5

This book is also available on the World Wide Web as an eBook.
Visit www.abc-clio.com for details.

Praeger
An Imprint of ABC-CLIO, LLC

ABC-CLIO, LLC
130 Cremona Drive, P.O. Box 1911
Santa Barbara, California 93116-1911

This book is printed on acid-free paper ∞
Manufactured in the United States of America

This book is dedicated to my mother, Mabel E. Price, for being my inspiration.

—Byron E. Price

This book is dedicated to my wife, Elizabeth Dashiell Morris, for her love and support.

—John C. Morris

Contents

Acknowledgments

Editing a three-volume book series is, without a doubt, a group effort, and the end result is the culmination of the work of many people. We wish to thank Michael Wilt, Valentina Tursini, and Beth Ptalis, our editors at ABC-CLIO, for their help and endless patience in dealing with questions, changes, and technical issues. We are very grateful for their support. We would also like to thank our copyeditor, Betsy Crist, for her tireless work in turning this manuscript into a reality.

We are also very grateful to our many contributors who not only wrote the chapters in this volume but also endured many rounds of edits and changes, and who waited patiently while we brought the project to fruition. We would also like to thank Matt Gable for his wonderful technical support and Katie Neill for her meticulous editing. We also thank Brittni McCrimmon and Casey Smith for their help keeping the many versions of manuscripts organized and available to us along with the team at BookComp, Inc. who put this book into pages. Without the support of all these people, this project would have forever remained an idea in our minds. We are indebted to all of you.

—Byron E. Price and John C. Morris

Introduction

The Political Climate
of Prison Privatization

Byron E. Price and John C. Morris

The prison privatization debate is just as much a political debate as it is an economic debate. In many respects, the arguments are one and the same, because economics often drive the decision-making processes of political institutions. The economic underpinnings of the debate are grounded in ideology. Arguments made from the economic perspective regarding support for privatization usually claim that privatization saves money: it fosters competition, which facilitates efficiency, and efficiency saves money. In addition to the idea that prison privatization saves money, the following themes drive the discussion about privatization in this volume: the role of advocacy in influencing the privatization decision; incentives to privatize once the coercive power of the state is ceded to a for-profit prison provider; accountability; the creation of a powerful elite that drives policy choices; and the idea that profit and public policy have competing values. Each of the themes will be discussed briefly in this introduction, and each chapter will be briefly summarized to provide a framework for the reader to evaluate the arguments on face value.

Advocacy is as American as apple pie, and all interest groups engage in political advocacy for the purpose of gaining a favorable outcome regarding issues they deem important to their interests. Most citizens see lobbying and political advocacy as a benefit to our pluralistic system in that it is tangible evidence of the ability of Americans to have input into their government. On the other hand, the pro-privatization and pro-incarceration advocacy engaged in by for-profit providers of prisons has been deemed harmful by opponents of prison privatization because they see profits being made from the suffering of citizens. Moreover, for many opponents, it is problematic that a prison lobby has developed to advocate for policy favorable to that industry. The prison lobby effort that causes the most concern for opponents of privatization is the lobbying for laws that incapacitate people for longer periods of time for the purpose of ensuring high rates of incarceration—private prisons make money by housing prisoners, and the more prisoners they have, the more money they make. The pros and cons of pro-privatization and pro-incarceration advocacy and the issue of turning over a public function to a private entity that benefits from punishment are recurring threads of debate throughout this volume.

Another theme that courses through the volume is the idea of accountability, a value central to democratic ideals. When a function is public, the public enjoys the benefits and efforts of the function's successes and has a voice in how the agencies manage the functions. Once privatized, however, the deliverer of the service is viewed to be no longer accountable to the public. Thus, accountability—a central tenet to democratic values—is viewed as being lost. This perceived erosion of democratic values creates considerable angst among purists in regards to how government should function. Thus, this debate is a central issue in the decision to consider prison privatization.

Another important theme that appears in this volume is the idea that elite exercise of power manifests itself in elite deviance when the power elite, through lobbying and campaign contributions, convince policy makers to expand the market for private prisons. Based on the disproportionate ability of the elite to influence policy through campaign contributions and lobbying, ordinary citizens believe campaign contributions undermine equitability in the process of having their voices heard. These concerns are concomitant with the accountability concerns that are raised when privatization is embraced.

A final theme in this volume is the belief that private profit and public policy values compete, and when public policy loses out to profit, there is an erosion of accountability, transparency, democracy, and public confidence. As long as profit competes with democratic values, the issue regarding the pursuit of privatization will remain a controversial one.

Chapter 1 of this volume examines the impact of public and private prison lobbies. Volokh examines such questions as, does an increase in private sector advocacy decrease public sector advocacy? This is a critical line of inquiry given that most research focuses on private prison lobbying and tends to give less attention to lobbying by public interest groups, such as unionized correctional officers. Volokh believes privatization reduces advocacy by public prison lobbies by breaking up the government monopoly of prisons. He contends that this action creates a collective action problem. His chapter offers an interesting look at a rarely considered aspect of prison privatization: that like private prison interest groups, public prison employees also lobby for laws that favor their industry and protect their jobs.

In chapter 2, Heitzeg explores the interests aligned against private prisons. According to Heitzeg, many of these interests are bonded by a shared perception that the prison industry operates in such a way as to systematically discriminate against minority and disadvantaged groups. The author contextualizes her argument by tracing the history of inmate labor exploitation, the development of prison industries, and the inimical impact of pro-privatization and pro-incarceration movements to illustrate how powerful organizations have formed to advocate against private prisons. She concludes that profit, crime, and punishment have been linked throughout history and that all factors have been important in extracting labor from the poor in our society.

Chapter 3 examines whether private providers of prisons inherit the same protections accorded government-run prisons, especially with respect to liability claims that arise from prisoner abuse cases. Gordon and Shelton-Quinn discuss the case law governing the issue of qualified immunity, the idea that government actors are protected from civil suits that arise from frivolous lawsuits. Furthermore, this chapter delves into the legal rights of prisoners, the requirement to indemnify private prisons, and how private providers of prisons are required by the public agencies with whom they contract to protect themselves from frivolous lawsuits.

Chapter 4 builds on the chapter 3 discussion of qualified immunity but examines the issue in terms of constitutional violations and legal accountability concerns. This chapter introduces the idea that profit and public policy have competing values. Hargis considers whether private actors, acting as agents of the government, are shielded from legal accountability when managing a facility for the government. Moreover, this chapter discusses how the issue of qualified immunity emerged using case law to trace the development of this concept.

Inman introduces in chapter 5 the idea that elites influence public policy by using such strategies as lobbying and campaign contributions to get policies passed that expand their market share. Furthermore, through the positions they hold in society, elites are disproportionately influential in the political and policy-making arenas, thus raising questions regarding equal representation and citizen voice in a democratic society. The private prison industry appears to enjoy such influential status, and Inman characterizes the practice of lobbying by private prison companies to expand their market share as elite deviance. Because of their ability to be more influential via campaign contributions, the author asserts that public confidence is undermined by elite deviance.

In chapter 6, Blessett also advances the idea that elites benefit from prison privatization and juxtaposes this argument with the issue of prison privatization as a political and economic decision. Blessett argues that politics shape public policy. A brief discussion of the competing values of private profit and public policy is undertaken to place in perspective what many who are against prison privatization believe: that profit undermines the democratic system.

Discussing the grassroots organizations that have formed to antagonize private prisons, chapter 7 explores the perceived vested interests private prisons have to incarcerate. Black also discusses the impact of pro-incarceration advocacy and the grassroots efforts to mitigate the pro-incarceration advocacy. Much of the chapter chronicles the efforts of various community and national groups committed to and working for prison reform. Black makes an argument in this chapter regarding the loss of accountability the public suffers when a prison becomes private. The chapter closes with a brief summary of successful grassroots campaigns that have thwarted the efforts of private prisons to expand their market share.

Another underexplored area regarding the state's transfer of its prison operations and management duties to a private provider involves the constitutional implications raised when coercive power is used by an actor other than the state itself. In chapter 8, Hargis discusses the constitutional implications of using private prisons and looks at inmates' rights under this arrangement. To determine the constitutional implications of private prisons, Hargis researches case law to see where the courts stand on the issue of accountability and whether the government is relieved of responsibility when it contracts out prison operations and management. She asserts that this situation represents shared control and decision making with an outside agency and not the removal of its responsibility. The chapter suggests that

there are three main constitutional implications of private prisons: delegation of public functions to private actors, constitutional rights of inmates,
and liability and accountability for private prison employee actions.

Along with several other chapters in this volume, chapter 9 looks at an
area in which very little research has been done in order to assess the realities
of the competing claims of private and public providers of prisons. Lee-
Thomas and Myers attempt to compare education in public prisons to education in private prisons. Implicit in this comparison is the belief that education
could help both entities reduce the recidivism rate. The authors find that private prisons provide fewer educational programs than public prisons. The
authors conclude with a discussion on the dearth of research regarding recidivism rates as a measure of success.

The crux of the debate surrounding the superiority of prison privatization
versus public management of prisons can be found in chapter 10, which discusses subjecting prisons to performance measurement. Many of the claims
made by private and public prisons regarding the superior effectiveness of
each are baseless, given that very few impartial studies exist that subject
either party's claim to adequate scrutiny. This chapter discusses the difficulty of applying performance measurement to corrections and debunks the
idea that comparisons of private and public prisons are easily made.
Furthermore, Montgomery finds that not only is it difficult to compare performance between the two, but it is also challenging to determine if private
prisons actually operate prisons more cheaply. Because states have difficulty in determining the marginal cost to operate a prison, many are not in a
position truly to assess whether a private prison can operate more efficiently
than a public prison.

Chapter 11 informs the reader of the various kinds of privatization that
most agencies pursue. The most used form of privatization, according to
McDowell and Morris, is contracting out. This is a popular form of privatization because of the potential cost savings offered by private prisons in
comparison to public management of prisons. McDowell and Morris discuss
how contracts can provide an accountability mechanism for states who contract out their prisons. One of the main concerns and criticisms of private
prisons is that accountability is lost when public prisons become private.
Thus, writing a good contract has the potential to mitigate the loss of
accountability opponents of prison privatization fear. The authors discuss the elements of a contract and present a case study of the State of

Mississippi's use of contracts when dealing with private prisons. Finally, the chapter closes with important issues for policy makers to consider when contracting for prison services.

Chapter 12 closes out this volume with a discussion of the future of private prisons. An examination of growth patterns for private prisons at the local, state, and federal levels is reviewed to ascertain whether certain trends lend themselves to future growth of private prisons. Issues such as a changing penal philosophy, immigration reform, the use of private prisons for economic development, and other salient factors are explored to gauge their future impact on private prison expansion. Finally, Price demonstrates that the growth of private prisons could ebb and flow given the right confluence of factors, as was seen in the 1980s with the war on drugs, get-tough-on-crime campaigns, increasingly punitive penal policies, and the drive toward privatization ushered in by President Reagan.

1

The Effect of Privatization on Public and Private Prison Lobbies[1]

Alexander Volokh

Private prison firms are often accused of lobbying for incarceration because, like a hotel, they have "a strong economic incentive to book every available room and encourage every guest to stay as long as possible" (Schlosser 1998, 51–64; see also Dolovich 2005; Sarabi and Bender 2000; Shichor 1995). This accusation has little support, either theoretical or empirical. At worst, the political influence argument is backward: privatization will in fact *decrease* prison providers' pro-incarceration influence. At best, the argument is dubious: its accuracy depends on facts that proponents of the argument haven't developed.

First, self-interested pro-incarceration advocacy is already common in the public sector—chiefly from public sector corrections officers' unions. The most active corrections officers' union, the California Correctional Peace Officers Association, has contributed massively in support of "tough on crime" positions on voter initiatives and has given money to crime victims' groups, and similar unions in other states have endorsed candidates for their tough-on-crime positions. Private firms would thus enter a heavily populated field and partly displace some of the existing actors.

Second, there's little reason to believe that increasing privatization would increase the amount of self-interested pro-incarceration advocacy. In fact, it's even possible that increasing privatization would *reduce* such advocacy. The intuition for this perhaps surprising result comes from the economic theory of public goods and collective action.

The political benefits that flow from prison providers' pro-incarceration advocacy are a "public good," because any prison provider's advocacy, to the extent that it's effective, helps every other prison provider. When individual actors capture less of the benefit of their expenditures on a public good, they spend less on that good; and the "smaller" actors, who benefit less from the public good, free ride off the expenditures of the "largest" actor.

Today, the largest actor—the actor that profits the most from the system—tends to be the public sector union, because the public sector provides the lion's share of prison services, and public sector corrections officers benefit from wages significantly higher than those of their private sector counterparts. The smaller actor is the private prison industry, which not only has a smaller proportion of the industry but also doesn't make particularly high profits.

By breaking up the government's monopoly of prison provision and awarding part of the industry to private firms, therefore, privatization can reduce the industry's advocacy by introducing a collective action problem. The public sector unions will spend less because under privatization they experience less of the benefit of their advocacy, while the private firms will tend to free ride off the public sector's advocacy. This collective action problem is fortunate for the critics of pro-incarceration advocacy—a happy, usually unintended side effect of privatization.

This is the simplest form of the story, but one can also tell more complicated versions in which privatization doesn't *necessarily* decrease total industry-expanding political advocacy. After presenting my main model, I introduce some realistic complications. Some of them don't change the basic result of the model; others make the effect of privatization ambiguous—increasing private sector advocacy but also decreasing public sector advocacy. Either way, we don't unambiguously predict that privatization increases advocacy. There is thus no reason to believe an argument against prison privatization based on the possibility of self-interested pro-incarceration advocacy—unless the argument takes a position on how lobbying, political contributions, and advocacy work, and why any increase in private sector advocacy would outweigh the decrease in public sector advocacy. Either this argument against prison privatization is clearly false, or it's only true under certain conditions that the critics of privatization haven't shown exist.

Advocacy as a Public Good

When a good is private, everyone pays for, and enjoys, only his or her own consumption. By contrast, industry-increasing advocacy is a public good; those who benefit from it care about the *total* amount (Oakland 1987). Privatizing part of the industry therefore introduces a collective action problem: unless everyone in the industry cooperates with each other, they will in aggregate spend less on industry-increasing advocacy than a single firm would if it covered the whole industry, because a portion of their expenditures will benefit their competitors.

The Basic Model

A monopolist is willing to lobby to increase the size of its industry. To determine how much to spend, it weighs the benefit its money can buy against the cost of the lobbying. It's reasonable to think that spending money on advocacy is subject to decreasing marginal returns, so each additional dollar gives less and less benefit. The cost of a dollar's worth of advocacy, on the other hand, is always $1. As long as the benefit of an advocacy dollar is greater than $1, the monopolist continues to spend until that benefit falls to $1. Say the resulting amount of spending is $1 million.

Now suppose we split up the industry so the large firm has 90 percent of the market and a competitor has the other 10 percent. The previous optimal amount of spending, $1 million, is no longer optimal for the larger firm: the cost of that last dollar was $1, and although the benefit of the dollar is $1 for the whole industry, the 90 percent firm only sees 90 cents of that benefit. The split-up has the same effect on the large firm as a 10 percent tax. Thus, the large firm spends less. As it cuts back, the benefit of the last dollar spent rises; it stops cutting back as soon as the total benefit to the industry of the last dollar spent reaches about $1.11 (which is a $1 benefit to the large firm). Say the new amount is $900,000. The competitor, which has 10 percent of the industry, does a similar calculation to find the point where the marginal expected benefit to the whole industry is $10, which gives the firm $1. Say this point is at $300,000.

The story so far is incomplete. The large firm doesn't want the amount spent to be exactly $900,000; it would be thrilled if other people happened to contribute more. It's just that it isn't *personally* willing to put another dollar into the pot if the pot already contains $900,000: if the benefit of a dollar only depends on the total amount spent, and if the 900,000th dollar had a total benefit worth $1.11 (and thus a benefit to the large firm worth $1), then the 900,001st dollar has a benefit worth slightly less than $1.11. The 10 percent competitor, by a similar reasoning, wants the total amount spent to be at least $300,000 and will not put a 300,001st dollar into the pot.

This leads to two conclusions. First, the total amount spent will be equal to the larger firm's threshold—in this case, $900,000. If it were less, the larger firm would want to spend more money. And if it were more, the larger firm would want to take some money out of the pot. Second, there's no reason for the smaller competitor to spend anything. It is unwilling to spend any dollar beyond the 300,000th, because its marginal benefit to the industry is under $10 and its marginal benefit to the firm is under $1. Suppose the larger firm were going to spend $600,000 and the smaller firm were going to spend $300,000. These would not be equilibrium actions: given that the larger firm is already spending more than $300,000, the smaller firm wouldn't be willing to spend even a single dollar. The only equilibrium is where the larger firm spends $900,000 and the smaller firm spends $0. The smaller actor entirely free rides off the larger one. The result is what Mancur Olson (1965, 29) calls the "systematic tendency for 'exploitation' of the great by the small."

Industry Shares versus Real Shares

If one accepts the assumption that the probability of success only depends on the total amount of money in the pot, this simple model can accommodate many institutional details of privatization. The total free-riding result happens whenever one actor has a lower threshold than the other, for whatever reason. In the original story, the two firms were identical except that one had 90 percent of the industry and the other had 10 percent. But one's threshold could be lower for other reasons as well.

For instance, suppose the government not only breaks up the monopoly but also subjects its revenues to a 50 percent tax. The 90 percent firm will act as though it controlled 45 percent of the industry, and the 10 percent competitor, if subject to the same tax, will act as though it controlled 5 percent. These new percentages—call them "real" shares—no longer need to add up to 100 percent, but they convey the idea that firms' spending thresholds are lower when, for whatever reason, their benefits decrease.

After we determine everyone's real shares, the same analysis applies as before: the dominant firm does all the advocacy, and the other firm is a free rider. The difference is that dominance is determined by looking not at market proportions but at shares of total industry revenue. Thus, if the 90 percent firm's revenues are taxed at a 90 percent rate, it acts as though its share is 9 percent; and if the 10 percent competitor is exempt from the tax, it acts as though its share is the full 10 percent. The apparently smaller firm has become dominant, and the free-riding relationship reverses itself.

Anything that affects one's revenues affects one's real share. Suppose, for instance, that the 90 percent firm is actually a monopoly over 90 percent of a geographic area, while the remaining 10 percent of the area is divided among 100 competitors who act according to the textbook perfect competition model in which everyone makes zero economic profits. Then those competitors—and thus that entire 10 percent of the market—act as though they had a 0 percent share of the industry.

Or, as a final example, suppose the 10 percent firm is better at advocacy, so that each dollar it spends on advocacy is twice as effective as each dollar spent by the 90 percent firm. Then it acts as though its share is 20 percent, and its threshold goes up accordingly. All these considerations affect the firms' real shares for purposes of choosing how much to spend on advocacy.

Does Privatization Always Reduce Advocacy in This Model?

This model applies straightforwardly to privatization: partial privatization splits an industry into public and private sectors, much as one can split a monopolist into competing firms. To be sure, the public sector isn't a profit maximizer like a private firm. But the concept of profit maximization needn't be interpreted in a narrow financial sense. Heads of government agencies still pursue goals of some sort and obtain *some* benefit when their agency provides a service.

Moreover, agencies aren't the only actors. The employees of the agencies, through their unions, also enjoy some benefit from public provision of the service, and they also participate in political advocacy. The challenge is to determine who the relevant actors are and what benefits they might plausibly seek to maximize.

The model implies, at a minimum, that *some* privatization will decrease advocacy, for two reasons. First, as long as privatization doesn't exceed a critical threshold, the public sector will dominate the private sector in terms of real share. Therefore, the model predicts that, up to that threshold, the private sector's advocacy will be zero. Second, as privatization increases, the size of the public sector falls, and thus the aggregate benefits of service provision to the public sector fall. Because the public sector is smaller, its advocacy falls accordingly.

How far can we continue to privatize before advocacy stops falling? As privatization increases, the second step always holds—by definition, privatization shrinks the public sector. The first step, however, doesn't hold for large enough levels of privatization. With enough privatization, the private sector dominates the public sector, at which point the private sector does all the advocacy, with the public sector acting as a free rider. From then on, privatization *increases* advocacy. We may call the threshold level of privatization at which advocacy stops falling an "advocacy-minimizing privatization level."

For instance, suppose a firm is divided into two firms whose profit is proportional to their share of the industry. Then the advocacy-minimizing breakup is an equal split of the industry. If a split in the industry creates a splinter firm that is twice as profitable as the incumbent firm, or perhaps twice as slick, then the advocacy-minimizing split is 67 percent to 33 percent, again allocating each firm an equal real stake in the system.

Applying This Model to the Real World

What Does the Model Predict about Prisons?

Now let's apply the theory to prisons, where "industry-expanding lobbying" means "pro-incarceration advocacy." I use the term "advocacy" broadly to include any use of political influence, licit or illicit, including endorsements, political contributions, lobbying, and bribes. And I use the term "incarceration" as shorthand to include the criminalization of a greater range of behavior, more active enforcement, greater reliance on imprisonment, longer sentences, and less parole—anything that increases person-years in prison. Endorsing a politician for being tough on crime, donating money to a three-strikes initiative, or testifying in favor of a "truth in sentencing" law all presumptively count as advocating incarceration.

Consider the main political actors in the prison industry: the private prison firms and the public corrections officers' union. I only focus on these two actors here because the other potential prison-based actors—private sector employees and departments of corrections—don't participate in pro-incarceration advocacy. Private sector workers aren't unionized, which makes it hard for them to act collectively (Dolovich 2005; Shichor 1995), and public departments of corrections actually want *fewer* prisoners (Allen 2006; Huppke 2006; Woodford 2006). I also assume that the private sector acts as a bloc (instead of competitively, and instead of, at the opposite extreme, cooperating with the public sector in a grand prison coalition) because cooperation within a concentrated oligopoly isn't that difficult. Firms interact with each other a lot and have ample opportunity to punish each other for noncooperative behavior (Ayres 1987). Moreover, private sector firms interact with each other more than they do with the public sector, so enforcing cooperation across the whole prison industry would be harder than merely doing so among private firms. (However, it turns out that how the industry cooperates, or whether it cooperates at all, doesn't make much of a difference for the main result.)

Without privatization, the public sector is the monopoly provider of prison services, and the corrections officers' union enjoys the benefits that flow from serving the whole system. As explained in the general model earlier, as part of the system is privatized, the public sector's advocacy decreases, while the private sector free rides off the public sector. This will remain true *provided the public sector stays the dominant sector.* And at current levels of privatization, the public sector is indeed dominant. It has a larger industry share and extracts more benefit from the system than does the private sector.

We can perform some rough estimates to verify this. (I assume, following much of the economic literature on firms and unions, that firms maximize profits, and that unions maximize total "union rents"—that is, here, the difference between public sector and private sector wages times the size of the public sector. See Farber 1986.)

- *Industry share*: The private sector has a smaller share of the industry. Of the 1.5 million prisoners under the jurisdiction of federal or state adult correctional authorities in 2004, 7 percent were held in private facilities (14 percent of federal prisoners and 6 percent of state prisoners). Among the 34 states with some privatization, the median percentage of private prisoners was 8 to 9 percent. If we're interested in the private share of marginal prisoners—that is, how likely a prisoner is to go to a private prison if convicted today—the private share becomes larger, mainly because private firms have absorbed much of the recent growth in federal incarceration. A reasonable estimate of the private share of marginal prisoners over the period 2000–2005 yields 6 percent for state systems, 54 percent for the federal system, and 22 percent overall (U.S. Department of Justice 2004, 2005).

• *Private sector profitability*: The profits of the private sector aren't high; 10 percent would be a generous estimate (Volokh 2007).

• *Public sector rents*: Public sector correctional officers' wages are quite a bit above—by about 30 to 65 percent—the wages of their private sector counterparts (Criminal Justice Institute 2000a, 2000b). This is a lot of money, because wages are about 60 to 80 percent of most prisons' operating expenses (Dolovich 2005; Donahue 1989; Logan 1990; Schlosser 1998; Shichor 1995).

These numbers are merely suggestive, not rigorous. But it should be intuitively plausible that public sector actors extract substantially more benefit from any given prison than do private firms. It's likewise clear that the public sector unions have a greater share of the industry than do private firms. Thus, overall, the public sector actors enjoy a greater benefit from prison provision than the private sector actors do, perhaps by an order of magnitude. This model predicts that the public sector unions should be doing all of the pro-incarceration advocacy, and the private firms should be entirely free riding.

Is This Realistic?

The theoretical model and rough numerical estimates predict that pro-incarceration advocacy should come from the public sector, not the private. Are such simple, highly stylized models realistic? In the case of prisons, the simple model may be close to true. As I document later, there's a lot of hard evidence of pro-incarceration advocacy by public corrections officers' unions (though a small part of union advocacy cuts the other way). But there's *virtually no evidence* of private sector pro-incarceration advocacy. This may simply mean that the private sector advocates incarceration secretly. But, in light of the theory, it may be more plausible that the private sector simply is a free rider, saving its political advocacy for policy areas where the public good aspect is less severe—*pro-privatization* advocacy.

But this model doesn't need to be literally realistic. Advocacy needn't be an entirely public good, and the smaller actors in the industry needn't be *complete* free riders. The point is merely that these assumptions are plausible, perhaps even likely. Advocacy has some public-good aspects, and free riding happens to some extent in the world. If people act enough like this model, privatization can still, on balance, reduce total pro-incarceration advocacy.

This plausible scenario rebuts the simple anti-privatization claim that privatization *does* increase pro-incarceration advocacy. (The extended models presented later on, in which the effect of privatization on advocacy is ambiguous, further rebut the simple unidirectional claim.) This scenario also points out a potential irony in the position of some incarceration opponents who, so as to avoid "reinforc[ing] the incarceration boom by introducing the profit motive into incarceration" (Sarabi and Bender 2000), would make common cause with public corrections officers' unions, who *concededly* are active lobbyists for incarceration.

Public Corrections Officers' Unions

Corrections officials were once politically aligned with liberal groups (Berk, Brackman, and Lesser 1977), but by the 1970s, correctional unions were already advocating incarceration (Wynne 1978). This activism continues today—for instance, through the California Correctional Peace Officers Association (CCPOA) (Pens 1998). The CCPOA gives twice as much in political contributions as the California Teachers Association—only the California Medical Association gives more in the state. CCPOA spends more than $7.5 million per year on political activities. It contributes to political parties and candidates, and it hires lobbyists, public relations firms, and polling groups.

Although some of its contributions are general, many are directly pro-incarceration:

- In 1994, the CCPOA gave more than $100,000 to California's Three Strikes Initiative, Proposition 184, making it the second-largest contributor.

- It gave at least $75,000 to the opponents of Proposition 36, the 2000 initiative that replaced incarceration with substance abuse treatment for certain nonviolent offenders.

- From 1998 to 2000, it gave more than $120,000 to crime victims' groups, who present a more sympathetic face to the public in their pro-incarceration advocacy.

- It spent more than $1 million to help defeat Proposition 66, the 2004 initiative that would have limited the crimes that triggered a life sentence under the three-strikes law (Warren 2004).

- And in 2005, it killed Governor Schwarzenegger's plan to "reduce the prison population by as much as 20,000, mainly through a program that diverted parole violators into rehabilitation efforts: drug programs, half-way houses and home detention" (Mendel 2006).

CCPOA doesn't always favor increasing incarceration, but the bulk of its advocacy has been in this direction.

Though corrections officers' unions outside California aren't as active as the CCPOA, many do advocate incarceration. One can see this in Florida (Deslatte 2006), Michigan (Gurwitt 1991), New York City (Murphy 2002), New York State (Falk 2003), and Rhode Island (Whitehouse 2006).

In some states, corrections officers are also affiliated with generalized public sector unions like the American Federation of State, County, and Municipal Employees (AFSCME). But the evidence that AFSCME Corrections United, AFSCME's corrections arm, has specifically advocated incarceration is weak: AFSCME did lobby in favor of the 1994 crime bill, which civil libertarians opposed because of its emphasis on incarceration, but AFSCME plausibly attributed its support of the bill to its grants for correctional facilities, corrections officer training provisions, and the like.

Private Prison Firms

Private prison firms depend, for their livelihood, on two policies: privatization and incarceration. Indeed, they admit as much to the world in their annual financial reports. It's thus natural to suspect that prison firms may advocate both privatization and incarceration in the public square. Their political advocacy mainly takes the forms of contributions to politicians and participation in the American Legislative Exchange Council (ALEC; a conservative organization that drafts model legislation), though they also lobby on particular bills, testify before Congress, and present arguments in the popular press. But while it's clear that these firms advocate *privatization*, it's unclear that they advocate *incarceration* to any significant extent.

In the discussion of corrections officers' unions earlier, I focused on advocacy that was specifically pro-incarceration; generalized contributions to candidates or support for multipurpose legislation, unlike targeted activities like contributions to single-issue voter-initiative campaigns, can't be traced back to any *specific* goal, like pro-incarceration advocacy. The same caveat is appropriate for private prison firms. Some commentators note private prison firms' advocacy without distinguishing between pro-privatization and pro-incarceration advocacy (Sarabi and Bender 2000), but this blanket approach is a mistake, unless one is attacking all political involvement by prison firms. The industry's contributions to politicians may not be pro-incarceration at all, or they may be multipurpose, for privatization and for incarceration. This is an important distinction, as merely advocating increased privatization arguably raises quite different concerns than advocating changes in the criminal law itself, and it may not implicate the same sorts of legitimacy values.

Because the industry's public statements virtually all favor privatization rather than incarceration, there's little hard evidence on the basis of which to attribute part of their political contributions to a pro-incarceration motive. Indeed, the Association of Private Correctional and Treatment Organizations (APCTO), the industry's trade group (now mostly inactive), speaking for its member firms, flatly denies that the industry lobbies for increased penalties. On the contrary, APCTO has frequently endorsed alternatives to incarceration, treatment programs, and other measures to reduce recidivism (some of which would also benefit its member firms financially) (Doucette 2006a, 2006b, 2006c, 2006d). Even if one ignores the industry association's official statements as self-serving and dismisses their anti-incarceration positions as mere public relations, at most, generalized political contributions are soft evidence of pro-incarceration advocacy. The most we can say empirically based on such evidence is that maybe pro-incarceration lobbying happens and maybe it doesn't. Perhaps the hard evidence is missing because the industry covers its tracks, or perhaps the hard evidence is missing because there's nothing to cover up.

As stated earlier, prison firms also participate in ALEC. Over the years, the Corrections Corporation of America (CCA) has participated in (and two of its executives have chaired) ALEC's Criminal Justice Task Force, which drafted, among other things, a "Truth in Sentencing Act" and a "Habitual Violent Offender Incarceration Act" (Dolovich 2005; Sarabi and Bender 2000; Talvi 2006). The ALEC critique has recently resurfaced in connection with alleged CCA involvement with the drafting of the text that became SB 1070, Arizona's controversial immigration law (Justice Policy Institute 2011, 30).

The inner workings of ALEC are hazy, and some commentators argue that the private prison industry expressly seeks out channels that are "conveniently out of public view" and "behind closed doors" to promote its pro-incarceration agenda (Dolovich 2005, 434–542). The trouble with this view is that we can also presume that prison firms work within ALEC on *privatization* issues: prison privatization is one of the major issues of the very same Criminal Justice Task Force; the task force has a Subcommittee on Private Prisons and a model "Housing Out-of-State Prisoners in a Private Prison Act," and CCA is known to have talked to the task force on the subject. Therefore, this, too, is soft evidence; we don't know that they also work on sentencing or incarceration issues. Indeed, CCA asserts that it hasn't participated in, voted on, or endorsed any stand on model legislation for sentencing or crime policies within ALEC (see, e.g., Grant 2010).

Apparently, the only CCA official to have ever publicly taken a stand on sentencing is J. Michael Quinlan, formerly director of the Federal Bureau of Prisons and (as of 2010) a CCA senior vice president, who, after he joined CCA in 1993, told a House subcommittee that mandatory minimum sentences "are unnecessary for non-violent, non-serious offenses" and "pose[] a severe threat to prison discipline and management" (Crime Prevention and Criminal Justice Reform Act 1994).

Nor does there seem to be a smoking gun of pro-incarceration lobbying if we examine the industry's explicit lobbying on particular bills. For instance, in 2010, CCA lobbied on several bills before Congress (Justice Policy Institute 2011, 23). One was the Private Prison Information Act of 2009, which would have extended the Freedom of Information Act to private prisons holding federal prisoners; clearly one expects private prison firms to lobby to reduce their own regulation. Another was the Safe Prisons Communication Act of 2009, which would have allowed prisons to jam cell phones—a public safety issue of interest to all prisons. The other bills were appropriations acts for the Department of Homeland Security and other departments that pay CCA's contract fees and miscellaneous bills to keep the government running or related to economic stimulus.

At the state level, one can similarly point, for instance, to CCA's contribution to California's failed Proposition 6 in 2008 (which would have enhanced some criminal penalties but also substantially increased law enforcement spending, including correctional spending) and GEO's lobbying in favor of Jessica's Law in Kansas in 2006 (which enhanced penalties for sex offenders but also—until the controversial language was dropped before the legislative vote—would have authorized private prison construction).

Of course, any lobbying for funding plays some part in keeping the system as a whole going, but this is a far cry from lobbying for stricter criminal penalties.

I've only found two pieces of evidence of arguably pro-incarceration advocacy by private firms. In 1995, Wackenhut chairman Timothy P. Cole testified in favor of certain amendments to the Violent Crime Control and Law Enforcement Act of 1994. The main point of his testimony was to boost privatization and to make sure his corporation could get a share of certain prison funds. But during this testimony, he also said the following:

- "Our proposed amendment . . . would help to assure that these grants will help the states incarcerate more violent criminals and not make the state governments more dependent on federal tax dollars in the long term."

- "By passing 'truth-in-sentencing' laws, states have begun to restore a fundamental sense of justice and fairness to our system of crime and punishment."

- "The new grant program [under the 1994 Act, without the proposed amendments] is available for 'alternative correctional facilities' and does not recognize the urgent need for more cells in secure facilities."

- "Current law encourages billions to be spent on new or retrofitted facilities that are not large enough, secure enough or efficient enough to keep the maximum number of violent criminals in prison for the least cost" (Overhauling the Nation's Prisons 1995).

This isn't great evidence—Cole was primarily advocating for funding priorities and privatization-friendly decision making. Cole's request to divert money from alternative facilities, his kind words for truth-in-sentencing laws, and his positive attitude toward locking up violent criminals are hardly a pro-incarceration smoking gun.

More serious is the story, which broke in 2009, that two Pennsylvania state judges received kickbacks to send teenagers to two privately run youth detention centers (Urbina and Hamill 2009). But this example, reprehensible though it is, stands out for being extraordinary. Even though private industry might have an advantage over the public sector when it comes to corruption, outright judicial corruption, at least in the United States, is not a major problem.

These two cases are the best I've found. Private prison firms may have made other statements or taken other actions that are arguably pro-incarceration, but I haven't found any, and to my knowledge, privatization critics haven't brought them to light.

Sometimes No Smoke Means No Fire

What do we make of the absence of hard evidence that private firms advocate for stricter criminal laws? As I've suggested earlier, perhaps they do so secretly. Or perhaps this simple model is basically right, and the private firms are actually spending their money on a form of advocacy where the public good aspect isn't important—*pro-privatization advocacy*.

Pro-privatization advocacy is an area where, obviously, the private sector can't free ride off the public sector, because the public sector is their enemy on that issue. If the private firms cooperate with each other, they reap all the benefits of their pro-privatization advocacy. Even if they don't cooperate with each other, an individual firm's pro-privatization contribution may benefit it directly to the extent that the contribution (perhaps improperly) increases the likelihood that the firm will obtain a particular contract.

Complicating the Model

The theoretical model presented earlier was highly simplified. It's therefore not surprising that its central prediction—that smaller actors would do no advocacy at all, and that privatization (up to the advocacy-minimizing level) would unambiguously decrease the level of industry-expanding advocacy—was also simple. Here, I complicate the model in various ways.

First, there are complications that, although realistic, don't change the result of the model significantly. First, I drop the assumption that money only buys victory for a given reform or candidate and introduce the possibility that money can also change the substance of the reform or the candidate's position. This doesn't significantly alter the conclusion. Next, I drop the assumption that anti-incarceration political advocacy is fixed. I find that pro-incarceration advocacy still falls with privatization, though the effect of privatization on anti-incarceration advocacy is ambiguous.

Afterward, I show how privatization may have an ambiguous effect on pro-incarceration advocacy. First, I relax the assumption that money is fungible and that only the total amount in the pot matters. If public sector and private sector money have different effects, privatization has an ambiguous effect on total pro-incarceration advocacy: private advocacy rises, but public advocacy falls. Next, I introduce the possibility that the pattern of privatization, as we observe it today, is already the result of a political process where strong unions have successfully opposed privatization while weak unions haven't. I find that exogenously increasing privatization in such an environment would likewise have an ambiguous effect on pro-incarceration advocacy; the effect depends on the correlation between actors' influence in privatization politics and their influence in incarceration politics.

The bottom line is that, if one wants to argue that privatization will *increase* pro-incarceration advocacy, one must argue either, from outside the model, that the model is wrong or, from inside the model, why privatization would increase private sector advocacy more than it would decrease public sector advocacy.

Allowing Money to Change Candidates' Positions

So far, I've taken the political agenda as a given; I didn't explain the source of the proposed reform. Thus, I've assumed that money is important only because it buys victory. But money can also change the substance of the agenda. It turns out, though, that the analysis in this case is similar.

A monetary contribution to a candidate or cause, when money can affect the substance of the proposed reform, has the following effects (Ball 1999; Grossman and Helpman 1996):

1. *Electoral influence.*

    a. As before, the contribution pays for persuasion, directly increasing the probability that the initiative prevails.

    b. But the contribution also moves the initiative in a more pro-incarceration direction.

2. *Substantive influence.* Finally, the contributor benefits if the initiative prevails, because the policy is better for the contributor than it would have been without the contribution.

A prison provider considering how much to contribute still follows the same framework as before: it contributes until the benefit of an extra dollar falls to $1. The benefit of an extra dollar is more complicated than it was in the earlier model because it now includes all three effects listed here, rather than just the first. The basic idea, however, remains the same. And the effect of privatization also remains the same as in the simpler model.

Anti-Incarceration Advocacy

This model focused only on *pro*-incarceration advocacy, taking *anti*-incarceration advocacy as a given. But it's plausible that pro- and anti-incarceration forces respond strategically to each other's expenditures. This suggests two questions.

First, does anti-incarceration advocacy change the basic conclusion about the effect of privatization on pro-incarceration advocacy? No: privatization still makes pro-incarceration advocacy decrease.

Second, how does privatization change *anti*-incarceration advocacy? After all, some anti-incarceration advocacy is as plausibly self-interested as prison providers' pro-incarceration advocacy. Proposition 66, which would have limited California's three-strikes law, was partly funded by "Sacramento businessman Jerry Keenan whose son Richard is serving time for manslaughter after crashing his car while driving drunk and killing two passengers" (Institute of Governmental Studies 2004). Proposition 36, California's drug treatment diversion initiative, was supported by dozens of drug treatment providers and 17 medical and public health organizations (National Families in Action 2000). And, as mentioned earlier, state departments of corrections generally advocate against incarceration. Perhaps those who are concerned about self-interest coloring people's positions on criminal justice should be concerned about this self-interested anti-incarceration advocacy as well.

It turns out that the privatization-induced decrease in pro-incarceration advocacy has an indirect effect on anti-incarceration advocacy. Unfortunately, we can't say anything a priori about the direction of this effect. On the one hand, pro-incarceration advocacy decreases the effectiveness of anti-incarceration advocacy by counteracting it. A decrease in pro-incarceration advocacy, therefore, makes anti-incarceration advocacy more effective, which would tend to increase it. On the other hand, a decrease in pro-incarceration advocacy also makes anti-incarceration advocacy less necessary, which would tend to decrease it. There's no theoretical way to know how these conflicting effects would balance out.

What this means normatively depends on one's attitude toward anti-incarceration advocacy. If one opposes pro-incarceration advocacy because there's already too much incarceration, then there's nothing wrong with advocacy the other way. But if one opposes pro-incarceration advocacy because it's assumed to be self-interested and because self-interested arguments are illegitimate in penal policy, then perhaps anti-incarceration advocacy is just as bad if it comes from boot camps, halfway houses, drug treatment providers, and other presumptively self-interested parties. Because there's no clear theoretical effect of privatization on *total* advocacy, privatization is thus normatively ambiguous on this dimension.

Relaxing the Assumption of Fungible Money

In the main model, free riding was *total*, because all dollars were equal; all that mattered was the total amount of money in the pot. A dollar from a public actor had the same effect as a dollar from a private firm. This can be plausible—for instance, dollars are fungible in buying advertising, or a politician may adopt the view of whatever policy-position supporter contributed the most to his or her war chest. But some alternative assumptions may also be plausible. For example, one group might be attractive only to Democrats, while another might be attractive only to Republicans. More generally, perhaps politicians are just sensitive to the variety of voices in a coalition, believing (rightly or wrongly) that having a wide variety of groups shows that a policy has wide support. Then neither group's contributions totally crowd out the other's. Your 500,001st dollar still has less benefit than your 500,000th dollar—there are still decreasing marginal returns—but (unlike in the previous model) it doesn't have the same benefit as your first dollar added on to your competitor's 500,000th. Therefore, the total free-riding effect from the simple model no longer occurs. There are many ways in which private and public spending *could* interact. For instance, the effect of a public dollar could be the same regardless of the level of private spending, and vice versa. Or, alternatively, public and private spending could be complementary if politicians are eager to endorse a policy supported by actors from both the public and private sectors. This is an empirical question to be answered by future research.

In this context, privatization may have two opposing effects. First, it increases the private sector share, so private sector advocacy goes up. Second, it decreases the share of the public sector, so public sector advocacy goes down. We can't say anything a priori about whether the first effect outweighs the second. Because the empirical effect of privatization is ambiguous, the normative effect of privatization is also ambiguous if one opposes pro-incarceration advocacy.

Strong and Weak Unions

Recall that an industry's effectiveness at advocacy is relevant to its real share for purposes of this analysis. For instance, if your competitor, with a 10 percent share, is twice as slick a lobbyist as you, meaning that his marginal dollars produce twice the benefit of yours, he will act as though his share is 20 percent. Which way this cuts isn't clear, as we don't know which sector is more effective at lobbying in favor of incarceration. The CCPOA, as we have seen, is highly effective, but corrections officers' unions are much less active outside California, and perhaps this is because they are less effective. It's hard to say how effective private prison firms are at lobbying in favor of incarceration, because, as we have seen, there's little evidence that they do this at all, and if they do it secretly, it's likewise hard to gauge how effective they are.

But suppose that one's effectiveness at lobbying for *incarceration* is correlated with one's effectiveness at lobbying for (or against) *privatization*. For simplicity's sake, let's suppose that they're *perfectly* correlated. Consider the states with high levels of privatization. We may conclude that those states have high privatization because their corrections officers' unions weren't effective at opposing privatization; the private industry was just too strong for them. When that relatively weak public sector was partly displaced by a relatively strong private sector, a weak pro-incarceration voice was similarly displaced by a strong pro-incarceration voice. Pro-incarceration advocacy, then, may plausibly have increased.

Similarly, consider the states with low levels of prison privatization or no privatization at all, like California, New York, or Rhode Island. The unions in those states, on this view, must have been stronger than the industry, or else we would see privatization there now. If privatization were introduced, total pro-incarceration advocacy would go down, but privatization is unlikely to be introduced there, so we will not see that happen.

This is a story where—contrary to my implicit assumption so far—privatization is endogenous: the states where privatization has gained a foothold aren't randomly chosen; rather, privatization emerges where corrections officers' unions are weak and fails to emerge where the unions are strong. Thus, past privatization may have, on balance, increased pro-incarceration advocacy. If one could somehow eliminate prison privatization (despite the confluence of powerful political forces that established it to begin with), one would reestablish the rule of the ineffective corrections officers' unions in those states where they were ineffective—to the benefit of those who oppose pro-incarceration advocacy. By a similar logic, one should *introduce* privatization where it's currently absent: if it's currently absent, it's because it was not a powerful enough political force to win on its own, which means it will also be an ineffective political force in fighting for incarceration.

In fact, the assumption here—that the effectiveness of pro-incarceration advocacy is perfectly correlated with the effectiveness of pro- or anti-privatization advocacy—implies that pro-incarceration advocacy is already as high as it can get, because the slick advocates, who were already slick enough to establish themselves in the industry, are now plying their slickness in the incarceration policy field. Adding a thumb to the privatization scales in either direction would tend to support the victory of the less persuasive party and would therefore reduce the total amount of pro-incarceration advocacy.

This story may be plausible, but it requires more fleshing out. For one thing, the assumption may not be right. Low-privatization states need not be high-union-strength states. Although antipathy to privatization and the strength of public sector unions are probably correlated, a very Democratic state may plausibly oppose privatization even if, for whatever reason, its corrections officers' union is weak.

Moreover, actors in the prison industry may not be similarly effective in the privatization debate as in the incarceration debate. Although one's effectiveness at advocacy probably depends on one's general characteristics, like goodwill, persuasiveness, and slickness, the specific subject matter of the advocacy also plays a big role. The incarceration debate is peopled by different interest groups than the privatization debate. For instance, prosecutors, police officers, victims' rights groups, and rural communities are interested in incarceration policy but not so much in privatization policy. Conversely, prison privatization is a matter of interest even to interest groups without a direct interest in prisons, such as, on one side, generalized public employee unions and, on the other side, small-government advocates, who assume (probably sensibly enough) that a victory for privatization in any field is a victory for the general privatization movement. Moreover, the appeal of incarceration arguments, which connect to fears of drugs and crime and concerns over civil liberties, seems to have a very different source than the appeal of privatization arguments, which relate to taxes, spending, and the effectiveness of government services.

We are back, then, to a general state-by-state analysis. In the first set of models—where the effectiveness of advocacy only depended on the total amount of money in the pot—everything was driven by the dominant actor, where the term "dominant" also takes effectiveness into account. I've given arguments as to why the private sector is currently probably the smaller actor. The slickness adjustment described here might change that in some places, but it's an empirical question. As is by now familiar, privatization increases the private sector share but decreases the public sector share. This slickness adjustment may change the de facto shares of the different sectors, but it doesn't change the qualitative result. The effect of privatization is theoretically ambiguous.

Conclusion

The current formulation of the political influence challenge to privatization is inadequate. Privatization may not worsen any political influence problem and might even alleviate it. The model here was simplified, so my specific conclusions here are tentative. My discussion here is meant to stimulate and discipline further debate, not end it.

But what isn't tentative is that this sort of analysis is necessary if one is to make the political influence argument properly, whether in the prison context or more generally. As Mancur Olson (1965, 2) (somewhat hyperbolically) observed, "the customary view that groups of individuals with common interests tend to further those common interests appears to have little if any merit." Critics of privatization who have charged that privatization increases industry-expanding advocacy haven't explained what it is about the lobbying world that would make this happen. Either they're unambiguously wrong, or they're only right under a particular set of empirical assumptions that they must spell out.

The surprising moral of this story shouldn't be that surprising. Indeed, the central insight here was also an important argument in favor of the antitrust laws. Discussing the conditions that preceded the enactment of those laws, William Howard Taft (1914, 4) wrote that "business methods and plans . . . directed to . . . suppressing competition . . . had resulted in the building of great and powerful corporations which had, many of them, intervened in politics and through use of corrupt machines and bosses threatened us with a plutocracy." The argument is plausible, and it's likewise plausible that privatization, by fragmenting an industry into at least two chunks (and more if private firms don't cooperate on advocacy), may similarly reduce that industry's political power.

In a roundabout way, then, privatization is a form of antitrust, and antitrust is a form of campaign finance regulation. It may not be worthwhile to privatize industries—or break up large corporations—merely to reduce their political advocacy, but at the very least this may count as an unintended—and possibly happy—side effect of privatization that, if real, should be taken into account in future analysis.

Note

A version of this chapter previously appeared in the *Stanford Law Review* at 60 Stan. L. Rev. 1197 (2008). When possible and appropriate, please cite to that version. For information, visit http://lawreview.stanford.edu. More details can also be found in Volokh (2010) and Volokh (2007).

References

Allen, R. F. 2006. "Inflow of Inmates Must Be Slowed." *Montgomery Advertiser*, July 17, A5.

Ayres, I. 1987. "How Cartels Punish: A Structural Theory of Self-Enforcing Collusion." *Columbia Law Review* 87 (2): 295–325.

Ball, R. 1999. "Opposition Backlash and Platform Convergence in a Spatial Voting Model with Campaign Contributions." *Public Choice* 98 (3/4): 269–286.

Berk, R. A., Harold Brackman, and Selma Lesser. 1977. *A Measure of Justice: An Empirical Study of Changes in the California Penal Code, 1955–1971.* New York: Academic Press.

Crime Prevention and Criminal Justice Reform Act: Hearing before the Subcommittee on Prisons and Criminal Justice, 103rd Congress. 1994. Statement of Michael Quinlan. 1994 WL 214215.

Criminal Justice Institute. 2000a. *2000 Corrections Yearbook: Private Prisons.* Middletown, CT: Criminal Justice Institute.

Criminal Justice Institute. 2000b. *2000 Corrections Yearbook: Adult Corrections.* Middletown, CT: Criminal Justice Institute.

Deslatte, A. 2006. "Crist Courts Voters with Positive Focus." *Florida Today*, August 16, A1.

Dolovich, S. 2005. "State Punishment and Private Prisons." *Duke Law Journal* 55 (3): 437–546.

Donahue, J. D. 1989. *The Privatization Decision: Public Ends, Private Means.* New York: Basic Books.

Doucette, P. 2006a. "Juvenile Justice: Legislature Should Invest More in Young." Letter to the editor. *Fort Pierce Tribune*, May 10, A6.

Doucette, P. 2006b. "Ohio Prisons Are Full." *Cincinnati Post*, August 8, A9.

Doucette, P. 2006c. "In Juvenile Justice, Florida Gets Just What It Pays For." Letter to the editor. *Palm Beach Post*, October 1, 4E.

Doucette, P. 2006d. "State Prison System Reaching Capacity." Letter to the editor. *Denver Post*, October 2, B7.

Falk, J. 2003. "Fiscal Lockdown Part II: Will State Budget Cuts Weaken the Prison-Industrial Complex—Or Strengthen It?" *Dollars & Sense* 250:32–35.

Farber, H. S. 1986. "The Analysis of Union Behavior." In *Handbook of Labor Economics*, vol. 2, edited by O. Ashenfelter and R. Layard, 1039–1089. Amsterdam: North-Holland.

Grant, Louise. 2010. Letter to Laura Sullivan and Susanne Reber, National Public Radio, November 16. http://www.cca.com/static/assets/CCA_letter_to_NPR_11_16_10_final.pdf.

Grossman, G. M., and E. Helpman. 1996. "Electoral Competition and Special Interest Politics." *Review of Economic Studies* 63 (2): 265–286.

Gurwitt, R. 1991. "The Growing Clout of Prison Guards." *Governing*, December, 37.

Huppke, R. W. 2006. "Rehabilitation or Recycling?" *Chicago Tribune*, March 12, 1.

Institute of Governmental Studies. 2004. "Election Results Update." November 2. http://igs.berkeley.edu/library/research/quickhelp/elections/2004general/htThreeStrikesProp66.html.

Justice Policy Institute. 2011. *Gaming the System: How the Political Strategies of Private Prison Companies Promote Ineffective Incarceration Policies*. http://www.justicepolicy.org/uploads/justicepolicy/documents/gaming_the_system.pdf.

Logan, C. H. 1990. *Private Prisons: Cons and Pros*. New York: Oxford University Press.

Mendel, E. 2006. "Governor May Act on Crisis in Prisons." *San Diego Union-Tribune*, September 2, A1.

Murphy, K. 2002. "Labor Helps Patakis [sic] Re-election Battle." *Stateline.org*. May 20. http://www.stateline.org/live/ViewPage.action?siteNodeId=136&contentId=14817.

National Families in Action. 2000. "A Guide to Drug-Related State Ballot Initiatives: California Proposition 36 Proponents." http://www.nationalfamilies.org/guide/california36-endorsements.html.

Oakland, W. H. 1987. "Theory of Public Goods." In *Handbook of Public Economics*, vol. 2, edited by A. J. Auerbach and M. Feldstein, 485–535. Amsterdam: North-Holland.

Olson, M. 1965. *The Logic of Collective Action: Public Goods and the Theory of Groups*. Cambridge, MA: Harvard University Press.

Overhauling the Nation's Prisons: Hearing on the Violent Crime Control and Law Enforcement Act of 1994 before the Senate Committee on the Judiciary, 104th Congress. 1995. Statement of Timothy P. Cole. 1995 WL 449225.

Pens, D. 1998. "The California Prison Guards' Union: A Potent Political Interest Group." In *The Celling of America: An Inside Look at the U.S.*

Prison Industry, edited by D. Burton-Rose with Dan Pens and Paul Wright, 134–139. Monroe, ME: Common Courage Press.

Sarabi, B., and E. Bender. 2000. *The Prison Payoff: The Role of Politics and Private Prisons in the Incarceration Boom*. Western States Center and Western Prison Project. November. http://www.safetyandjustice .org/review-status/story/450.

Schlosser, E. 1998. "The Prison-Industrial Complex." *Atlantic Monthly*, December, 51–77.

Shichor, D. 1995. *Punishment for Profit*. Thousand Oaks, CA: Sage Publications.

Taft, W. H. 1914. *The Anti-Trust Act and the Supreme Court*. New York: Harper and Brothers.

Talvi, S. J. A. 2006. "Follow the Prison Money Trail." *In These Times*, September 4, 12.

Urbina, I., and S. D. Hamill. 2009. "Judges Plead Guilty in Scheme to Jail Youths for Profit." *New York Times*, February 12, A22.

U.S. Department of Justice. 2004. *Prisoners in 2004*. Washington, DC. http://www.ojp.usdoj.gov/bjs/pubalp2.htm#Prisoners.

U.S. Department of Justice. 2005. *Prison and Jail Inmates at Midyear 2005*. Washington, DC. http://www.ojp.usdoj.gov/bjs/pubalp2.htm#pjmidyear.

Volokh, A. 2007. *Privatization, Free Riding, and Industry-Expanding Lobbying: Additional Materials*. Georgetown Law & Economics Research Paper No. 969789. May 8. http://ssrn.com/abstract=969789.

Volokh, A. 2010. "Privatization, Free Riding, and Industry-Expanding Lobbying." *International Review of Law and Economics* 30 (1): 62–70.

Warren, J. 2004. "Guards Union Is Giving Prisons Chief Hard Time." *Los Angeles Times*, November 15, A1.

Whitehouse, S. 2006. "Rhode Island Brotherhood of Correctional Officers Endorses Whitehouse." Press release, August 25.

Woodford, J. S. 2006. "Hard Time: Why I Quit the Prison System." *Los Angeles Times*, August 6, M1.

Wynne, J. M., Jr. 1978. *Prison Employee Unionism: The Impact on Correctional Administration and Programs*. Washington, DC: National Institute of Law Enforcement and Criminal Justice, U.S. Department of Justice.

2

The High Cost of Profit: Racism, Classism, and Interests against Prison Privatization

Nancy A. Heitzeg

The recent reemergence of private prisons for profit simply offers a new twist on an old story. Private profit from imprisonment has a long-standing history in the United States; from the outset, private interests have amassed great fortunes from imprisoned labor, be they slaves or convicts. Labor by imprisoned black slaves was the economic centerpiece of the plantation economy, and after the Civil War, slavery was de facto perpetuated via prison farms, the convict lease system, and the chain gang. The result was "slavery by another name" (Blackmon 2008). Inmate labor, almost exclusively by blacks and poor whites, built corporate fortunes in agriculture and industry as well the public infrastructure of railroads, highways, levees, and dams.

Although the most extreme versions of these practices were phased out by the mid-20th century, the profit motive as an underpinning of our prison system has returned in full force. Profiting from prisons was transformed yet again by what is often referred to as the prison-industrial complex, and this "new plantation" was supported by a host of policies that result in the "New Jim Crow" (Alexander 2009). The rise of the prison-industrial complex and the corresponding explosion in U.S. incarceration rates has created new opportunities for profiting from mass incarceration. As before, there is both public and private profit from inmate labor—which is still overwhelming provided by blacks, browns, and poor whites. But in addition, corporate and government interests now profit from prison via the provision of inmate services, job creation, construction contracts, and more. Increasingly, the lines between publically operated prisons and private interests are blurred; federal and state-run prisons allow corporate contracts for inmate labor and services, and private correctional corporations, such as the GEO Group and Corrections Corporation of America (CCA), are contracted to operate existing public prisons and to build and manage new private prisons. The private prison then is just the most explicit in a series of multifaceted schemes that allow for profit to be garnered from imprisonment, and any critique of the private prison must be located in the larger context of profiteering from imprisonment.

Now, as then, vast profits are made from exploited inmate labor. Furthermore, the profit is derived from an immense imprisoned population that is disproportionately people of color and disproportionately poor. Now, as then, private profiteering from imprisonment has been resisted because of economic interests and job loss to cheaper labor; this pattern has been further resisted on grounds of human rights and civil rights. For small businesses and unions, the interest against private prisons are almost exclusively economic. For others—grassroots organizations, civil and human rights nonprofits, and churches—the critiques of private prisons are those raised historically about the role of all imprisonment in the United States; these are rooted in resistance to racism, classism, slavery, brutalization, and exploitation.

Profiteering from Prisons: Plantations, Convict Lease Labor, and Chain Gangs

The history of prison in the United States is simultaneously a history of private profit from a captive labor force. The early colonial practice of transportation allowed imported prisoners to work as indentured servants on plantations (Sellin 1975). They were later replaced by the even more profitable traffic in African slaves. Both slavery and indentured servitude continued and expanded in the new United States. Before the Civil War, the bulk of the imprisoned labor in the United States was slave labor, which was the undisputed centerpiece of the South's agricultural economy. Private–public partnerships were in place at the outset of the early U.S. penal system; New York's Auburn Penitentiary, for example, awarded a private contract for the creation of a prison factory in 1817 (Sellin 1975). In the North, prison labor was also widely used à la Auburn, with inmates expected to produce goods as part of a regime of discipline and punishment rather than rehabilitation. As Shelden (2005a) notes:

> It can also be said that the use of inmates as a form of cheap labor has been part of the capitalist system from the beginning, as owners seek to maximize profits however they can, including using the cheapest form of labor, whether it be slaves, immigrant labor, or inmates. In fact, taking advantage of those imprisoned (in various forms, including slavery) has been common among nations for centuries.

The use of prisons as a source of private profit solidified after the Civil War with the introduction of a number of practices that continue, albeit in slightly altered forms, to this day: the plantation prison, which profited from neo-slave inmate labor; the convict lease system, which sold those convicted and even those acquitted of crimes to individuals and corporations for labor on farms, logging enterprises, and mines; and chain gangs. The South's loss of its vast pool of unpaid slave labor led to immediate legal efforts to re-enslave newly freed blacks. Davis (2003, 29) traces the initial expansion of the penitentiary system to the abolition of slavery, noting that "in the immediate aftermath of slavery, the southern states hastened to develop a criminal justice system that could legally restrict the possibilities of freedom for the newly released slaves." There was a subsequent transformation of the Slave Codes into the Black Codes and later Jim Crow laws. These laws echoed the restrictions associated with slavery and criminalized a range of activities only if the perpetrator were black. The libratory promise of the Thirteenth Amendment—"Neither slavery nor involuntary servitude shall exist in the United States"—contained a dangerous loophole: *except as a punishment for crime.*" This allowed for the conversion of the old plantations to penitentiaries—the 18,000-acre Louisiana Penitentiary at Angola is a case in point—and the creation of prison farms, such as Parchman in Mississippi and the infamous Tucker Prison Farm and Cummins Prison Farm in Arkansas. Entire prisons were leased out to private contractors that literally worked thousands of prisoners to death. These prisoners were largely black; in the post–Civil War South, the racial composition of prison and jail populations shifted dramatically from majority white to majority black, and in many states increased tenfold. As Davis (2003, 31) notes, "the expansion of the convict lease system and the county chain gang meant that the antebellum criminal justice system defined criminal justice largely as a means for controlling black labor."

The introduction of the convict lease system allowed private individuals and businesses to continue to benefit economically from the unpaid labor of blacks. It also provided revenue for the states, because incarcerated workers were entirely in the custody of the contractors, who paid a set annual fee to the state (Nyasha 2007a; Sellin 1975). This system also allowed inmates literally to be sold directly to private individuals and industries and transported to work in fields; in logging; in road, levee, and railroad construction; and in mines. The conditions of this sort of incarceration have rightly been described as worse than slavery—because the inmates were not valued property, they were largely expendable and were frequently worked to death in addition to being subjected to brutal punishments, malnourishment, and disease (Blackmon 2008).

In addition to the convict lease system, many states, both North and South, adopted the use of the chain gang. The chain gang was "an extremely dehumanizing cruelty that chained men, and later women, together in groups of five . . . originated to build extensive roads and highways. The first state to institute chain gangs was Alabama, followed by Arizona, Florida, Iowa, Indiana, Illinois, Wisconsin, Montana, and Oklahoma" (Nyasha 2007b). Chain gangs effectively rebuilt significant portions of the post–Civil War South and worked to produce public projects such as roads and railways; in some cases, they were also leased to private contractors.

The convict lease system persisted in many states well into the 20th century and, in many respects, is the precursor to the private prisons of today. Because of increased public scrutiny and pressure from organized labor, the convict lease system was largely abolished by the mid-1930s. Nyasha (2007b) observes that

> [t]he loss of outside jobs and the inherent brutality and cruelty of the lease system sparked resistance which eventually brought about its demise. One of the most famous battles was the Coal Creek Rebellion of 1891. When the Tennessee Coal, Iron and Railroad locked out their workers and replaced them with convicts, the miners stormed the prison and freed 400 captives; and when the company continued to contract

prisoners, the miners burned the prison down. The Tennessee leasing system was disbanded shortly thereafter. But it remained in many states until the rise of resistance in the 1930s.

By the late 1920s, mounting pressure from organized labor led Congress to pass legislation limiting the sale of prison-made products. The Hawes-Cooper Act, Public Law 669, 70th Congress (1929) provided that prison-made goods transported into another state would be governed by the laws of the recipient state, which effectively precluded the export of goods into states where organized labor had been able to push for adoption of the state-use doctrine. The Ashurst-Sumners Act, Public Law 215, 74th Congress (1935) prohibited transportation carriers from introducing prison-made goods into any state in violation of the laws of that state; it also required that prison-made goods be labeled. The bill also placed a $10,000 limit on sales of prison-made goods to the U.S. government (Nyasha 2007b). As a result, the long unfettered ability of private companies to profit from prison labor was dampened for the next several decades.

Of course, neither prison labor nor private profit from prison labor ceased. Prison industries still flourished, now under the oversight of UNICOR, Federal Prison Industries, Inc., a federal corporation created in 1934. State prison industries also continued to operate and expanded use of the chain gang (which was finally phased out nationwide by 1955 but recently restored in several states) (Shelden 2005c). Still, the Ashurst-Sumners Act made large-scale profit unattainable because of barriers on interstate sale of prison-made products or large government orders. For a brief time, the notion of inmate labor was even promoted as a rehabilitative tool that might offer inmates vocational skills that would benefit their reintegration upon release, but this was short-lived (Nyasha 2007b; Sellin 1975). By the late 1970s, however, the declining power of U.S. labor unions and the increased trend toward a corporate-dominated global economy led to the easing of these restriction and paved the way for the rise of the prison-industrial complex. The Justice System Improvement Act of 1979, which created the Prison Industries Enhancement Program (PIECP), lifted the ban on interstate transportation and sale of prison-made products, permitting a for-profit relationship between prisons and the private sector and prompting a dramatic—and still escalating—increase in both inmates and potential profit (Price 2006).

Profiteering from Prisons Redux: The New Plantation and the Prison-Industrial Complex

The passage of the Justice System Improvement Act of 1979 again paved the way for privatization and large-scale profit—not only from prison labor but also from private sector service contracts. Although prisons had been primarily a burden on taxpayers, the prison-industrial complex now became a source of corporate profit, governmental agency funding, cheap neo-slave labor, and employment for economically depressed regions. This complex now includes more than 3,300 jails, more than 1,500 state prisons, and 100 federal prisons in the United States. Nearly 300 of these are private for-profit prisons. More than 2.4 million persons are in state or federal prisons and jails—a rate of 751 out of every 100,000 people—and another 5 million are under some sort of correctional supervision, such as probation or parole. The United States, which has less than 5 percent of the world's population, has 25 percent of its prisoners. This is the highest incarceration rate in the world (Pew Center on the States 2008).

Much like its namesake, the military-industrial complex, "the prison industrial complex is not a conspiracy, but a confluence of special interests" (Silverstein 1997, 10). Indeed, "the prison industrial complex is a self-perpetuating machine where the vast profits . . . and perceived political benefits . . . lead to policies that are additionally designed to insure an endless supply of 'clients' for the criminal justice system" (Brewer and Heitzeg 2008, 45–65). Profits are generated via corporate contracts for cheap inmate labor (at wages ranging from 2 cents to 2 dollars per hour), private and public supply and construction contracts, job creation for criminal justice professionals, and continued media profits from exaggerated crime reporting and the use of crime/punishment as ratings-grabbing news and entertainment. The perceived political benefits include reduced unemployment rates because of job creation and imprisonment of the poor and unemployed, "get tough on crime" and public safety rhetoric, and funding increases for the police and for criminal justice system agencies and professionals.

Any discussion of prisons and privatization cannot be neatly disentangled from this larger correctional context. Increasingly, there is a blur between the private and public sectors in the oversight of prisons, including the direct, day-to-day management of prisons and prison programs and the privatized oversight of key prison services. The renewed trend toward privatization includes the takeover of existing public facilities by private operators, the contracting to private providers for the provision of some direct services to public facilities, contracting for private provider access to inmate labor to produce products for private profit, and the building and operation of new prisons by for-profit prison companies. The private prison is simply the most extreme example from a network that creates multiple pathways for private profit via mass imprisonment, and it is part of a confluence of special interests that includes the PIECP; privatized industry self-regulation via the National Correctional Industry Association; the private prison industries, most notably the GEO Group and CCA; a long list of corporations that are now free to exploit inmate labor; and the lobbying influence of the American Legislative Exchange Council (ALEC).

Of course, those who profit from such incarceration will do what they must to ensure a steady and ever-expanding supply of new labor. It is no surprise that the rise of the prison-industrial complex is made possible by many varieties of legislation that guarantee to ensnare more and increasingly younger offenders; incarcerate nonviolent offenders, primarily via the war on drugs; increase sentence length; and set up released inmates for failure and recidivism. The prison-industrial complex then is linked with a host of policies and practices designed to ensure a steady flow of inmates into the system (Hallett 2005; Heitzeg 2009).

The result is a tenfold increase in the U.S. prison population over the past 40 years, and with an overrepresentation of people of color and the poor as the captive labor force. This collusion between governmental agencies and private corporations in pursuit of profit from prisons is extensive and entangled. The prison is again—as it has been throughout U.S. history—a site where profit, not justice, is at the center.

Profiteering from Prison: Interests against Privatization

Like its predecessors—slavery, the plantation prisons, the convict lease system, and the chain gang—the prison-industrial complex is a joint venture between governmental agencies and the private sector. The private for-profit prison is the most blatant manifestation of a profit motive that pervades the operation of nearly all prisons and jails. Although crime control and corrections are the ruse, the bottom line is profit, and profit is obtained at the expense of a captive labor pool that is disproportionately poor and disproportionately people of color. As before, such arrangements represent a threat to the economic interests of small businesses and workers who cannot compete with neo-slave prison wages and the resulting cheap products. And, as always, the partnership of profit and prison produces and reproduces a situation of criminal injustice, where civil rights and human rights are sacrificed to the bottom line.

The proliferation of prisons and privatization has not been without resistance from many fronts. There has been consistent opposition to the profit motive in imprisonment and the policies designed to ensure mass incarceration from labor interest and human/civil rights organizations such as the American Federation of State, County and Municipal Employees (AFSCME), the Sentencing Project, the Prison Moratorium Project, Critical Resistance, Families Against Mandatory Minimum Sentencing, Amnesty International, Human Rights Watch, Grassroots Leadership, and the Prison Activist Resource Center. These groups have opposed the expansion of privatization on multiple grounds, including corporate domination, political collusion, and human and civil rights violations.

Corporate Domination: Jobs and Economic Interests

Prison labor provides huge profits for a range of private interests: private prison corporations, private contractors, state correctional industry agencies, foreign correctional industry agencies, city and county jail industry programs, and the Federal Prison Industries Program (known as UNICOR). Profits total in the hundreds of billions of dollars (*Business Wire* 2010). The list of private companies profiting from inmate labor contains the cream of U.S. corporate society: AT&T Wireless, Boeing, Compaq, Dell, Hewlett-Packard, Honeywell, IBM, Intel, Levy, Lucent Technologies, Macy's, Microsoft, Motorola, Nordstrom's, Nortel, Northern Telecom, Pierre Cardin, Revlon, Starbucks, Target Stores, Texas Instrument, 3Com, TWA, Victoria's Secret, and more (Nyasha 2007b). In addition, prison labor is the major supplier for the U.S. military, ranking among the top 50 suppliers for the army alone (Nyasha 2007b). According to Nyasha (2007b),

the federal prison industry produces 100% of all military helmets, ammunition belts, bullet-proof vests, ID tags, shirts, pants, tents, bags, and canteens. Along with war supplies, prison workers supply 98% of the entire market for equipment assembly services, 93% of paints and paint-brushes, 92% of stove assembly, 46% of body armor, 36% of home appliances, 30% of headphones/microphones/speakers, and 21% of office furniture, airplane parts, medical supplies, and much more. Prisoners are even raising seeing-eye dogs for blind people. By 2007, the overall sales figures and profits for federal and state prison industries had skyrocketed into the billions. Apparently, the military industrial complex and the prison industrial complex (PIC) have joined forces.

In addition to the profits from inmate labor, vast corporate profits are generated from the provision of prison services. These include food service (Sodexho is the largest provider); phone service; privatized health care and treatment provided by managed care corporations, such as Prison Health Services and Correctional Medical Services; and even conservative Christian religious programming from the likes of Corrections Concepts, Inc., Prison Fellowship Ministries, Glorystar Satellite Systems, and Trinity Broadcasting Network (Nyasha 2007b; Price 2006).

The loosening of restrictions on private profit from prison labor also paved the way for the rise of the private prison corporations in the 1980s. The two largest private prison corporations in the United States, GEO (formerly Wackenhut) and CCA, are multinational corporations. Both are top performers on the New York Stock Exchange and boast of investors such as Chevrolet, Exxon, Ford, General Motors, Hewlett-Packard, Texaco, UPS, Verizon, and Wal-Mart (Nyasha 2007b). CCA has an annual revenue of $1.7 billion, and in 2010, the GEO Group completed a $730 million merger with Cornell Companies that created joint revenues of approximately $1.5 billion (*Business Wire* 2010). These for-profit giants manage private prisons, state and federal prisons, and detention centers for the Bureau of Prisons and Immigration and Customs Enforcement (ICE); they also provide prison services in at least 13 states and several foreign countries, including Australia, Canada, South Africa, and the United Kingdom.

Under the Justice Assistance Act of 1979, Congress authorized the federal PIECP to certify that local or state prison industry programs meet all the necessary requirements to be exempt from federal restrictions on prisoner-made goods in interstate commerce. The Crime Control Act of 1990 (P.L. 101-647) authorized the program to continue indefinitely. Currently, 37 state and

4 county-based certified correctional industry programs operate in the United States, and these programs manage at least 175 business partnerships with private industry (Bureau of Justice Assistance 2010).

According to the Bureau of Justice Assistance, the legislative intent of the PIECP was to develop a partnership between prison industries and corporations to provide employment opportunity to prison inmates via vocational training that would presumably increase prisoners' potential to secure meaningful employment upon release. In reality, PIECP has done little for prisoners. The program has enabled prisons to partner with private firms to market products on a wider scale. Participating industries must comply with federal regulation that state inmates must be paid the prevailing local minimum wage for similar work and receive worker's compensation. In reality, about 80 percent of this money—in the hundreds of millions—goes to costs for keeping the prisoner, victim restitution, and help for victims' families (Bureau of Justice Assistance 2010).

In order to protect small businesses and ostensibly inmates, Congress included nine mandatory criteria for participants to abide by if they wished to participate in the PIECP (Bureau of Justice Assistance 2010). These mandatory requirements included stipulations that were designed to protect small businesses from unfair competition, to ensure that inmates were paid prevailing wages, and to ensure that programs were initiated only after consultation with both labor unions and private businesses.

Despite the presence of these regulations, conflict of interest in their oversight has rendered them ineffective and largely unenforced. As of 1995, the Department of Justice's Bureau of Justice Assistance outsourced to the National Correctional Industries Association (NCIA) the responsibility for auditing and certifying compliance, applications, reviews, and noncompliance investigations in accordance with several mandatory criteria/requirements Congress introduced (Price 2006). The NCIA, however, is doing much more than just auditing and certifying program participants for compliance with program requirements. As the organization's website states:

> National Correctional Industries Association is an international nonprofit professional association whose members represent all 50 state correctional industry agencies, Federal Prison Industries, foreign correctional industry agencies and city/county jail industry programs. Private sector companies that work in partnership with correctional

industries both as suppliers/vendors and as partners in apprenticeship and work programs are also members.... In addition, NCIA administers the Training and Technical Assistance Project of the Privat Sector/ Prison Industry Enhancement Certification Program (PIECP) for the U.S. Department of Justice, Bureau of Justice Assistance. Activities under the PIECP grant program include: conducting reviews of PIECP programs and cost accounting center; providing technical support to PIECP applicants and programs via electronic means and our website. (NCIA 2010)

Because NCIA now regulates the very programs that its members profit from, it is no surprise that watchdogs have uncovered a long list of ongoing PIECP violations. The program violations website (http://www.piecp-viola tions.com/) frequently reports the PIECP violations of the mandatory criteria for participants (Sloan 2010). Following is a list of violations documented as of April 2010:

- Failing to consult with local labor unions and groups or with private industry before establishing the program; this oversight resulted in the closure of other private sector businesses and the termination of private sector employees.

- Failing to pay prevailing wages to inmate workers.

- Avoiding PIECP requirements by using subassembly parts to avoid paying the state's minimum hourly wage and, instead, paying standard prison industry wages of between 20 and 50 cents per hour.

- Failing to identify PIECP-participating industries to the Bureau of Justice Assistance, which has contributed to the inability to track, evaluate, and review procedures at participating prison industries.

- Failing to identify industry orders as PIECP by arguing that the private sector is not required to pay PIE wages to inmates when the products are being shipped to customers within the state.

Of course, these violations allow investors in inmate labor to maximize profit, particularly by suppressing inmate wages. Cheap inmate labor, as low as 21 cents per hour, produces everything from blue jeans to auto parts, electronics and toys, computer circuit boards, and packaged plastic eating utensils for fast-food restaurants (Nyasha 2007b). The result has been a situation that unfairly hinders the ability of small businesses to compete with cheaply produced prison products and has undercut labor. Union opposition to privatization is based not only on claims of unfair wage competition but also on the failure of privatization to create the promised quality jobs in private prisons. AFSCME Corrections United, a union that represents prison guards, is opposed to privatization because private prisons have not hired qualified and unionized correctional officers. Corrections officers are paid substantially less in private facilities, and as AFSCME (2006, 8) notes, "[t]he poor pay undoubtedly contributes to the high turnover that exists in private prisons, a whopping 52.2 percent, compared to 16 percent in publicly run prisons." This trend, as will be discussed later, also hampers safety and security for inmates and staff.

Corporate Domination and Undue Political Influence

The trend toward privatization is also opposed by those who resist corporate domination of the political process. ALEC is at the center of this debate and has been a major force behind legislation that ensures the steady supply of inmates. ALEC represents many conservative political interests, and representatives of CCA and the GEO Group have served as board members. According to Hodai (2010), a

> 501(c)(3) nonprofit organization, ALEC bills itself as "the nation's largest bipartisan, individual membership association of state legislators" and as a public-private legislative partnership. As such, ALEC claims as members more than 2,000 state lawmakers (one-third of the nation's total legislators) and more than 200 corporations and special-interest groups.
>
> The organization's current corporate roster includes the Corrections Corporation of America (CCA, the nation's largest private jailer), the Geo Group (the nation's second largest private jailer), Sodexho Marriott (the nation's leading food services provider to private correctional institutions), the Koch Foundation, Exxon Mobil, Blue Cross and Blue Shield, Boeing, Wal-Mart and Rupert Murdoch's News Corporation, to name just a few.

ALEC has several task forces whose role is to design model legislation—this in spite of a ban on nonprofits engaging in legislative activity.

The Criminal Justice Task Force, in particular, has played a key role in promoting legislation that guarantees increased incarceration and lengthy sentences. In the early 1990s, ALEC's Criminal Justice Task Force was cochaired by an employee of CCA. During those years, the National Rifle Association, which also had a member on the task force, initiated a campaign to introduce two pieces of ALEC-inspired legislation at the state and federal level: the truth-in-sentencing and three-strikes laws. Truth in sentencing called for all violent offenders to serve 85 percent of their sentences before being eligible for release. Three strikes called for mandatory life imprisonment for a third felony conviction. Most recently, ALEC has been a strong supporter of Arizona's controversial anti-immigrant legislation (SB 1070), which is designed to increase incarceration of (and thus profits from) those with insufficient documentation (Hodai 2010). The connections between ALEC and industry interests demonstrate how legislation is crafted to enrich key players in the prison-industrial complex. As AFSCME (2006, 5) observes, this contributes to injustice: "Privatizing the corrections system creates perverse incentives. Since companies are paid on a per diem basis, there are incentives for private operators to increase inmates' sentences and offer fewer services to reduce recidivism." Laws enacted by these groups are partly responsible for the massive increase in incarceration rates nationwide—while crime rates are down across the board. They have also modeled legislation that furthers the tendency toward prison privatization (Price 2006).

Civil Rights Violations

Profit from prisons and the privatization of many aspects of incarceration have resulted in a perversion of the purposes of prisons: punishment is no longer designed to fit the crime and the role of prisons to "correct" the offender is lost. Rather, the purpose is to ensure a steady supply of labor. As Donzinger (1996, 87) aptly notes,

> Companies that service the criminal justice system need sufficient quantities of raw materials to guarantee long-term growth in the criminal justice field, the raw material is prisoners.... The industry will do what it must to guarantee a steady supply. For the supply of prisoners to grow, criminal justice policies must insure a sufficient number of

incarcerated Americans whether crime is rising or the incarceration is necessary.

The rise of the prison-industrial complex and privatization then is associated with a range of policies that have little to do with justice and everything to do with ever-escalating incarceration rates. These policies are designed to ensure this steady supply of inmates. They include enhanced police presence in poor neighborhoods and communities of color, racial profiling, decreased funding for public education combined with zero-tolerance policies and increased rates of expulsion for students of color, increased rates of adult certification for juvenile offenders, mandatory minimum and three-strikes sentencing, draconian conditions of incarceration, a reduction in the type of prison services that contribute to the prevention of recidivism, and collateral consequences that nearly guarantee continued participation in crime and a return to the prison-industrial complex after initial release; all of these are designed to ensnare both new and repeat offenders back into the pool of profitable prison labor (Brewer and Heitzeg 2008; Heitzeg 2009).

The dramatic escalation of the U.S. prison population can be traced almost exclusively to the war on drugs and the rise of lengthy mandatory minimum prison sentences for drug crimes and other nonviolent felonies. On average, nonviolent offenders now make up more than 70 percent of the U.S. prison population. Nonviolent offenders, who were once supervised in the community via probation, are now imprisoned for lengthy terms, despite evidence that prison is the most expensive and least effective approach for reducing recidivism (Davis 2003).

Punitive policies extend beyond prison time served. In addition to the direct impact of mass criminalization and incarceration, there is a plethora of what Mauer and Chesney-Lind (2002) refer to as "invisible punishments." These additional collateral consequences further decimate communities of color politically, economically, and socially. The current expansion of criminalization and mass incarceration is accompanied by legislation that further limits the political and economic opportunities of convicted felons and former inmates. Collateral consequences are now attached to many felony convictions and include voter disenfranchisement; denial of federal welfare, medical, housing, or educational benefits; accelerated timelines for loss of parental rights; and exclusion from any number of employment opportunities. Collateral consequences are particularly harsh for drug felons, who represent the bulk of the recently incarcerated. Drug felons are permanently barred from receiving public assistance such as Temporary Assistance for Needy Families, Medicaid, food stamps, Supplemental Security Income, federal financial aid for education, and federal housing assistance. These policies dramatically reduce the successful reintegration of former inmates and increase the likelihood of recidivism and return to prison.

A similarly repressive trend has emerged in the juvenile justice system, which has shifted sharply from its original rehabilitative, therapeutic, and reform goals. Recent changes have turned the juvenile justice system into a "second-class criminal court that provides youth with neither therapy nor justice" (Feld 2007). Throughout the 1990s, nearly all states and the federal government enacted a series of legislation that criminalized a host of what were termed "gang-related activities," made it easier (and in some cases mandatory) to try juveniles as adults, lowered the age at which juveniles could be referred to adult court, and widened the net of juvenile justice with blended sentencing options that included sentences in both the juvenile and adult systems (Heitzeg 2008; Podkopacz and Feld 2001; Walker, Spohn, and DeLone 2012). The superpredator youth and rampant media coverage of youth violence provided the alleged justification for this legislation and for additional federal legislation such as the Consequences for Juvenile Offenders Act of 2002 (first proposed in 1996) and the Gun-Free Schools Act of 1994, which provides the impetus for zero-tolerance policies in schools and the school-to-prison pipeline (Advancement Project 2005; CDF 2007; NAACP 2005). The school-to-prison pipeline is a consequence of schools that criminalize minor disciplinary infractions via zero-tolerance policies, have a police presence at the school, and rely on suspensions and expulsions for minor infractions. What were once disciplinary issues for school administrators are now called crimes, and students are either arrested directly at school or their infractions are reported to the police. Students are criminalized via the juvenile and/or adult criminal justice systems. The risk of later incarceration for students who are suspended or expelled and arrested is also great. For many, going to school has become literally and figuratively synonymous with going to jail. Future generations are being prepared not for college or careers but, instead, for prison.

Beyond the sheer numbers of those imprisoned, the question of race, class, and gender disparity in incarceration rates looms. Unsurprisingly, mandatory minimums for drug violations, three-strikes laws, increased use of imprisonment as a sentencing option, lengthy prison terms, adult certification for juveniles, and the school-to-prison pipeline all disproportionately affect the poor and people of color. Quigley (2010) notes that "the biggest crime in the U.S. criminal justice system is that it is a race-based institution where African-Americans are directly targeted and punished in a much more aggressive way than white people." Indeed, this has been the history of the U.S. criminal justice system from the outset; the poor, and especially people of color, have been disproportionately policed, prosecuted, convicted, disenfranchised, imprisoned, and executed. Davis (2003, 95) traces the historical links between current practices and the policies that emerged during the post–Civil War era, noting that vast amounts of black labor

> became increasingly available for use by private agents precisely through the convict lease system . . . and related systems such as debt peonage. . . . This transition set the historical stage for the easy acceptance of disproportionately black prison populations today. . . . The racial composition of the incarcerated population is approaching the proportion of black prisoners to white during the era of the southern convict lease and country chain gang systems. Whether this human raw material is used for purposes of labor or for the consumption of commodities provided by a rising number of corporations directly implicated in the prison industrial complex, it is clear that black bodies are considered dispensable within the "free world" but as a source of profit in the prison world.

Despite no statistical differences in rates of offending, the poor, the undereducated, and people of color, particularly African Americans, are overrepresented in these statistics at every phase of the criminal justice system. African Americans, who are 13 percent of the population and 14 percent of drug users, represent 37 percent of the people arrested for drug offenses and 56 percent of the people in state prisons for drug offenses (Mauer 2009). Approximately 50 percent of all prisoners are black, 30 percent are white, and 17 percent are Latino, and the incarceration rate for black women is increasing at the most rapid pace. Although 1 of every 35 adults is under correctional supervision and 1 of every 100 adults is in prison, 1 of every 36 Latino adults, 1 of every 15 black men, 1 of every 100 black women, and 1 of every 9 black men ages 20 to 34 are incarcerated (Pew Center on the States 2008).

The racial disparities are even greater for youth. African Americans, while representing 17 percent of the youth population, account for 45 percent of all juvenile arrests. Again, despite no differences in rates of offending, black youth are two times more likely than white youth to be arrested, to be referred to juvenile court, to be formally processed and adjudicated as delinquent, or to be referred to the adult criminal justice system. They are also three times more likely than white youth to be sentenced to out-of-home residential placement. Nationally, one in three black boys and one in six Latino boys born in 2001 are at risk of imprisonment during their lifetime (Walker, Spohn, and DeLone 2012). Although boys are five times as likely to be incarcerated as girls, girls are at increasing risk. This rate of incarceration is endangering children at younger and younger ages via the school-to-prison pipeline (Heitzeg 2009; NAACP 2005).

The connection between the profit motive and prison has always been linked to the denial of civil rights. Unduly harsh sentences for nonviolent offenses are an injustice, but in all aspects of criminal justice, particularly imprisonment, disparities by class and race are more severe. The parallels have not been lost on observers. Alexander (2009, 15) describes current criminal justice policies as the "New Jim Crow":

> I came to see that mass incarceration in the United States had, in fact, emerged as a stunningly comprehensive and well-disguised system of racialized social control that functions in a manner strikingly similar to Jim Crow.
>
> In my experience, people who have been incarcerated rarely have difficulty identifying the parallels between these systems of social control. Once they are released, they are often denied the right to vote, excluded from juries, and relegated to a racially segregated and subordinated existence.
>
> Through a web of laws, regulations, and informal rules, all of which are powerfully reinforced by social stigma, they are confined to the margins of mainstream society and denied access to the mainstream economy. They are legally denied the ability to obtain employment, housing, and public benefits—much as African Americans were once forced into a segregated, second-class citizenship in the Jim Crow era.

Human Rights Violations

Prison for profit translates into inhumane treatment and denial of basic human rights. These violations range from denial of medical care, religious freedom, and educational services to brutal conditions of confinement resulting from overcrowding, the warehousing of the mentally ill, and the dehumanization of inmates. Conditions in U.S. prisons rise to the level of torture, and these practices are magnified by the profit motive (Amnesty International 1998; Davies 2005; HRW 2000, 2003; Nyasha 2007a; Shelden 2005c).

Amnesty International and Human Rights Watch have documented decades-old patterns of human and civil rights abuses by local and federal police and law enforcement officers as well as prison, jail, and ICE detention officials. These abuses are exacerbated by the profit motive (AFSCME 2006; Gainsborough 2003; Gorman 2010). These include a variety of abusive police and correctional officer practices (e.g., racial profiling; excessive use of force, including kicking and beatings of restrained suspects with fists, batons, and flashlights; excessive use of dangerous chokeholds, hog-ties, and other restraints that have resulted in death; excessive use of tasers and chemical sprays; excessive use of deadly force; inappropriate use of strip searches; and use of sexual abuse and torture) and prison procedures (e.g., dangerous use of restraints, including four-point restraints, the rail, and the restraint chair, which have resulted in multiple deaths; the shackling of pregnant inmates; use of nudity, strip searches, and sexual humiliation and assault as a source of social control; failure to curtail sexual assaults on both male and female inmates by other inmates and guards; beatings by guards; denial of medical care or treatment; use of dogs, tasers, and chemical sprays; excessive use of supermax and isolation confinement; and denial of rights on religious freedom, communications, and right to counsel) (Amnesty International 1998; Davies 2005; HRW 2000, 2003; Nyasha 2007a; Shelden 2005c).

International nonprofit human rights organizations have consistently claimed that these U.S. police and prison practices violate several international treaties and protocols, including, but not limited to, the Geneva Convention, the International Covenant on Civil and Political Rights, the Convention against Torture, the International Convention on the Elimination of all Forms of Racial Discrimination, the United Nations (UN)

Universal Declaration of Human Rights, the UN Body of Principles for the Protection of All Persons Under Any Form of Detention, the UN Standard Minimum Rules for the Treatment of Prisoners, the UN Code of Conduct for Law Enforcement Officials, and the UN Basic Principles on the Use of Force and Firearms by Law Enforcement Officials (Nyasha 2007a; Shelden 2005b).

Private prisons and privately provided prison health care have the worst records. Prison Health Services and Correctional Medical Services provide services to a variety of facilities in 41 states. Despite years of lawsuits; investigative reports exposing horrific problems in South Carolina, New York, Texas, Vermont, and other states; and an occasional lost contract, these companies continue to flourish (Allen 2009). CCA's more than 20-year history has been marred by a series of lawsuits and investigations regarding wrongful deaths and staff-on-inmate violence (Gainsborough 2003); complaints have ranged from rapes to staff-on-inmate assaults, suicides, and deaths due to lack of medical care. In a recent investigative report, Gorman (2010) examines recent scandals in GEO-run prisons and detention centers in Texas and, among other GEO violations, notes this:

> The Reeves County complex is touted as the largest private prison in the world. A little over a year ago it was the site of two major riots, the second of which burned large areas of the complex. The inmates who did it were not killers or hardened criminals. Most were immigrants whose only crime was illegally re-entering the United States after having been deported. And they and their families said they were rioting because of medical care so poor that some of them were dying from it. . . . Since 2008, five inmates have died there—three from inadequate medical care, according to the inmates, and two allegedly by suicide.

The story is repeated nationwide in Florida, Arizona, California, and Mississippi, where prison services are privatized. Safety and security for inmates and staff also suffer as corners are cut. Inmate-to-staff ratios in private prisons are higher, as are violent incidents. The following examples are illustrative (AFSCME 2006, 6):

> [P]rivate prisons had 50 percent more inmate-on-staff assaults and two-thirds more inmate-on-inmate assaults. In just a year's time, four

inmates and a private prison guard were killed in the GEO Group's two New Mexico prisons. In a little over a year, 20 inmates were stabbed and two were murdered at a CCA facility in Youngstown, Ohio. And the GEO Group closed one of its juvenile facilities after the U.S. Department of Justice said that the facility's conditions were "life-threatening." In 2004, Colorado spent an estimated $386,000 quelling a major riot at the CCA-operated Crowley County Correctional Facility. A DOC [Department of Corrections] investigation found that CCA chronically understaffed the facility and the private prison guards were inadequately trained and ill-equipped to prevent the riot or regain order. CCA had a staffing ratio of 34 inmates per officer compared to a ratio of five inmates per officer in state-operated prisons. CCA prison guards made about two-thirds that of state corrections officers—$1,818 per month, compared with $2,774 per month—and CCA's staff turnover was about twice the rate as in state prisons. During the riot, inmates were severely beaten, cells were ransacked and set on fire, and a female librarian was trapped with dozens of convicts.

Inmates are now as expendable as they were in the era of convict lease labor, and underpaid, undertrained staff fare little better. Inmates are in prison for one purpose now—and that purpose is profit. To the extent the costs of humane treatment threaten the profit margin, basic human rights will be denied.

Conclusion

Although profitable for some, the nation's experiment in mass incarceration is a costly one; it proceeds at the expense of taxpayers, social programs, entire communities, and current and future generations—and it proceeds at the expense of the lives of the millions lost to its vast machinery. Imprisonment costs an average of $25,000 per inmate per year, and the costs sometimes approach $50,000 per year (Bureau of Justice Statistics 2009). Local, state, and federal governments expend nearly $150 billion per year on corrections. Comparatively, community correctional options such as probation have one-third of the costs and twice the success rate, as measured by rearrests within a 12-month period (Bureau of Justice Statistics 2010).

The proliferation of prisons and privatization has not been without resistance from labor and human rights vantage points. Organizations such as AFSCME, the Sentencing Project, the Prison Moratorium Project, Critical Resistance, Families Against Mandatory Minimum Sentencing, Amnesty International, Human Rights Watch, Grassroots Leadership, and the Prison Activist Resource Center have successfully linked a large and growing body of research with a critique of current practices and a call for legislative and policy change. Additionally, as states face fiscal crises on many fronts, high correctional costs and discussions of alternatives to prison have reemerged in public discourse. For the first time in 40 years, state prison populations overall have experienced a slight decline, and the U.S. prison population increased only slightly because of additional federal inmates. Costs and budget challenges are cited as the major impetus behind rethinking ever-escalating incarceration rates (Pew Center on the States 2010). As expected, CCA and GEO are ready too and have plans to expand their services into halfway houses, additional youth prisons, drug treatment programs, housing, or job placement programs that help prisoners reenter society (Cook 2010). When clients fail to reintegrate as a result of inadequate services, these companies are prepared to triple profit as the revolving door returns the recidivists right back to prison.

Profit, crime, and punishment are inextricably linked here. The historical trajectory from slavery to slavery by another name with a new plantation and a new Jim Crow reveals a deep race and class dynamic. The prison—in fact the entire criminal justice system—cannot be disentangled from its foundations in profiteering from captive labor, mostly poor and disproportionately black, in a cycle that repeats perpetually. Although organized labor has long opposed private prisons on more narrow economic grounds, interests against private prisons are ultimately interests against the prison itself, and against the racist and classist underpinnings that make the prison possible. As Davis (1998, 105) points out:

> We must give serious consideration to abolitionist strategies to dismantle the prison system . . . which preserves existing structures of racism as well as creates new ones . . . this is no more outlandish than the fact that race and economic status play more prominent roles in shaping the practices of social punishment than does crime.

Perhaps reform is finally insufficient, and now, as in the face of slavery and Jim Crow, the renewed call must be for abolition.

References

Advancement Project. 2005. *Education on Lockdown: The School to Jail-house Track,* Washington, DC: Advancement Project.

Alexander, Michelle. 2009. *The New Jim Crow: Mass Incarceration in the Age of Colorblindness.* New York: New Press.

Allen, Terry J. 2009. "Death by Privatization: For-profit Prison Healthcare System Implicated in Death of Inmate." *In These Times,* December 8.

American Federation of State, County and Municipal Employees (AFSCME) Corrections United. 2006. *Prison Privatization: Don't Be a Prisoner to Empty Promises.* Washington, DC: AFSCME.

Amnesty International. 1998. *United States of America: Rights for All.* London: Amnesty International Publications.

Blackmon, Douglas. 2008. *Slavery by Another Name: The Re-Enslavement of Black People in America from the Civil War to World War II.* New York: Doubleday.

Brewer, Rose M., and Nancy A. Heitzeg. 2008. "The Racialization of Crime and Punishment: Criminal Justice, Color-Blind Racism and the Political Economy of the Prison Industrial Complex." *American Behavioral Scientist* 51:45–65.

Bureau of Justice Assistance. 2010. Prison Industry Enhancement Certification Program (PIECP). http://www.ojp.usdoj.gov/BJA/grant/piecp.html.

Bureau of Justice Statistics. 2009. Prison Statistics. http://www.ojp.usdoj.gov/bjs/prisons.htm.

Bureau of Justice Statistics. 2010. Annual Probation Survey. http://bjs.ojp.usdoj.gov/content/pub/pdf/cj8_08.pdf.

Business Wire. 2010. "The GEO Group and Cornell Companies Announce $685 Million Merger." April 24. http://www.businesswire.com/news/home/20100419006086/en/GEO-Group-Cornell-Companies-Announce-685-Million.

Children's Defense Fund (CDF). 2007. *America's Cradle to Prison Pipeline.* Washington, DC: CDF.

Cook, Nancy. 2010. "How the Recession Hurts Private Prisons." *Newsweek,* June 30.

Davies, Deborah. 2005. "Torture Inc. America's Brutal Prisons." March 28. BBC.co.uk.

Davis, Angela. 1998. "Racialized Punishment and Prison Abolition." In *The Angela Y. Davis Reader*, edited by J. James, 96–110. New York: Blackwell.

Davis, Angela. 2003. *Are Prisons Obsolete?* New York: Seven Stories Press.

Donzinger, S. 1996. *The Real War on Crime: Report of the National Criminal Justice Commission*. New York: Perennial.

Feld, Barry C. 2007. "Juvenile Justice in Minnesota: Framework for the Future." In *Justice Where Art Thou?* Minneapolis, MN: Council on Crime and Justice. http://www.crimeandjustice.org/researchReports/FINAL%20 REPORT%2010.4.07.pdf.

Gainsborough, Jenni. 2003. "The Truth about Private Prisons" *Alternet*, December 15. http://www.alternet.org/story/17392/.

Gorman, Peter. 2010. "Private Prisons, Public Pain: Despite a Long Record of Abuses, GEO Is Still Running Texas Prisons." *Fort Worth Weekly*, March 10. http://www.fwweekly.com/index.php?option=com_content &view=article&id=2897%3Aprivate-prisons-public-pain&catid=30%3 Acover-story&Itemid=375.

Hallett, M. 2005. *Private Prisons in America: A Critical Race Perspective.* Champaign: University of Illinois Press.

Heitzeg, Nancy A. 2008. "Race, Class and Legal Risk in the United States: Youth of Color and Colluding Systems of Social Control." *Forum on Public Policy*, Summer. http://forumonpublicpolicy.com/summer08papers/ migdivsum08.html.

Heitzeg, Nancy A. 2009. "Education or Incarceration: Zero Tolerance Policies and the School to Prison Pipeline." *Forum on Public Policy*, Summer. http://forumonpublicpolicy.com/summer09/issuesineducation.html.

Hodai, Beau. 2010. "Corporate Con Game: How the Private Prison Industry Helped Shape Arizona's Anti-immigrant Law." *In These Times*, June 21. http://www.inthesetimes.com/article/6084/corporate_con_game/.

Human Rights Watch (HRW). 2000. *Out of Sight: Super-Maximum Security Confinement in the United States*. New York: HRW.

Human Rights Watch (HRW). 2003. *Ill-Equipped: U.S. Prisons and Offenders in the United States*. New York: HRW.

Mauer, Marc. 2009. *The Changing Racial Dynamic of the War on Drugs.* Washington, DC: Sentencing Project. http://www.sentencingproject.org/ doc/dp_raceanddrugs.pdf.

Mauer, M., and M., Chesney-Lind, eds. 2002. *Invisible Punishment: The Collateral Consequences of Mass Imprisonment.* NY: New Press.

NAACP. 2005. *Interrupting the School to Prison Pipeline.* Washington, DC: NAACP.

National Correctional Industries Association (NCIA). 2010. "Who We Are." http://www.nationalcia.org.

Nyasha, Kiilu. 2007a. "American Torture Chambers: A Report on Today's Prisons and Jails Part I." *Black Commentator*, February 1. http://black commentator.com/215/215_american_torture_chambers_prisons_nyasha .html.

Nyasha, Kiilu. 2007b. "Slavery on the New Plantation: A Report on Today's Prisons and Jails Part I." *Black Commentator*, February 15. http:// blackcommentator.com/217/217_american_torture_chambers_prisons_2_ nyasha.html

Pew Center on the States. 2008. *One in 100: Behind Bars in America 2008.* Washington, DC: Pew Center on the States.

Pew Center on the States. 2010. *Prison Count 2010.* Washington, DC: Pew Center on the States.

Podkopacz, Marcy Rasmussen, and Barry C. Feld. 2001. "The Back-Door to Prison: Waiver Reform, Blended Sentencing, and the Law of Unintended Consequences." *Journal of Criminal Law and Criminology* 91: 997–1072.

Price, Byron. 2006. *Merchandizing Prisoners: Who Really Pays for Prison Privatization?* Santa Barbara, CA: Greenwood.

Quigley, Bill. 2010. "Fourteen Examples of Racism in the Criminal Justice System." *Huffington Post*, July 26. http://www.huffingtonpost.com/ bill-quigley/fourteen-examples-of-raci_b_658947.html.

Sellin, Thorsten. 1975. *Slavery and the Penal System.* New York: Elsevier.

Shelden, Randall. 2005a. "Slavery in the Third Millenium Part I." *Black Commentator*, June 9. http://www.blackcommentator.com/141/141_ slavery_1.html.

Shelden, Randall. 2005b. "Slavery in the Third Millenium Part II." *Black Commentator*, June 16. http://blackcommentator.com/142/142_slavery_ 2.html.

Shelden, Randall. 2005c. "Slavery in the Third Millenium Part III." *Black Commentator*, June 23. http://www.blackcommentator.com/143/143_ slavery_3.html.

Silverstein, K. 1997. "America's Private Gulag." *Prison Legal News*, June.

Sloan, Bob. 2010. *PIECP Program Violations Web Site.* http://www
.piecp-violations.com/index.html.

Walker, S., C. Spohn, and M. DeLone. 2012. *The Color of Justice: Race,
Ethnicity and Crime In America*. 5th ed. Belmont, CA: Wadsworth.

3

Privatized Prisons and Indemnification: A Revisit to *Richardson v. McKnight*

Trina M. Gordon and Anitra D. Shelton-Quinn

In an age where the number of private prisons has grown steadily since the 1980s, private prison officials have been looking for ways to maintain their private status, yet still obtain state and government privileges when convenient for them. One such area where for-profit prisons are seeking privilege is on the issue of indemnification. Indemnification is a legal exemption from penalty and liability for perceived wrongdoing. There are governmental provisions for qualified immunity from prosecution for federal and state correctional officers and prison staff. Qualified immunity, as defined by *Harlow v. Fitzgerald* (1982), refers to the protection of government officials from the liability of civil damages brought forth by a plaintiff, providing the official's actions did not violate statutory or constitutional rights of which a reasonable person would have known.

From a public policy stance, one would ask the question: Should courts and public policy allow private prisons to have the same qualified immunity if they are working as an agent of the government? Legal scholars have debated this issue of qualified immunity (indemnification) for private prisons over the past 13 years since the Supreme Court decided *Richardson v. McKnight* (1997). According to the court, correctional officers employed by for-profit prisons are not entitled to qualified immunity, although they may be under contract with a state or federal government agency. This chapter will present a brief history of private prisons, the history and purpose of indemnification for government and state agents, the case law regarding indemnification issues and private prisons, and an overview of public policy issues to consider when discussing private prisons and indemnification.

History of Private Prisons and the United States

The debate since the incorporation of private entities in the correctional system has always centered on the economy and economic necessity. To help understand the debate, one must understand the dynamics of political policies and Reaganomics during the 1980s. During the 1980s, President Ronald Reagan was a strong believer in less government. He declared that too much government was the problem, and his goal was to outsource and privatize as many government functions as possible, including privatizing prisons and correctional facilities (Selman and Leighton 2010).

State and federal prison populations more than quadrupled between 1980 and 2008, going from approximately 320,000 inmates to more than 1.5 million inmates (Selman and Leighton 2010). The rise in the inmate population can be attributed to the relentless "tough on crime" initiatives that led to an increase in harsher penalties and punishments for crimes that were once seen as minimal. The war on drugs also helped contribute to the inmate population due to harsher sanctions for drug crimes. The increases in inmates eventually led to overcrowding. Thus, inmates began filing lawsuits against the prisons claiming that their Eighth Amendment right against cruel and unusual punishment was being violated. Faced with the economic realities and shrinking state and federal budgets, policy makers began looking for new and innovative ways to handle the growing inmate population; thus, modern-day prison privatization was born (Price 2006).

The pressures of increased prison and jail populations and rising inmate costs encouraged the reintroduction of privatization to correctional institutions. As time continued, the "follow the money" trend tended to encourage the increase of private prison expansion (Selman and Leighton 2010). As a result, the government believed it was their duty to control for overcrowding and increasing correctional costs by outsourcing inmates to private prisons. Although private prison operators are not responsible for the incarceration binge, they contributed to the binge by supporting legislation that enforces tough-on-crime initiatives and by making promises to state and government officials touting the cost-effectiveness of private prisons through reductions in overhead costs and improvements in quality and management of prisons (DelFiandra 2000, 593).

The private prison industry is one of the fastest growing industries in the United States (Selman and Leighton 2010). Because of the expansion of prison privatization, the United States currently has the highest rate of incarceration in the world, with approximately 2.3 million inmates (West and Sabol 2009). Thirteen American companies are currently managing private correctional facilities for adults in the United States, and 31 states have incorporated the use of private prison entities (Zito 2003). Approximately 7 percent of all U.S. inmates are housed in private correctional institutions (West and Sabol 2009).

Prison privatization has a long-standing history in the United States, and it has undergone numerous changes in the face of economic realities. In all likelihood, prison privatization will continue to be viewed as a viable solution to prison overcrowding and shrinking state and federal budgets. Research on the benefits of prison privatization has been both positive and negative. Although contracting out inmates has provided fiscal relief for many states, it has not been without its problems. It is suggested that the government needs to have more accountability and a well-designed contract administration policy, along with a monitoring system to ensure quality and accountability from the contract awardees (Donahue 1989).

There is an ongoing debate regarding the degree of accountability or transparency required of governmental and state agencies; however, private agencies such as private prisons are not always held to the same standard. In 1997, Senator Joseph Lieberman, a Democrat at the time, introduced to Congress the Private Prison Accountability Act of 1997 (H.R. 1889). The Private Prison Accountability Act of 1997 required private prisons to disclose information regarding their operations to the public. The argument for the bill was that the public does not have the same type of access to information about private prisons as it does for federal prisons. Because of the large number of federal inmates being housed at private prison institutions, there is a perception of a lack of accountability regarding how taxpayer dollars are spent to house inmates in the private prison facilities. The legislation's goal with the bill was to help ensure that the public could be confident that abuse, neglect, and misconduct were not taking place in private prisons holding federal inmates. From the time the bill was introduced, it has been met with resistance from the "big three" private prison corporations: Corrections Corporation of America (CCA), the GEO Group, and Cornell Companies. In the next section, we will look at the historical background and purpose of indemnification and its relation to prisons and inmate rights.

History and Purpose of Indemnification for State and Government Prison Agents

As with most legal regulation in the United States, the issue of indemnification is derived from English law. Qualified immunity protects a select group of governmental and state employees (public and private) from potentially frivolous lawsuits being brought against them. The rationale behind qualified immunity is to protect the government and/or public official's ability to conduct their job functions effectively without the threat of litigation (*Wyatt v. Cole* 1992). However, the issue of qualified immunity also helps to strike a balance between protection of the government official and compensation protection to the injured party against any injury caused by misconduct by government officials (Carter 1998, 612). In order for a government official to claim qualified immunity, the official's actions must not violate any constitutional or statutory right for which a "reasonable" person would have known (*Harlow v. Fitzgerald* 1982, 800). Furthermore, if the official is entitled to qualified immunity, there needs to be a determination that (1) a specific right has been allegedly violated, (2) the right is clearly established, and (3) a reasonable person would believe his or her conduct was lawful (*Alexander v. City and County of San Francisco* 1994, 1363–1364).

At the onset of private prison inclusion in the criminal justice system in America, promises were made regarding their ability to maintain lower costs associated with the incarceration of inmates, thus releasing the government of any indemnification for the federal inmates in their custody. Historically, states created contracts with private prisons under the contractual assumption that the facility was fully indemnified (Price 2006, 46–47). As problems such as riots, escapes, and serious assaults began to occur at the for-profit prisons, however, the state agencies learned that, in most cases, the prisons were not fully indemnified. An illustrative example of unclear indemnification was the case in Youngstown, Ohio. In 1997, CCA contracted with the District of Columbia to take control of its inmates for the 1,500-bed, medium-security prison that was located at the Northeast Ohio

Correctional Center (NOCC) in Youngtown. At the time the prison opened, there were no Ohio state laws to regulate private prisons. In May 1997, the first 900 inmates from the District of Columbia arrived at NOCC. The contract between CCA and the District of Columbia specified that the inmates would be medium-security inmates; however, the inmates who arrived were not all considered medium security (five had been convicted of murder). In addition, CCA did not receive the requested transfer packet, and no one from CCA complained or checked the classifications for these inmates to ensure that they were truly medium-security inmates. The prison was filling at such a rapid rate that paperwork, such as medical records, did not always follow the inmates, and no one assumed responsibility for checking on paperwork. By the spring of 1998, approximately 20 inmates had been stabbed, 2 inmates had been murdered, 5 inmates had died of medical complications, and 6 had escaped. Inmates were also routinely subjected to a series of degrading strip and body cavity searches. To complicate matters, two inmates who had escaped from NOCC had done so two days after CCA told a federal judge that all dangerous inmates had been transferred to another facility (DelFiandra 2000, 594).

Because of the problems occurring at NOCC, the governor of Ohio called for the prison to be shut down, and a class action suit was filed by inmates approximately 10 weeks after the facility opened (Gerhardstein 2000, 186). Furthermore, as a result of the lawsuits and the District of Columbia's being a named defendant along with CCA and the state, the District of Columbia eventually sued CCA to force its compliance with the contract regarding indemnification for the District of Columbia (AFSCME 2010). In its suit, the District of Columbia claimed CCA refused to indemnify district officials and failed to obtain the required insurance policy naming the district as insured (AFSCME 2010).

According to the American Federation of State, County, and Municipal Employees (AFSCME 2010), there is growing evidence that for-profit prisons may be unable to obtain sufficient liability insurance. A 1999 Securities and Exchange Commission filing by Cornell Companies, a for-profit prison company, stated that it could not be properly insured because of "some unique business risks including riot and civil commotion or the acts of an escaped offender" (as cited in AFSCME 2010). Another example occurred between Hamilton County, Tennessee, and CCA in 1990. CCA signed a contract with Hamilton County that required the company to obtain a $25 million insurance policy to protect the county for any liability; however, Hamilton County learned after the contract was signed that CCA did not have the insurance policy, nor would they be able to obtain one (AFSCME 2010).

Federal Laws and Statutes Related to Indemnification and Prisons

In this section, we will discuss some key federal laws and statutes that help to build a foundation to the issue of indemnification and prisons in general. We will then move into the specific issue of private prisons and indemnification.

Fourteenth Amendment

Section 1 of the Fourteenth Amendment of the Constitution protects citizens from deprivation of life, liberty, and property without due process of the law. In addition, it says that all persons under the jurisdiction of the state are entitled to equal protections of the law. When applying these principles to inmates, it was once believed that inmates forfeited these rights as a consequence of their crimes because they were considered "slaves of the state" (*Ruffin v. Commonwealth* 1871, 790, 796). In 1948, the courts began to determine that the due process and equal protection clauses should apply to inmates to some extent (Cornell University Law School 2010). In *Cooper v. Pate* (1964), the court determined that state prisoners have constitutional rights, and they may sue state officials in federal court under section 1983.

In 1972, a more direct affirmation of the applicability of the Fourteenth Amendment's due process and equal protection clauses became apparent in the *Wolff v. McDonnell* (1974, 555–556) case, where the Supreme Court stated that "[t]here is no iron curtain drawn between the Constitution and the prisons of this county" (*Wolff v. McDonnell* 1974, 555–556). Thus, the door to inmate litigation against prison officials began to flourish under section 1983 of the United States Code.

Section 1983 of the Civil Rights Act of 1871

The threat of constitutional liability on private prisons began to take form from 42 U.S.C. §1983, one of the most influential sections of the Civil

Rights Act of 1871. The Civil Rights Act of 1871 was brought forth as a protection for black southern former slaves against their treatment by the Ku Klux Klan and against violations of their civil liberties. Section 1983 (42 U.S.C. §1983) states:

> Every person who, under color of any statute, ordinance, regulation, custom, or usage, of any State or Territory or the District of Columbia, subjects, or causes to be subjected, any citizen of the United States or other person within the jurisdiction thereof to the deprivation of any rights, privileges, or immunities secured by the Constitution and laws, shall be liable to the party injured in an action at law, suit in equity, or other proper proceeding for redress, except that in any action brought against a judicial officer for an act or omission taken in such officer's judicial capacity, injunctive relief shall not be granted unless a declaratory decree was violated or declaratory relief was unavailable. For the purposes of this section, any Act of Congress applicable exclusively to the District of Columbia shall be considered to be a statute of the District of Columbia.

The creation of section 1983 helped to enforce individual rights already incorporated into the Constitution (Morris 1999, 497). The original intent of section 1983 was to create an action against unconstitutional acts made by state officials, not federal officials. It was not until later cases during the 1960s and 1970s that section 1983 was extended to the actions of federal agents. According to Carter (1998, 611), section 1983 is a "tort-like remedy" to protect individuals from harm at the hands of government officials or anyone acting "under the color of the law" or as a "state agent" of the law. From its original inception, section 1983 was considered a "weapon against state policies" not against action of individual state actors (Carter 1998, 611). However, inmates used section 1983 more often against individual state officials than against state policies.

Two-Pronged Tests of Section 1983
In order for a claim under section 1983 to be successful, the plaintiff must prove (1) that a person subjected the plaintiff to conduct that occurred under the color of the law and (2) that the conduct deprived the plaintiff of rights, privileges, and/or immunities under federal law and the Constitution

(Morris 1999, 497). Early decisions made by the Supreme Court made forms of qualified immunity available to section 1983 defendants; however, the rationale and scope of those immunities were often unclear and inconsistent (Carter 1998, 612). As Morris (1999, 497) points out:

> Federal courts are authorized to hear cases brought under section 1983 pursuant to two statutory provisions: 28 U.S.C.A. § 1343(3) (1948) and 28 U.S.C.A. § 1331 (1948). The former statute permits federal district courts to hear cases involving the deprivation of civil rights, and the latter statute permits federal courts to hear all cases involving a federal question or issue. Cases brought under section 1983 may therefore be heard in federal courts by application of both jurisdictional statutes.

Monroe v. Pape (1961)

The Supreme Court expanded the scope of section1983 in the case of *Monroe v. Pape* (1961). In the *Monroe* case, plaintiffs alleged that 13 Chicago police officers broke into their home and engaged in an illegal search of their belongings. The plaintiffs were required to stand in the living room naked during the time of the search, and the father, Mr. Monroe, was arrested and taken to the police station for questioning about a two-day-old murder. Monroe filed suit against the City of Chicago and the police department for a violation of his, and his family's, civil rights, and argued that the officers should be held liable under section 1983. According to case records, the Chicago police officers did not have a search or arrest warrant for their actions; however, they acted under the "color of the statutes, ordinances, regulation, and customs" of the State of Illinois and the City of Chicago. In *Monroe*, the court held that section 1983 "could reach individual state officers even if their actions were not sanctioned by state police" (Morris 1999, 498).

Prisoner's Litigation Reform Act of 1997

In 1997, Congress implemented the Prisoner's Litigation Reform Act (PLRA) in an effort to decrease the number of frivolous lawsuits filed by prison inmates and limit the court's involvement in prison conditions unless constitutional rights were in question. The PLRA has two main provisions that fall under the broad categories of prospective relief and prisoner litigation provisions (42 U.S.C. § 1997e). The prospective of relief provision refers to "civil actions in regards to prison conditions" or acts of government officials that may affect the lives of those incarcerated (42 U.S.C. § 1997e). The prospective of relief provision does not include any issue regarding habeas corpus challenges to the actual confinement of an individual in a prison setting. For the purposes of the present chapter, we will focus mainly on the second broad category of PLRA: prisoner litigation. The prisoner litigation component of the PLRA applies to civil actions brought by prisoners. The act indicates that an inmate may not bring forth a legal suit against a prison or prison agents unless all administrative remedies have been exhausted (Gerhardstein 2000, 192).

The PLRA also applies to private prison inmates, as indicated in *Roles v. Maddox* (2006), which involved an inmate, Roles, who was incarcerated at the Idaho Correctional Center, operated by CCA under contract with the Idaho Department of Corrections. According to Roles, a CCA corrections officer confiscated magazines from his cell after he kept them for more than six months. Roles filed a PLRA complaint asserting that Idaho law and his constitutional rights against unlawful seizure were violated due to the confiscation of the magazines. According to Roles, the confiscation of his magazines did not fall under the umbrella of a "prison condition." The question in Roles's appeal was whether he adhered to the required exhaustion rule and prisoner grievance process outlined in the PLRA. The district court dismissed the case because Roles did not follow the correct procedures by not exhausting all administrative remedies, such as filing grievances within the prison before filing his lawsuit. Roles argued that the PLRA exhaustive rule did not apply to this situation and lawsuit because he is housed in a private prison, not a state or federal prison.

Gerhardstein (2000) questioned whether the Prison Litigation Reform Act applies to private prisons. According to Gerhardstein (2000, 192), section 802 (g)(5) of the PLRA seems to exclude private prisons based on the provision that a "prison is any federal, state, or local facility that incarcerates or detains juveniles or adults accused of, convicted of, sentenced for, or adjudicated delinquent for, violations for criminal law." There is very little documentation and few congressional findings related to PLRA claims and private prisons. It appears that before the Roles case in Idaho, there was little basis to exclude private prisons from PLRA claims, and obviously for-profit prisons are not arguing against inclusion.

Case Law and Prison Indemnification

In its decisions regarding immunity of government officials, the Supreme Court has recognized the role that some private parties have in acting as a "state actor" under the color of the law and may be subject to section 1983 liability (Carter 1998, 613). A private individual is a state actor when the state delegates that person to perform duties and functions that are "traditionally governmental in nature" (Carter 1998, 613). As the prison system moved forward in its existence and maintained custody of federal and state inmates, the Supreme Court was asked whether or not private prison officials have the same protection of liability and are immune from section 1983 claims. Legal scholars have debated this issue since the Supreme Court decision in *Richardson v. McKnight* (1997). We will address this issue of the Supreme Court's stance on extending immunity and indemnification rights to private prisons by examining case law regarding the issue of private prisons and indemnification.

Richardson et al. v. McKnight **(1997)**

The legal case of *Richardson v. McKnight* (1997) was pivotal in the applicability of section 1983 and indemnification for private prison officials. South Central Correctional Center (SCCC), a private for-profit prison facility managed by CCA, attempted to obtain qualified immunity from prosecution for two of its correctional officers, Daryll Richardson and John Walker. At the time of the lawsuit, CCA was under contract with the State of Tennessee to manage state inmates. An inmate, Ronnie McKnight, sued officers Richardson and Walker after filing a section 1983 claim that his Eighth Amendment constitutional right of freedom from cruel and unusual punishment was violated when the officers refused to loosen his restraints. According to McKnight, his restraints were "too tight for his 302 pound frame" (*McKnight v. Rees* 1996, 417–418). According to the complaint filed by McKnight, the restraints caused him serious medical injury, and he was hospitalized for impaired circulation and swelling in his hands and feet. In addition, McKnight asserted that the officers ignored his complaint and taunted him as he asked for the restraints to be loosened to ease the pain (Gillette and Stephan 2000, 107).

As a result of the lawsuit, CCA, Richardson, and Walker filed a motion to dismiss the case because of their perceived ability to invoke qualified immunity because they were acting in the scope of their job duties and acted under the "color of state law." The federal district court dismissed their claim of qualified immunity because the guards were employed by a private entity. The guards appealed the case to the Sixth Circuit Court of Appeals, which agreed with the district court's decision, stating that the guards did not meet the criteria for claiming indemnification from section 1983 claims. The guards submitted their case to the Supreme Court and the court granted a case review. The Supreme Court upheld the lower court decisions and in a 5–4 decision concluded that Richardson and Walker were not entitled to qualified immunity under section 1983 because they were employees of a private agency.

In the majority opinion, the justices based their decision on three main reasons. First, Justice Breyer wrote the majority opinion using a functional rational, claiming that although the guards may have acted under the color of state law, employees of private firms compete against each other to contract with government and state agencies (Gillette and Stephan 2000, 107; Van Duizend 1998, 1481). Private prisons do not operate under the same principles, as they face marketplace pressures to retain state and governmental contracts and have embedded incentives to "encourage sound decision making" and "overcome excessive timidity" (Gillette and Stephan 2000, 108).

The majority opinion further argued whether the underlying purpose of the immunity clause would warrant an extension to private prison officials. The court maintained that the purpose of immunity was to ensure that public officials would engage in "principled and fearless decision-making" without fear of lawsuits (Trant 1999, 578). The defendants in *Richardson* argued that "since private prison guards perform the same work as state prison guards . . . they must require immunity to the same degree" (*Richardson v. McKnight*, 1997, 408). The second important issue raised by the majority was that private firms are able to provide "comprehensive insurance," which increases the likelihood of employee indemnification and fear of unwarranted liability (Trant 1999, 578; Van Duizend 1998, 1481). Private firms are not "bound by civil law restraints" and can offset employee liability risk by offering bonuses, extra benefits, or higher pay, unlike state and government agencies. Lastly, the majority concluded that the distractions that may exist because of the lawsuits do not necessitate sufficient evidence to justify granting immunity (Trant 199, 578; Van Duizend 1998, 1481).

Future of Indemnification and Private Prisons

Since the creation of the United States penal system, there have been many changes in its infrastructure. Although the issue of privatization has been around since the Middle Ages, we will continue to see a number of legal cases and challenges brought forth by different private prison entities as they seek equal privileges as state and governmental officials. As indicated in *Richardson*, the Supreme Court did not believe private prison entities should be afford the same indemnification practices as state and federal prison officials. Legal scholars appear to differ on the issue, with some advocating for private prisons to be given the same privileges as the state and government and others arguing against it. The major issue to look at when determining a stance on either side of the argument is to evaluate the rationale private prison officials use to fight for the same indemnification rights when they are performing the same job functions as a surrogate agent of the state or federal government. If private prisons are seeking the same rights and privileges when they are working in a state or federal government capacity, there needs to be better communication between the states, federal government, and private prison entities to find a viable solution to this debate. McCain (2001, 401) wrote a compelling argument regarding extending immunity to private entities, stating that

> since the contractor is already used to facing liability exposure under ordinary rules of law while it is engaged in its private work, there is little reason to give it special protection in every instance when it happens to be on government time ... if immunity were the rule and not the exception for such contractors, their wrongful behavior might be under-deterred and victims of their wrongful acts might be under compensated.

The issue of whether for-profit prisons are eligible for qualified immunity will continue to be a hotly debated issue. Agencies in favor of indemnification for private prisons and entities against the inclusion of private prisons may not reach a viable solution if both parties are not willing to discuss the benefits of inclusion and potential consequences for exclusion in protection against litigation. The answer to that question lies in the true intentions of the for-profit prison.

References

Alexander v. City and County of San Francisco, 29 F.3d, 1363–1364 (9th Cir. 1994).

American Federation of State County and Municipal Employees (AFCME). 2010. "The Record — For-profit Private Prisons Do Not Provide Measurable Cost Savings." http://www.afscme.org/news/publications/ privatization/the-evidence-is-clear-crime-shouldnt-pay/the-record-for-profit-private-prisons-do-not-provide-measurable-cost-savings.

Carter, B. 1998. "*Richardson v. McKnight*: The Rise and Fall of Private Prison Guards' Qualified Immunity." *University of Memphis Law Review* 28:611–632.

Civil Rights Act of 1871, 42 U.S.C. § 1983.

Cooper v. Pate, 378 U.S. 546 (1964).

Cornell University Law School. 2010. CRS Annotated Constitution. Legal Information Institute. www.law.cornell.edu/anncon/html/amdt14efrag10_ user.html.

DelFiandra, D. J. 2000. "The Growth of Prison Privatization and the Threat Posed by 42 U.S.C. §1983." *Duquesne Law Review* 38:591–612.

Donahue, J. D. 1989. *The Privatization of Decision: Public Ends, Private Means*. New York: Basic Books.

42 U.S.C. § 1997e of the Prison Litigation Reform Act.

Gerhardstein, A. 2000. "Private Prison Litigation: The Youngstown Case and the Theories of Liability." *Criminal Law Bulletin* 36 (3): 183–199.

Gillette, C. P., and P. B. Stephan. 2000. "*Richardson v. McKnight* and the Scope of Immunity after Privatization." *Supreme Court Economic Review* 8:103–126.

Harlow v. Fitzgerald, 457 U.S. 800, 818 (1982).

McCain, D. L. 2001. "*Malesko v. Correctional Services Corp.* In the Second Circuit: Pursuing Damages for Constitutional Violations by the Private Prison Industry." *Howard University Law Journal* 44:399–420.

McKnight v. Rees, 88 F.3d, 417–418 (1996).

Monroe v. Pape, 365 U.S. 167 (1961).

Morris, H. 1999. "The Impact of Constitutional Liability on the Privatization Movement after *Richardson v. McKnight*." *Vanderbilt Law Review* 52: 489–513.

Price, B. E. 2006. *Merchandizing Prisoners: Who Really Pays for Prison Privatization?* Westport, CT: Praeger Publishers.

Private Prison Accountability Act of 1997 (H.R. 1889).

Richardson v. McKnight, 521 U.S. 399 (1997).

Roles v. Maddox, 439 F.3d 1016 (9th Cir. 2006).

Ruffin v. Commonwealth, 62 Va. 790 (1871).

Selman, D., and P. Leighton. 2010. *Private Prisons, Big Business, and the Incarceration Binge.* Lanham, MD: Rowman and Littlefield Publishers.

Trant, R. 1999. "*Richardson v. McKnight*: Are Private Prison Operators Engaged in State Action for the Purposes of 42 U.S.C. § 1983?" *New England Journal on Criminal and Civil Confinement* 25:577–605.

Van Duizend, A. 1998. "Should Qualified Immunity Be Privatized? The Effect of *Richardson v. McKnight* on Prison Privatization and the Applicability of Qualified Immunity under 42 U.S.C. § 1983." *Connecticut Law Review* 30:1481–1506.

West, H. C., and W. Sabol. 2009. "Prisoners in 2008." NCJ 228417. http://bjs.ojp.usdoj.gov/index.cfm?ty=pbdetail&iid=1763.

Wolff v. McDonnell, 418 U.S. 539, 555–556 (1974).

Wyatt v. Cole, 504 U.S. 1589 (1992).

Zito, M. 2003. *Prison Privatization: Past and Present.* http://www.ifpo.org/articlebank/prison_privatization.html.

4

Private Prisons and Qualified Immunity

H. Jessica Hargis

Throughout the study of public policy, outsourcing[1] has been a topic of discussion for politicians, scholars, and economists alike. In this and other works on the subject, contracting out, in its most basic form, is a means of implementing public policy. Implementation is done by contracting for-profit, not-for-profit, or government organizations to deliver services, including the supply of technical, support, welfare, and administrative services (Greve 2001; Kettl 1993; Lavery 1999; Rosenbloom, Carroll, and Carroll 2004; Wise 1985).

The literature in the field finds consensus that alignment and delivery through outsourcing is accomplished in three stages: pre-contract, development and bidding of a contract, and post-contract management (Brown, Potoski, and Van Slyke 2006; Cohen 2001; Crawford and Krahn 1998; Fernandez, Rainey, and Lowman 2006; Kettl 1993, 1997, 2000; Lavery 1999; Megginson and Netter 2001; Shetterly 2000; Siegel 1999; Van Slyke and Hammonds 2003; Wallin 1997; Wise 1985). When faced with providing services, public resource managers must carefully consider conditions that influence outcomes and outputs in each stage. Along with practical considerations, which in the past few decades have been focused on efficiency and cost-effectiveness, democratic considerations play a part in this deliberation. What is missing from the field is a frank discussion of the lack of legal accountability for constitutional violations within the privatization structure.

The complexity of government outsourcing and the goal of efficient, effective, and democratic delivery of government services are evident in the area of law and order. Both national and state governments in the United

States of America use private sources to confine, detain, and supervise prison inmates (DiIulio 1990; McFarland, McGowan, and O'Toole 2002; Price 2006; Shichor 1996; Swanson 2002). This chapter examines the Supreme Court's role in creating a dichotomous understanding of legal accountability for violations of constitutional rights concerning public and private agents engaged in correctional services. Doing so requires an examination of both privatization and qualified immunity. The chapter begins with a brief analysis of practical and democratic considerations that led to government privatization and, more specifically, prison privatization. Next, it summarizes relevant immunity case law to demonstrate the evolution of the doctrine of qualified immunity for public and then private actors. Finally, the chapter provides concluding remarks for public managers and private prisons to help understand their legal accountability.

Privatization

Reading the literature, one finds that the phenomenon of contracting out is not new (Brown and Potoski 2003; Brown, Potoski, and Van Slyke 2006; Crawford and Krahn 1998; Freeman 2000, 2003; Gore 1993; Kettl 1993; Lavery 1999; Megginson and Netter 2001; Van Slyke and Hammonds 2003; Wallin 1997; to name a few). Throughout the years, the subject of contracting out has been examined from the standpoint of both practical and democratic considerations. Some scholars seek to evaluate the types of services that should be outsourced (Bozeman 1988; Henig 1989–1990; Moe 1987; Pynes 2006); others study how privatization affects workforce morale (Ewoh 1999; Fernandez, Rainey, and Lowman 2006). From a management perspective, contracting out is evaluated to identify necessary skills and knowledge bases (Behn and Kant 1999; Brown and Potoski 2003; Brown, Potoski, and Van Slyke 2006; Crawford and Krahn 1998; Fernandez, Rainey, and Lowman 2006; Kettl 1993; Lavery 1999), and from a legal standpoint, contracting out is examined for constitutional and legislative consequence (Freeman 2000, 2003; Lindquist 2003; Lindquist and Bitzer 2002). Contextually, some of these perspectives are practical and others are democratic.

Practical and Democratic Considerations

Practical considerations include political and social environments that influence how or why policy processes change in particular situations. Practical considerations develop in response to environmental conditions and political mandates, and they have a dominant influence over decision making. For example, the use of private entities to deliver government services changes based on which political party is in power. Led by the president, the political agenda in the 1980s saw a push for reduced government size (Bozeman 1988; Henig 1989–1990). A call to reinvent government came from the Clinton administration (Gore 1993; Hill and Hupe 2002; Moe 1994; Thompson 2000). President George W. Bush vowed to rid the government of excessive and inefficient civilian government jobs (Stevenson 2002). To be effective, managers must understand how these practical considerations interact with democratic considerations.

Democratically, there are competing opinions on the impacts and influences of outsourcing government functions. Opponents of privatization have argued that it diminishes democratic values by removing fundamentally governmental functions from public control (Brown and Potoski 2003; Lawther 2004; Moe 1994; Reinke 2006). Proponents claim that privatization enhances democratic values by raising the quality of service and lowering costs to citizens (Bennett and Dilorenzo 1987; Lavery 1999; Lawther 2004). In essence, democratic considerations include judgments relating to values, quality, and core democratic beliefs of liberty, freedom, and equality (Lawther 2004).

Practical and democratic considerations can complement one another (such as efficiency and service quality), but they can also conflict (being cost-effective while maintaining fairness). When dealing with privatization, there is a need for managers to not only understand how to balance practical and democratic considerations but also to become more involved throughout the bidding, hiring, and contract management phases (Hargis 2009; Kettl 1993; Lavery 1999; Lawther 2004; Rosenbloom 2000, 2002; Shichor 1996) to ensure proper distribution of legal accountability. Responsibility for production is ultimately in the hands of managers and does not end with the decision to privatize.

Prison Privatization

Although private industry involvement in America's correctional service began in the 1800s (McDonald 1992; McFarland, McGowan, and O'Toole 2002; Shichor 1995, 1996), the modern era of prison privatization began during a Reagan administration push toward privatization of government services (McFarland, McGowan, and O'Toole 2002; Shafritz, Ott, and Jang 2005; Shichor 1995, 1996). After a tumultuous 1970s that included inflation, elevated interest rates, high unemployment, and poor economic growth, President Ronald Reagan blamed a seismic increase in government for the nations' problems (Durant 1987; Henig 1989–1990; Hill and Hupe 2002; McFarland, McGowan, and O'Toole 2002; Poole and Fixler 1987). Reagan's presidential campaign included promises to shrink the size of government, reorganize the structure, reduce personnel, and cut budget expenditures (Durant 1987; Freeman 2003; Hargis 2009; Hill and Hupe 2002; McDonald 1992).

Once in office, the Reagan administration supported reduction of government by pushing for the privatization and outsourcing of many government services (Durant 1987; Hargis 2009; Henig 1989–1990; Hill and Hupe 2002; McFarland, McGowan, and O'Toole 2002; Shichor 1995). Hill and Hupe (2002, 93) describe this era in the Reagan administration as functionally businesslike because government agencies became centers for operations with minimal capability to provide service delivery. Together with stricter laws, the war on drugs, and efforts to combat illegal immigration during the 1980s, prison overcrowding became an overwhelming dilemma (Austin and Coventry 2001; Chang and Thompkins 2002; McDonald 1992; McFarland, McGowan, and O'Toole 2002; Price 2006; Shichor 1995, 1996). As crime rates grew, the ensuing result was prison population growth beyond the capacity of federal and state prisons, opening the door for private industry to participate in prison ownership (Austin and Coventry 2001; McDonald 1992; McFarland, McGowan, and O'Toole 2002; Pelaez 2008; Shichor 1996). The Reagan administration's call for privatization was to reduce the cost incurred by continuing to build and operate prisons.[2] The mandate for privatizing government services continued under President George H. W. Bush. In 1992, Bush issued Executive Order 12803, which encouraged the use of private prisons for local, state, and federal needs. The trend has continued, and by the end of 2005, 151 of the 1,821 state and federal correctional facilities were privately operated.[3]

Immunity

As part of the Bill of Rights, the Fifth Amendment maintains that no person shall "be deprived of life, liberty, or property, without due process of law."

In so doing, the Constitution established specific limitations on the federal government's ability to intrude on a person's right to equality and fairness under the law, thereby, ensuring that the government does not usurp individual rights. After the Civil War, due process protections expanded into the state governments with the ratification of the Fourteenth Amendment in 1868. In three sweeping statements, section one of the Fourteenth Amendment declares that no "State shall make or enforce any law which shall abridge the privileges or immunities of citizens of the United States; nor shall any State deprive any person of life, liberty, or property without due process of law; nor deny to any person within its jurisdiction the equal protection of the laws." Finally, Congress has the authority to "make all Laws" (Article I, section 8) and "to enforce, by appropriate legislation," (Fourteenth Amendment, section 5) these constitutional amendments.

To support this position, Congress passed numerous civil rights acts in the late 1800s. The Civil Rights Act of 1871 contains a now vital decree in Title 42, section 1983, which states:

> Every person who, under color of any statute, ordinance, regulation, custom, or usage, of any State or Territory or the District of Columbia, subjects, or causes to be subjected, any citizen of the United States or other person within the jurisdiction thereof to the deprivation of any rights, privileges, or immunities secured by the Constitution and laws, shall be liable to the party injured in an action at law, suit in equity, or other proper proceeding for redress, except that in any action brought against a judicial officer for an act or omission taken in such officer's judicial capacity, injunctive relief shall not be granted unless a declaratory decree was violated or declaratory relief was unavailable. For the purposes of this section, any Act of Congress applicable exclusively to the District of Columbia shall be considered to be a statute of the District of Columbia.[4]

Although the goal of the act was racial equality by placing constitutional restraints on states' rights, early Supreme Court cases over constitutional violations by government actors did not support congressional intent. It was not until the emergence of the modern administrative state[5] that the Court used section 1983 to define public administrator accountability for constitutional violations (Cooper 2007; Rosenbloom 1983a, 1983b, 1983c, 1987; Rosenbloom, Carroll, and Carroll 2004).

Over the course of several cases, the Supreme Court created the doctrine of absolute immunity from prosecution under section 1983 and identified a right to such immunity for judges (*Pierson v. Ray*, 386 U.S. 547, 1967), prosecutors (*Imbler v. Pachtman*, 424 U.S. 409, 1976), and legislators (*Butz v. Economou*, 438 U.S. 478, 1978).[6] Other public administrators have qualified immunity when "exercising discretionary functions" (*Procunier v. Navarette*, 434 U.S. 555, 1978; see footnote 7). The rule or principle that forms the basis for qualified immunity[7] cannot be found in any one constitutional right or statutory law. To all intents and purposes, the United States Supreme Court developed the doctrine of qualified immunity over the course of many years through its interpretation of Title 42, section 1983, of the Civil Rights Act of 1871. Focusing on several key phrases in the act, the Court shaped immunity for public officials by defining and redefining the applicability of section 1983's phrases "Every person" and actions "under color of" state. In effect, this immunity shields public officials from legal accountability for constitutional violations otherwise sought through section 1983 suits. Private prison employees, however, do not share the same immunity, and their legal accountability for constitutional violations remains unclear.

To examine the lack of legal accountability for constitutional violations by private prison employees, this section begins with a discussion of key United States Supreme Court[8] decisions that helped shape the doctrine of qualified immunity for state actors. Next is a discussion of how the doctrine applies to privatization, and finally, this section concludes with case law dealing specifically with private prisons. This chapter is not a comprehensive history of all Court cases related to privatization or immunity. Instead, it examines the doctrine of qualified immunity, the extent to which the Court's construction of immunity affects private corporations providing public services, and the importance of legal accountability for constitutional violations by both private and public service providers.

Case Law and Immunity

When ruling on early immunity issues, the United States Supreme Court reconciled constitutional issues by narrowly defining public servants' range of personal legal accountability. Six significant Supreme Court cases that exemplified the constitutional conflict between constitutional rights and legal accountability are *Pierson v. Ray* (386 U.S. 547, 1967), *Bivens v. Six*

Unknown Agents of Federal Bureau of Narcotics (403 U.S. 388, 1971), *Wood v. Strickland* (420 U.S. 308, 1975), *Procunier v. Navarette* (434 U.S. 555, 1978), *Harlow v. Fitzgerald* (457 U.S. 800, 1982), and *Anderson v. Creighton* (483 U.S. 635, 1987). Although many other cases embody the Court's examination of legal accountability for constitutional violations, these cases epitomize the type and character of legal immunity issues before the Court, thereby, accurately illustrating the emergence of the doctrine of qualified immunity for public officials.

In *Pierson v. Ray* (386 U.S. 547, 1967), the question before the Supreme Court was whether public employees could be held responsible for actions taken under an unconstitutional statute. The case included a section 1983 suit against both arresting officers and the local judge presiding over the case. Finding support in common law, Chief Justice Warren, writing for the majority, acknowledged a long-established doctrine of immunity for "judges from liability for damages for acts committed within their judicial jurisdiction" (386 U.S. 554, 1967).[9] Common law does not extend the same level of immunity to police officers. Instead, the Court acknowledges that police officer liability is judged on the basis of their actions so long as they base their actions in "good faith and probable cause" when making arrests (386 U.S. 555, 1967).[10]

An intriguing aspect of the *Pierson* case is the dissenting opinion penned by Justice Douglas. According to Douglas, the Court's decision is contrary to congressional intent with regard to the Civil Rights Act of 1871, Title 42, section 1983: "The congressional purpose seems to me to be clear. A condition of lawlessness existed in certain of the States under which people were being denied their civil rights. Congress intended to provide a remedy for the wrongs being perpetrated" (386 U.S. 559, 1967). Failure to allow citizens to assert their section 1983 rights against public employees of all branches of government is, Douglas argues, "a more sophisticated manner of saying 'The King can do no wrong'" (386 U.S. 556, 1967).

In 1971, the Court addressed the issue of liability and immunity for federal agents in the section 1983 claim of *Bivens v. Six Unknown Agents of Federal Bureau of Narcotics* (403 U.S. 388, 1971). Webster Bivens argued that Federal Bureau of Narcotics agents arrested him after entering and searching his home without a warrant and with no apparent probable cause. Although Bivens filed a claim for violation of federal rights under section 1983, the agents argued their actions were based in state law and, therefore, had no federal restraints. The purpose, the Court argued, of the Fourth Amendment is protection from government action, regardless of whether state actors proceed unconstitutionally or not. By arguing that federal restraints do not apply to agents of the state who act unconstitutionally, "they ignore the fact that power, once granted, does not disappear like a magic gift when it is wrongfully used. An agent acting—albeit unconstitutionally—in the name of the United States possesses a far greater capacity for harm than an individual trespasser exercising no authority other than his own" (403 U.S. 392, 1971). The Court went on to state that because there is no provision in the Fourth Amendment for "an award of money damages for the consequences of its violation . . . it is . . . well settled that, where legal rights have been invaded, a federal statute provides for a general right to sue for such invasion" (403 U.S. 396, 1971).

Although the Court's decision in *Bivens* appeared to emphasize a need for legal accountability by state actors when violating constitutional rights, it did not provide a guideline for identifying when violations occur. In its five to four decision in *Wood v. Strickland* (420 U.S. 308, 1975), the Court attempted to create a standard of review including both objective and subjective terms. Objectively, an action must violate a "basic, unquestioned constitutional right" (420 U.S. 322, 1975). Subjectively, one must examine the intent of a public employee. If intent can be characterized as good faith, the employee should hold some level of immunity. The Court's dissenters argued that the objective standard for knowledge of "settled, indisputable law" and "unquestioned constitutional rights" is unrealistic (420 U.S. 329, 1975). Justice Rehnquist, who penned the dissent, argues that a more correct standard for qualified immunity for government employees includes a "varying scope," which is "dependent upon the scope of discretion and responsibilities of the office and all the circumstances as they reasonably appeared at the time of the action on which liability is sought to be based" (420 U.S. 330, 1975).

Ignoring Rehnquist's call for situational immunity, the Court relied on the objective and subjective guideline outlined in *Wood* when deciding, in *Procunier v. Navarette* (434 U.S. 555, 1978), whether qualified immunity should be available to prison officials. *Procunier* arises from Apolinar Navarettes's claim that, while a resident in a California state prison, prison officials violated his First and Fourteenth Amendment rights when they interfered with his outgoing mail. The prisoner claimed that letters to legal assistance groups and law students never reached their intending recipients. Both acting prison officials and their supervisors asserted qualified immunity, claiming that they were not aware of any constitutional right against tampering with prisoner mail. The majority, written by Justice White, questioned whether the actions taken by prison officials were done in bad faith. The Court found that they were not. Justice White argued that in 1971 and 1972, when the mail was interfered with, prison officials could not have known, or reasonably known, that "the action [taken] within [their] sphere of official responsibility would violate the constitutional rights" of the prisoner (434 U.S. 562, 1978). As such, the Court found that the prison officials should be afforded qualified immunity. An important consequence of the Court's explanation of the immunity afforded "officer[s] of the executive branch" is it, in effect, identified the functions of correctional officers as never being exclusively public (434 U.S. 561–562, 1978).[11]

The Court continues to uphold its position in *Wood v Strickland* in the 1982 case of *Harlow v. Fitzgerald* (457 U.S. 800, 1982). In *Harlow*, aides to former President Nixon argued their close proximity to the president entitled them to absolute immunity from section 1983 claims. The majority disagreed with the blanket claim of absolute immunity to presidential advisers and aides but did acknowledge a need for qualified immunity. The Court held that "government officials performing discretionary functions, generally are shielded from liability for civil damages insofar as their conduct does not violate clearly established statutory or constitutional rights of which a reasonable person would have known" (457 U.S. 818, 1982). As such, the Court relied on the "the objective reasonableness of an official's conduct . . . measured by reference to clearly established law" as a means to reduce the cost and burden of litigation on public officials (457 U.S. 818, 1982).

The Supreme Court further strengthened its position with regard to an objective legal reasonableness standard in *Anderson v. Creighton* (483 U.S. 635, 1987). Delivering the opinion in *Anderson*, Justice Scalia focused on the sensibleness that any right being deprived must be "clearly established" so that "a reasonable official would understand that what he is doing violates that right" (483 U.S. 640, 1987). Although reasonableness does not afford automatic qualified immunity, it does imply that "unlawfulness must be apparent" (483 U.S. 640, 1987).

Turning from personal responsibility to municipal responsibility, *Oklahoma City v. Tuttle* (471 U.S. 808, 1985) addresses whether citizens can hold a municipality responsible for individual public employee violations of section 1983. The suit arose from the shooting death of Albert Tuttle by Oklahoma City police officer Julian Rotramel. In a suit against the officer and Oklahoma City for deprivations of constitutional rights, Mrs. Tuttle argued that inadequate police policies caused Officer Rotramel to shoot and kill her husband. The Court rejected Tuttle's argument that Oklahoma City is liable for individual police officer action based solely on their *respondeat superior*[12] relationship. According to the Court's majority, a municipality is responsible only if the violation of constitutional rights by a police officer happened directly from municipality authority. Otherwise, the municipality "is not responsible for the unauthorized and unlawful acts of its officers" (471 U.S. 808, 1985; see footnote 5). Ultimately, the Court found that "municipal liability should not be imposed when the municipality was not itself at fault" (471 U.S. 818, 1985).

Private Persons and Qualified Immunity

This section moves from general questions of liability and immunity provided public officials to liability and immunity afforded private entities providing government services. As previously stated, there are three stages to outsourcing government services: pre-contract, development and bidding of a contract, and post-contract management. However, before contracting out government work, public managers must identify whether a service is an inherently governmental function. The Court addresses this question, and the question of whether private entities can be held liable for constitutional violations, in four precedent setting cases, *Lugar v. Edmondson Oil Co., Inc.* (457 U.S. 922, 1982), *West v. Atkins* (487 U.S. 42, 1988), *Wyatt v. Cole et al.* (504 U.S. 158, 1992), and *Lebron v. National Railroad Passenger Corporation* (513 U.S. 374, 1995).

Addressing whether a person can seek section 1983 recovery for "state actions" that violate Fourteenth Amendment rights, but that occur indirectly "under the color of state law," is the Supreme Court case of *Lugar v. Edmondson Oil Co., Inc.* (457 U.S. 922, 1982).[13] According to the majority opinion, Congress intended section 1983 to cover only those actions typified as state action. As such, the Court acknowledged the importance of identifying not only if the claimed deprivation of right resulted from state action but whether private parties can be characterized as "state actors" (457 U.S. 939, 1982). In effect, the Court's majority ruled that "[p]rivate persons, jointly engaged with state officials in the prohibited action, are acting *'under color' of law for purposes of the statute. To act 'under color' of law does not require that the accused be an officer of the State. It is enough that he is a willful participant in joint activity with the State or its agents"* (italics in original; 457 U.S. 941, 1982).[14]

Writing scathing dissenting opinions, Chief Justice Burger and Justice Powell each disagreed with the characterization of private persons' using state laws to file legal claims as state action. Burger stated that the important factor for section 1983 claims is the "infringement of a federal right fairly attributable to the state" (457 U.S. 943, 1982). Powell argued that the Court's decision in *Lugar* recognizes actions by a private citizen, "who did no more than commence a legal action of a kind traditionally initiated by private parties, thereby engaged in 'state action'" (457 U.S. 945, 1982). Both dissenters agreed that the expansive depiction of state action would only cause confusion.

Burger and Powell's dissenting positions in *Lugar* became a majority decision in 1992's *Wyatt v. Cole et al.* (504 U.S. 158, 1992), when the United States Supreme Court struck down qualified immunity defenses for private persons in section 1983 suits as they relate to private parties using state laws. The decision in *Wyatt* identified congressional intent[15] as one of several reasons for refusing to extend private party immunities reserved for government officials. According to Justice O'Connor, who wrote for the majority, "the rationales mandating qualified immunity for public officials are not applicable to private parties" (504 U.S. 167, 1992). Relying on precedent, the Court acknowledged that the balance struck for a qualified immunity defense lies in the ability to compensate "those who have been injured by official conduct and protecting government's ability to perform its traditional functions" (504 U.S. 167, 1992). This balance, the Court continues, is not necessary in the private sector, even if private persons use state laws to guide their actions.

The Court recognized that its decision in *Wyatt* was not applicable to all private party section 1983 suits because of its limited focus on private party usage of state laws and not private party actions as a state actor. The Court addressed the later in 1995 with its decision in *Lebron v. National Railroad*

Passenger Corporation (513 U.S. 374, 1995). *Lebron* involves a suit against Amtrak for section 1983 violation of First Amendment rights of free speech.[16] The constitutional question raised by Michael Lebron, a creator of public issue billboards who contracted with Amtrak to display his creations, is whether an individual has the right to constitutional protection from private corporations. After an extensive history of government-created private corporations, Justice Scalia, writing for the majority, argued that although created as a "private, for-profit corporation," Amtrak is "an agency or instrumentality of the United States for the purpose of individual rights guaranteed against the Government by the Constitution because it is a 'device' of 'government'" (513 U.S. 402 and 394, 1995).

An important aspect of Scalia's opinion is how to derive whether a private corporation is engaged in state action. According to Scalia, three considerations are necessary to identify private actors as state agents. First, the judiciary may examine the public function provided by the private corporation and assess its actions as inherently governmental. Second, if the private corporation functions in a way that it is difficult to be extricated or separated from the government, it is likely acting on behalf of the state. Finally, when the government specifically encourages and/or authorizes a private corporation to act unconstitutionally, the private entity is carrying out a state action.[17] Justice O'Connor, in her solo dissent, agreed only with Scalia's final consideration, arguing that "unless the government affirmatively influenced or coerced the private party to undertake the challenged action, such conduct is not state action for constitutional purposes" (513 U.S. 411, 1995). According to O'Connor, private parties acting on their own private choice are "not subject to constitutional scrutiny" (513 U.S. 411, 1995).

Private Prisons and Qualified Immunity

By the late 1980s, the Supreme Court's jurisprudence on applying qualified immunity defenses to private actors was not only variable but also complex and inconsistent. Three cases, specifically involving the correctional function of government, demonstrate the multifaceted legal position espoused by the Court. Case law in this section includes *West v. Atkins* (487 U.S. 42, 1988), *Richardson v. McKnight* (521 U.S. 399, 1997), and *Correctional Services Corp. v. Malesko* (534 U.S. 61, 2001).

West v. Atkins (487 U.S. 42, 1988) questions whether a part-time physician, in this case Samuel Atkins, M.D., contracted by a state prison to treat inmates, acts "under color of state law" as outlined in section 1983. In this case, Quincy West, prisoner of a publicly run correctional facility, filed a suit against Atkins for failing to "provide adequate treatment" to an Achilles tendon tear (487 U.S. 42, 1988). As with *Lugar*, the Supreme Court held that "if a defendant's conduct satisfies the state action requirement of the Fourteenth Amendment, 'that conduct [is] also action under color of state law and will support a suit under [section] 1983'" (487 U.S. 49, 1988). The Court also argued that "acting under color of state law" means that an actor possessed power "by virtue of state law and made possible only because the wrongdoer is clothed with the authority of state law" (487 U.S. 49, 1988).

As to whether a private person contracted by the state can act on behalf of the state, the Court ruled that a private contractor's function "within the state system . . . determines whether his actions can fairly be attributed to the State" (487 U.S. 56, 1988). Liability for violating constitutional rights, the Court continued, is a matter of examining the relationship created between the parties, in this case, the relationship between the state prison, the physician contracted to provide medical care, and the prisoner. Ultimately, the majority ruled that the state is responsible for providing medical care for prison inmates. The state cannot, the Court asserted, concede its responsibility to uphold the constitutional rights of prisoners simply by choosing to contract that responsibility to a private physician. Based on his relationship with the prison, the Court found Atkins to be a state actor within section 1983 meaning.

In seeming contradiction to its decision in *West*, the Supreme Court ruled in 1997 that prison guards employed by private correctional facilities are not entitled to qualified immunity against section 1983 violations in *Richardson v. McKnight* (521 U.S. 399, 1997).[18] Evaluating the historical application of immunity, the Court held there was no support to extend coverage to private prisons. Relying heavily on their 1992 decision in *Wyatt*, the Court reiterated its position that the principle underlying qualified immunity for public actors is not relevant to private actors. After an exhausting examination of the history of immunity and privatization, Justice Breyer asserted the majority's opinion that there is "no evidence that the law gave purely private companies or their employees any special immunity from such suits" (521 U.S. 406, 1997). In the end, Justice Breyer dismissed the notion that the "mere performance of a governmental function" qualifies private companies for qualified immunity, particularly when the private company "performs a job without government supervision or direction" (521 U.S. 408–409, 1997).[19]

Ultimately, the Court skirts the most important issue—whether private prisons and their employees act "under color of state law" and, therefore, can be found liable under section 1983 for violations of constitutional rights (521 U.S. 413, 1997). The avoidance of ruling on the issue of liability, along with two other qualifications in the Court's decision—the generalization of its decision and whether a "special good-faith defense" applies to private actors (521 U.S. 413, 1997)—places considerable apprehension with respect to the Court's jurisprudence as it relates to private actors and immunity.

In competing judicial jurisprudence, a dissent from Justice Scalia asserted a doctrine of qualified immunity for prison officials, both public and private, emphasizing the need for consistency and relying on *Procunier* as precedent. Scalia chastises the majority for failing to acknowledge that private prison officials "perform the same duties as state-employed correctional officials, who exercise the most palpable form of state police power, and who may be sued for acting 'under color of state law'" (521 U.S. 414, 1997). Criticizing the majority's historical account of immunity decisions, Scalia points to two basic points made in all cases questioning application of the immunity defense: "immunity is determined by function, not status," and "private status is not disqualifying" (521 U.S. 416, 1997).

In 2001, the question of the applicability of section 1983 to private actors providing public services came before the Court yet again in *Correctional Services Corp. v. Malesko* (534 U.S. 61, 2001). This time, the constitutional question in *Correctional Services Corp.* was whether the Court should extend section 1983 liability to a private corporation, thereby allowing monetary recovery as permitted in *Bivens*. The majority said no.

The main point of the case arises from the cause of action asserted by John Malesko, an inmate of a prison operated by Correctional Services Corporation (CSC), a private corporation contracted by the federal government to manage incarceration of federal inmates. Malesko sued CSC after he succumbed to his heart condition and suffered a heart attack when prison guards forced him to climb the stairs to his cell, rather than use the elevator.[20] The Court found that the purpose of *Bivens* was "to deter individual federal officers from committing constitutional violations" (534 U.S. 70, 2001). Because the claim of action was against CSC, *Bivens* does not apply. "[I]f a corporate defendant is available for suit, claimants will focus their collection efforts on it, and not the individual directly responsible for the alleged injury" (534 U.S. 71, 2001).

Concluding Remarks

As evidenced throughout this chapter, the development of the doctrine of qualified immunity gave rise to a complex, multifaceted approach to section 1983 suits as they relate to public actions of both public and private actors. The United States Supreme Court has emphatically asserted that "[t]o state a claim under [section] 1983, a plaintiff must allege the violation of a right secured by the Constitution and laws of the United States, and must show that the alleged deprivation was committed by person acting under color of a state law" (*West v. Atkins*, 487 U.S. 48, 1988). In addition, the Court has asserted the purpose of section 1983 is protection from usurpation of constitutional rights by government actors, not private harm. Finally, the Supreme Court maintains that the doctrine of qualified immunity "strikes a balance between compensating those who have been injured by official conduct and protecting government's ability to perform its traditional functions" (*West v. Atkins*, 504 U.S. 167, 1992).

Part of the difficulty in assessing applicability of section 1983 liability and immunity is identifying not only when private contractors "act under color of state law," but also when said action is a traditional government function. In addition, the Court has implied that private parties performing public service functions on the states' behalf must also have "government supervision or direction" (*Richardson v. McKnight*, 521 U.S. 408-409, 1997). In its effort to be vigilant that not every tort becomes a question of constitutionality, the Court has narrowly defined the state action doctrine as applied to section 1983 suits. Doing so has limited private prison employee immunity against allegations of constitutional violations. It has also differentiated public and private administration of correctional facilities. If public managers seek to define legal accountability for privatized prisons, the Court has provided, through case precedent, a road map for public managers that emphasizes a better developed contract and diligent post-contract management.

Notes

1. For the purpose of this chapter, the terms "outsourcing," "privatization," and "contracting out" are used interchangeably. These terms refer to the delivery of government services to citizens on many different levels (i.e., federal, state, and local) and in many different areas (e.g., refuse collection, highway construction, prisons, social services).

2. Reagan era privatization supporters argued pragmatic principles of efficiency and cost savings, an argument that conformed to Republican-held ideological beliefs of lower taxes and limited government (Bennett and Dilorenzo 1987). Critics of privatization argued idealistic principles, including whether the worth, importance, or usefulness of government services would be lost in the endeavor to make delivery economical (Henig 1989–1990; Metzger 2003).

3. These statistics are from December 30, 2005, Bureau of Justice Statistics, accessible at http://bjs.ojp.usdoj.gov/index.cfm?ty=tp&tid=13.

4. The statute has been revised on two occasions. In 1874, Congress added the words "and laws"; and in 1979, Congress included reference to the District of Columbia and to territories.

5. Scholars identify Franklin D. Roosevelt's dramatic response to the Great Depression by pushing unprecedented and far-reaching social welfare legislation, under the heading of the New Deal, as the advent of the modern administrative state (Cooper 2007; Rosenbloom 2002; Shafritz, Hyde, and Parkes 2004; Skowronek 1982).

6. The Court afforded state legislators absolute immunity in *Tenney v. Brandhove* (341 U.S. 367, 1951) "as long as the deprivation of civil rights which they caused a person occurred while the legislators were acting in a field where legislators traditionally have power to act" (*Pierson v. Ray*, 386 U.S. 559, 1967).

7. See Alan K. Chen's "The Facts About Qualified Immunity" (2006) for a detailed discussion of the legal wherewithal of the doctrine of qualified immunity.

8. As one of five practices that explain how the Court evaluates constitutional questions, Rosenbloom, Carroll, and Carroll (2004) identify precedent as one of the most important functions the High Court holds in constitutional, administrative, and public law. Along with precedential approaches, Rosenbloom, Carroll, and Carroll (2004,

4–5) recognize that Supreme Court decision making takes account of historical, value-laden, structural, and textual approaches.

9. In a gripping dissent, Justice Douglas dismissed the arguments made by the majority opinion with regard to absolute immunity for judges stating that he did not "think that all judges, under all circumstances, no matter how outrageous their conduct, are immune from suit under" section 1983 (386 U.S. 558–559, 1967). Douglas argued that an independent judiciary does not require judges to be immune from prosecution, especially if their conduct demands accountability.

10. Chief Justice Warren pointed out that "[u]nder the prevailing view in this country, a peace officer who arrests someone with probable cause is not liable for false arrest simply because the innocence of the suspect is later proved" (386 U.S. 555, 1967).

11. In one of two dissenting opinions for *Procunier*, Justice Stevens argued that the majority erred in its application of qualified immunity by failing to follow the guidelines set forth in *Wood* properly. According to Stevens, a prison official "forfeit[s] his good faith defense by deviating from a reasonable performance of his job" (434 U.S. 571, 1978). Although prison officials did not know the constitutionality of interfering with prisoner mail, they did know the legality of interfering with a prisoner's right to legal counsel (434 U.S. 573, 1978). Deductively, officers of the executive branch should have reasonably known that their actions were violating prisoner rights.

12. *Respondeat superior* is a legal relationship between an employer and an employee where the employer is the principle and the employee the agent. In said relationship, the principle is ultimately responsible for employee actions if the employee is acting on behalf of the employer. Theoretically, the principle controls agent behavior and, therefore, assumes responsibility for agent actions. In the area of privatization, *respondeat superior* could be a valid argument for government accountability if the contract between public and private entities allows for a principle–agent relationship.

13. Edmondson Oil Company filed suit against Lugar for failing to pay rent payments on a truck stop. Before judgment on the suit, the court issued a writ of attachment against Lugar, stopping him from selling his personal property for the duration of the suit (457 U.S. 922, 1982).

14. Justice White, in footnote 14, underscored the importance of the joint action between the state and a private party by emphasizing that "whatever satisfies the state action requirement of the Fourteenth Amendment satisfies the 'under color of state law' requirement of the statute." Chief Justice Burger disagreed and, in his dissenting opinion, stated that the important factor for section 1983 claims is the "infringement of a federal right fairly attributable to the state" (457 U.S. 943, 1982). In this case, Burger argued that private action under a state statute does not constitute state action. Left unanswered was whether private actors using state action for "replevin, garnishment, and attachment statutes" can claim qualified immunity in section 1983 suits (*Wyatt v. Cole et al.*, 504 U.S. 158, 1992). The Court's decision in *Wyatt* answered this question in the negative, thereby narrowing a private persons' availability to qualified immunity (504 U.S. 169, 1992).

15. In the *Wyatt* opinion, Justice O'Connor claimed that "Congress did not intend to abrogate [qualified immunity] defenses when it enacted the Civil Rights Act of 1871" whether they "acted without malice and with probable cause" (504 U.S. 165, 1992), and therefore, the Court would not extend it.

16. This case is unique in that Amtrak is a private, government-owned corporation created by Congress. The president, subject to confirmation by the United States Senate, appoints members of the board of directors.

17. The courts identify these tests as the public function test, the state compulsion test, and the nexus test, respectively.

18. In *Richardson v. McKnight*, Ronnie Lee McKnight, a prisoner in a privately run Tennessee prison, filed a section 1983 claim against two prison guards. In his claim of action, McKnight alleged that the privately employed guards used excessive force in restraining him, thereby violating his constitutional rights.

19. I disagree with Breyer's position on this matter as it is evident through the cases listed throughout this chapter that the Court equates performance of state action "under the color of state law" (Title 42, section 1983) as the basis for section 1983 liability and immunity. Justice Scalia outlines historical support for this position in his *Richardson* dissent (521 U.S. 414–423, 1997).

20. Employees of the company enforced a corporate policy requiring all inmates to use the stairs for anyone housed on floors one through six.

References

Anderson v. Creighton. 1987. 483 U.S. 635. Legal Research, FindLaw. http://caselaw.findlaw.com.

Austin, James, and Garry Coventry. 2001. *Emerging Issues on Privatized Prisons*. Washington, DC: National Council on Crime and Delinquency for the Office of Justice Programs, U.S. Department of Justice.

Behn, Robert D., and Peter A. Kant. 1999. "Strategies for Avoiding the Pitfalls of Performance Contracting." *Public Productivity & Management Review* 22 (4): 470–489.

Bennett, James T., and Thomas J. Dilorenzo. 1987. "The Role of Tax-Refunded Politics." *Proceeding of the Academy of Political Science* 36 (3): 14–23.

Bivens v. Six Unknown Agents of Federal Bureau of Narcotics. 1971. 403 U.S. 388. Legal Research, FindLaw. http://caselaw.findlaw.com.

Bozeman, Barry. 1988. "Exploring the Limits of Public and Private Sectors: Sector Boundaries as Maginot Line." *Public Administration Review* 48 (2): 672–674.

Brown, Trevor L., and Matthew Potoski. 2003. "Contract-Management Capacity in Municipal and County Governments." *Public Administration Review* 63 (2): 153–164.

Brown, Trevor L., Matthew Potoski, and David M. Van Slyke. 2006. "Managing Public Service Contracts: Aligning Values, Institutions, and Markets." *Public Administration Review* 66 (3): 323–331.

Butz v. Economou. 1978. 438 U.S. 478. Legal Research, FindLaw. http://caselaw.findlaw.com.

Chang, Tracy, and Douglas Thompkins. 2002. "Corporations Go to Prisons: The Expansion of Corporate Power in the Correctional Industry." *Labor Studies Journal* 27 (1): 45–69.

Chen, Alan K. 2006. "The Facts About Qualified Immunity." *Emory Law Journal* 55 (2): 229–277.

Cohen, Steven. 2001. "A Strategic Framework for Developing Responsibility and Functions from Government to the Private Sector." *Public Administration Review* 61 (4): 432–440.

Cooper, Phillip J. 2007. *Public Law & Public Administration.* 4th ed. Belmont, CA: Thomson Wadsworth.

Correctional Services Corp. v. Malesko. 2001. 534 U.S. 61. Legal Research, FindLaw. http://caselaw.findlaw.com.

Crawford, John W., Jr., and Steven L. Krahn. 1998. "The Demanding Customer and the Hollow Organization: Meeting Today's Contract Management Challenge." *Public Productivity & Management Review* 22 (1): 107–118.

DiIulio, John J., Jr. 1990. "Prisons That Work: Management Is the Key." *Federal Prisons Journal* 1 (4): 7–15. http://www.bop.gov/news/PDFs/sum90.pdf.

Durant, Robert F. 1987. "Toward Assessing the Administrative Presidency: Public Lands, the BLM, and the Reagan Administration." *Public Administration Review* 47 (2): 180–189.

Ewoh, Andrew I. E. 1999. "An Inquiry into the Role of Public Employees and Managers in Privatization." *Review of Public Personnel Administration* 19 (Winter): 8–27.

Fernandez, Sergio, Hal G. Rainey, and Carol E. Lowman. 2006. "Privatization and Its Implications for Human Resource Management." In *Public Personnel Management: Current Concerns, Future Challenges,* edited by Norma M. Riccucci, 204–224. San Francisco, CA: Longman.

Freeman, Jody. 2000. "The Contracting State." *Florida State University Law Review* 28 (Fall): 155–214.

Freeman, Jody. 2003. "Extending Public Law Norms through Privatization." *Harvard Law Review* 116 (5): 1285–1352.

Gore, Al. 1993. *Creating a Government that Works Better and Costs Less. Accompanying Report of the National Performance Review.* Washington, DC: National Performance Review. www.fas.org/irp/offdocs/npr.

Greve, Carsten. 2001. "New Avenues for Contracting Out and Implications for Theoretical Framework." *Public Performance & Management Review* 24 (3): 270–284.

Hargis, H. Jessica. 2009. "Not to Be Overlooked: How the United States Supreme Court Shapes the Administrative State." PhD diss., University of Texas at Dallas.

Harlow v. Fitzgerald. 1982. 457 U.S. 800. Legal Research, FindLaw. http://caselaw.findlaw.com.

Henig, Jeffrey R. 1989–1990. "Privatization in the United State: Theory and Practice." *Political Science Quarterly* 104 (4): 649–670.

Hill, Michael, and Peter Hupe. 2002. *Implementing Public Policy*. Thousand Oaks, CA: Sage Publications.

Imbler v. Pachtman. 1976. 424 U.S. 409. Legal Research, FindLaw. http://caselaw.findlaw.com.

Kettl, Donald F. 1993. *Sharing Power: Public Governance and Private Markets*. Washington, DC: Brookings Institute.

Kettl, Donald F. 1997. "The Global Revolution in Public Management: Driving Themes, Missing Links." *Journal of Policy Analysis and Management* 16 (3): 446–462.

Kettl, Donald F. 2000. "The Transformation of Governance: Globalization, Devolution, and the Role of Government." *Public Administration Review* 60 (6): 488–497.

Lavery, Kevin. 1999. *Smart Contracting for Local Government Services: Processes and Experience*. Westport, CT: Praeger.

Lawther, Wendell C. 2004. "Ethical Challenges in Privatizing Government Services." *Public Integrity* 6 (2): 141–153.

Lebron v. National Railroad Passenger Corporation. 1995. 513 U.S. 374. Legal Research, FindLaw. http://caselaw.findlaw.com.

Lindquist, Stefanie A. 2003. "Privatization through Related Corporations: Liability Considerations." *Review of Public Personnel Administration* 23 (4): 323–327.

Lindquist, Stefanie A., and Michael Bitzer. 2002. "Government Contractors' Liability for Constitutional Torts: The Legal Implications of Privatization." *Review of Public Personnel Administration* 22 (3): 241–245.

Lugar v. Edmondson Oil Co., Inc. 1982. 457 U.S. 922. Legal Research, FindLaw. http://caselaw.findlaw.com.

McDonald, Douglas C. 1992. "Private Penal Institutions." *Crime and Justice* 16:361–419.

McFarland, Stephen, Chris McGowan, and Tom O'Toole. 2002. "Prisons, Privatization, and Public Values." Paper presented to Professor Mildred Warner, Privatization and Devolution CRP 612, Cornell University, December. http://government.cce.cornell.edu/doc/pdf/PrisonsPrivatization.pdf.

Megginson, William L., and Jeffry M. Netter. 2001. "From State to Market: A Survey of Empirical Studies on Privatization." *Journal of Economic Literature* 39 (2): 321–389.

Metzger, Gillian E. 2003. "Privatization as Delegation." *Columbia Law Review* 103 (6): 1367–1502.

Moe, Ronald C. 1987. "Exploring the Limits of Privatization." *Public Administration Review* 47 (6): 453–460.

Moe, Ronald C. 1994. "The 'Reinventing Government' Exercise: Misinterpreting the Problem, Misjudging the Consequences." *Public Administration Review* 54 (2): 111–122.

Oklahoma City v. Tuttle. 1985. 471 U.S. 808. Legal Research, FindLaw. http://caselaw.findlaw.com.

Pelaez, Vicky. 2008. "The Prison Industry in the United States: Big Business or a New Form of Slavery?" *Global Research*, March 10. http://www.globalresearch.ca/index.php?context=va&aid=8289.

Pierson v. Ray. 1967. 386 U.S. 547. Legal Research, FindLaw. http://caselaw.findlaw.com.

Poole, Robert W., Jr., and Philip E. Fixler, Jr. 1987. "Privatization of Public-Sector Services in Practice: Experience and Potential." *Journal of Policy Analysis and Management* 6 (4): 612–625.

Price, Byron E. 2006. *Merchandizing Prisoners: Who Really Pays for Prison Privatization?* New York: Praeger.

Procunier v. Navarette. 1978. 434 U.S. 555. Legal Research, FindLaw. http://caselaw.findlaw.com.

Pynes, Joan E. 2006. "Human Resources Management Challenges for Nonprofit Organizations." In *Public Personnel Management: Current Concerns, Future Challenges*, edited by Norma M. Riccucci, 225–242. San Francisco, CA: Longman.

Reinke, Saundra J. 2006. "When Worlds Collide: A Case Study of Ethics, Privatization, and Performance in Juvenile Corrections." *Public Performance & Management Review* 29 (4): 497–509.

Richardson v. McKnight. 1997. 521 U.S. 399. Legal Research, FindLaw. http://caselaw.findlaw.com.

Rosenbloom, David H. 1983a. *Public Administration and Law: Bench v. Bureau in the United States.* New York: Marcel Dekker.

Rosenbloom, David H. 1983b. "Public Administrative Theory and the Separation of Powers." *Public Administration Review* 43 (3): 219–227.

Rosenbloom, David H. 1983c. *Administrative Law for Public Managers: Essentials of Public Policy and Administration.* Boulder, CO: Westview Press.

Rosenbloom, David H. 1987. "Public Administrators and the Judiciary: The 'New Partnership.'" *Public Administration Review* 47 (1): 75–83.

Rosenbloom, David H. 2000. "Retrofitting the Administrative State to the Constitution: Congress and the Judiciary's Twentieth-Century Progress." *Public Administration Review* 60 (1): 39–46.

Rosenbloom, David H. 2001. "'Whose Bureaucracy Is This, Anyway?'" *Political Science and Politics* 34 (4): 773–777.

Rosenbloom, David H. 2002. *Building a Legislative-Centered Public Administration: Congress and the Administrative State, 1946–1999.* Tuscaloosa: University of Alabama Press.

Rosenbloom, David H., James D. Carroll, and Jonathan D. Carroll. 2004. *Constitutional Competence for Public Managers.* Belmont, CA: Wadsworth Group.

Shafritz, Jay M., Albert Hyde, and Sandra Parkes, eds. 2004. *Classics of Public Administration.* 5th ed. Belmont, CA: Wadsworth.

Shafritz, Jay M., J. Steven Ott, and Yong Suk Jang, eds. 2005. *Classics of Organizational Theory.* 6th ed. Belmont, CA: Wadsworth.

Shetterly, David R. 2000. "The Influence of Contract Design on Contractor Performance: The Case of Residential Refuse Collection." *Public Performance & Management Review* 24 (1): 53–68.

Shichor, David. 1995. *Punishment for Profit.* Thousand Oaks, CA: Sage Publications.

Shichor, David. 1996. "Private Prisons." In *Encyclopedia of American Prisons*, edited by Marilyn D. McShane and Frank P. Williams III, 364–672. New York: Garland Publishing.

Siegel, Gilbert B. 1999. "Where Are We on Local Government Service Contracting?" *Public Performance & Management Review* 22 (3): 365–388.

Skowronek, Stephen. 1982. *Building a New American State: The Expansion of National Administrative Capacities, 1877–1920.* Cambridge: Cambridge University Press.

Stevenson, Richard W. 2002. "Government May Make Private Nearly Half of Its Civilian Jobs." *New York Times*, November 15, A1.

Swanson, Meagan. 2002. "The Private Prison Debate: A Look at Efficiency of Private Prisons vs. Public Prisons." *Major Themes in Economics.* Spring. http://www.cba.uni.edu/economics/Themes/swanson.pdf.

Thompson, James R. 2000. "Reinvention as Reform: Assessing the National Performance Review." *Public Administration* 60 (6): 508–521.

Van Slyke, David M., and Charles A. Hammonds. 2003. "The Privatization Decision: Do Public Managers Make a Difference?" *American Review of Public Administration* 33 (2): 146–163.

Wallin, Bruce A. 1997. "The Need for a Privatization Process: Lessons from Development and Implementation." *Public Administration Review* 57 (1): 11–20.

West v. Atkins. 1988. 487 U.S. 42. Legal Research, FindLaw. http://caselaw.findlaw.com.

Wise, Charles. 1985. "Suits against Federal Employees for Constitutional Violations: A Search for Reasonableness." *Public Administration Review* 45 (6): 845–856.

Wood v. Strickland. 1975. 420 U.S. 308. Legal Research, FindLaw. http://caselaw.findlaw.com.

Wyatt v. Cole et al. 1992. 504 U.S. 158. Legal Research, FindLaw. http://caselaw.findlaw.com.

5

The Prison Doors Swing Both Ways: Elite Deviance and the Maintenance and Expansion of the Market of Prison-Industrial Complex

Benjamin R. Inman

We paraphrase what has been written about judges, that, above all things, integrity is their lot and proper virtue, the landmark, and he that removes it, corrupts the fountain. In this case, the fountain from which the public drinks is confidence in the judicial system—a fountain which may be corrupted for a time well after this case.
—Edwin M. Kosik

The corrupted fountain is an ideal analogy that aptly describes the current state of the private prison industry. The quote at the beginning of the chapter was taken from a proposed plea agreement between the United States and former judges Michael Conahan and Mark Ciavarella Jr. The plea agreement was rejected, and both judges were later convicted of illegal acts that were committed in the performance of their official judicial duties. The charges included accepting bribes from a private prison company in exchange for tougher sentencing and using their judicial power to close a public correction facility. After closing the facility, they assisted in brokering a 20-year contract with a private facility valued at $58 million. Although an isolated incident, the case demonstrates the great lengths to which the private prison industry will venture to ensure that the market for private prison services remains viable.

Privatizing the operations and ownership of prisons became popular policy during the 1980s and 1990s. The response to the widespread policy initiatives such as the war on crime and the war on drugs (Shelden 2004) promulgated a crackdown on crime in the United States (Shichor 1995). Driven by citizen support for the "get tough on crime" movement (Johnston 1990; Shelden 2004), strict sentencing guidelines for a wide variety of crimes became federally mandated, as seen in the Comprehensive Crime Control Act of 1984, the Anti-Drug Abuse Act of 1988, and the Violent Crime and Law Enforcement Act of 1994. The increase in minimum sentencing guidelines and the exponential growth of crime rates quickly exceeded the capacity of the corrections system to house the drastic increase in prisoners (Perrone and Pratt 2003; Shelden 2004; Shichor 1995). As the number of incarcerated drastically increased, prisons at all levels began to experience severe overcrowding and dramatic increases in the costs of providing service (Culp 2005). Nevertheless, although citizens favored the harsher sentencing guidelines, paying for the increase in incarceration costs required to confine convicted offenders was, and still is, unpopular. In many cases, the tax base could not support such growth in prison populations (Culp 2005). The increasing costs, the need for infrastructure growth and improvement to accommodate increased incarceration rates, and citizen dissatisfaction with tax increases prompted public prison systems to look at other options.

As Price (2006, xiv) noted, "Prison privatization continues to be one of the most controversial issues in public policy [and management]. Although steeped in 'public choice' rationalizations to save costs through competitive bidding, privatization may also be rooted in the sociopolitical atmosphere." There are concerns that the use of private (for-profit) prisons, in conjunction with tough-on-crime legislation and minimum sentencing guidelines, has prompted private prison companies to groom their market for service. This chapter will focus on lobbying groups, campaign contributions, and kickbacks/bribes. This research seeks to identify the market practices, legal or not, private prisons use to ensure that a market for private prison services is viable. Criminal justice and sociological theories of the power elite and elite deviance will be used to explain why private prison corporations may engage in morally unacceptable practices to ensure or maintain their market for service. Given that the private prison industry relies on privatization and incarceration policy outcomes, licit and illicit practices may be used to influence these outcomes (Volokh 2008). This is particularly important given that the current recession has seen private prisons in some states, including California, Oklahoma, and Colorado, become entirely vacant (Cook 2010) and has had a significant impact on the private prison industry's bottom line. Likewise, there are legislative pushes to decrease sentencing for nonviolent offenders and to permit early outs for those who may be currently incarcerated, which in turn would likely remove more offenders from the system.

Theoretical Framework

The 1980s brought significant change in the policy domain of prison privatization. The war on crime, the war on drugs, three-strikes laws, and the increase in minimum sentencing guidelines promulgated drastic increases in the populations of prisoners remanded to the correction systems. These policy initiatives were heavily supported, and are still favored, by the private prison industry through lobbying, campaign contributions, and other means. The surge in convicted criminals remanded to the corrections systems created poor living conditions, overcrowding, and increases in prisoner-on-prisoner violence, which garnered the media's attention. In many cases, judicial review of public prisons uncovered severe overcrowding, poor living conditions, and widespread violence. Under court order, some systems were required to provide better conditions, but often states could not fund or support the additional financial burdens to build new facilities or expand existing prisons to meet the judgments imposed by the courts. The increasing problem caused by limited financial resources, media scrutiny, and public outcry created a vacuum in the need for private prison services.

The Power Elite

The "Great Changes" in policy are not controlled by the everyday citizen, but rather, they are controlled by what C. Wright Mills (1956) describes as the power elite. The evolution of American democracy has witnessed the growth of strong political and corporate power elites that have the ability to influence the context of American public and international policy. In most cases, the power elite is the class of the wealthy, influential, and educated few of society. Most of those incarcerated in the American penal system tend to reflect the sociopolitical disadvantaged and minority groups that in no way, shape, or form represent the elites of society. According to Mills (1958), the American economy, or market, is dominated by large corporations that are politically connected and have the majority voice in economic decisions. Although Mills (1958) notes that the American economy is primarily dominated by the military-industrial complex, the implications for the current prison-industrial complex are increasingly relevant.

Violent crime in America continues to capture the headlines. Murder, assault, and other violent crime statistics are used to gauge the safest cities. We, as a people, shy away from the poor and downtrodden on the assumption that they mean to do us harm. As Robinson and Murphy (2006, 6) put it: "Americans are under the impression that the greatest threat to their personal safety and property comes from below—the poor. This is a myth! In reality, the greatest threats to health and welfare of American citizens comes from above—the wealthy." In short, street crimes are technically not as abundant and overarching as white-collar crime, or crimes committed by the power elite. For example, in 2005, there were 16,692 deaths from murder. On the other hand, there were approximately 100,000 deaths related to hospital error or negligence. In many cases, the harms perpetrated by the power elites remain outside the realm of the criminal; however, they do offend the moral sensibility of the American people. Simon (2002, 35) explains that "[m]oral harms are the deviant behavior of elites that forms a negative role model that encourages deviance, distrust, cynicism, and/or alienation among non-elites." Essentially, more people are affected by elite deviance than by traditional crime; however, the citizenry are either ill-informed or persuaded that violent crime affects them more than white-collar crime.

The actions of the power elite often fall into the category of what Mills (1956) calls the "higher immorality." Higher immorality refers to the often illegal or unethical practices of government officials; however, the term is also applicable to the private sector when it is performing an inherently public function. According to Hagan and Simon (1998, 244), "policy-making . . . is increasingly controlled by corporate financed polling organizations, lobbying organizations, public relations firms, and think tanks." These organizations are often founded or controlled by congresspersons and senators. Organizations such as these exert tremendous power and control over the policy process; specifically, they maintain the ability to influence the decisions of policy makers. The political composition of such organizations can influence the partisan nature and objectivity of the organization. Policy makers are inherently uninformed in the area of correction policy and must rely on subject matter experts provided by lobbying, public relations, and think tank organizations. Policy advisory councils (PACs) serve policy makers in an advisory capacity, and though in an ideal situation the PACs would provide unbiased policy advice, in the case of private prison policy, PACs often serve a biased conservative agenda and advocate policy initiatives that benefit the market. The use of PACs, lobbying, and other groups moves from higher immorality to elite deviance.

Elite Deviance

In the context of sweeping privatization reform, there is room for criminal justice theory to explore ways private companies engage in immoral behavior and borderline criminal actions to ensure that the use of private prisons remains viable. Research suggests that elite deviance is a key way private companies maintain their markets for service. The concept of elite deviance has its roots in Sutherland's (1949) study of white-collar crime. Significant research indicates that citizens are more likely to be harmed or killed by negligent or immoral behaviors (Friedrich 1996) that are not deemed illegal, rather than those that are considered criminal (Frank and Lynch 1992; Reiman 1996; Robinson 1999; Rosoff, Pontell, and Tillman 1998). The latter are generally considered to be excluded harms, which "are defined as harmful behaviors that either do not fall within the purview of the criminal law, or do but are not pursued vigorously by agencies of social control" (Robinson 1999).

Elite deviance is particularly important in addressing the methods by which private prison companies ensure a market for the provision of services. Specifically, elite deviance describes corporate crime, and research suggests that crimes of elite deviance affect more people than traditional street crime. Elite deviance encompasses private prison initiatives that involve the expansion of the private prison market. These deviant behaviors range from making political campaign contributions to support of tough-on-crime and harsher sentencing guidelines, providing (or failing to provide) rehabilitation to juvenile offenders in the hopes of increasing recidivism, and bribing members of the judiciary to impose harsher sentences for lesser offenses.

The power elite and elite deviance models demonstrate how corporations, specifically for-profit prisons, influence or groom the policy process by the use of immoral, illegal, and socially unacceptable methods to ensure that the private prison market remains viable. It should not be construed that private prison corporations are the only industry that practices market grooming. On the contrary, market grooming, or marketing a product, is an everyday practice for private industry. The problem with market grooming and the prison-industrial complex is that it straddles the line between acceptable business practices and unfair incarceration policy. Given the potential to create citizen distrust in one of the core functions of government, the methods used for grooming the private prison market need to be examined further.

Private Prison Elite Deviance Conceptual Model

Elite deviance in the private prison industry is predicated on several factors, including revolving doors between the public and private sector employees, campaign contributions, lobbying, and even outright illegal activities. As Gilham (1984, 339) asserts: "The corporate war chest includes many of the devices available to criminal syndicates—outright bribery, campaign contributions, PACs, and offers of post–public service employment—to influence government officials and employees." Figure 5.1 provides a simple model to reflect how each of these factors plays a role in the grooming of the private prison market. Likewise, elite deviance adequately explains how the private prison complex is able to shape the policy process by the use of unethical, morally unacceptable, and/or illegal practices. The historical justification for privatization is based on the argument that private prison companies are more efficient and effective at providing services than their public counterparts. This model adds variables of elite deviance (solid black arrows) to the current argument. Essentially, these methods can be attributed to the means by which private prison companies maintain, improve, or create markets for their services.

Methods for Grooming the Market

Lobbying

Perhaps the most troubling aspect—an excluded harm—of the private prison complex is the emergence of the private prison lobby. Private prisons

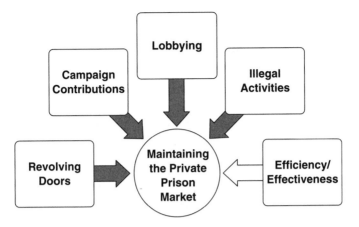

Figure 5.1

often lobby state legislators to influence and push pro-privatization policies. Coupled with their lobbying efforts to increase maximum sentencing guidelines, tough-on-crime legislation, and three-strikes laws, private prisons cover both ends of the spectrum. First, private prisons push to maintain their market through pro-privatization legislation. Second, they ensure present and future services by pushing harsher sentencing guidelines. There is the potential for private prisons to forgo the social welfare goals that government-run systems provide in search of increased fiscal and monetary reward. As Dolovich (2005, 524) explains, "[t]his would create the possibility that the state's sentencing policies, and thus the sentences imposed pursuant to them, are inconsistent with the priority of the most urgent interests and instead serve the financial interests of the private prison industry and the politicians who accept campaign contributions from industry members." Private prison companies have a vested interest in the sentencing guidelines and criminal justice legislation that affect their market. Private prisons are capable of grooming the private prison market by way of excluded harms on society. Differing significantly from other public policy arenas, criminal justice policy is largely determined not by the realities of crime but by its perception. The fear of crime can be a call to arms, or to the polls, for the citizenry, and politicians often take notice. Do private prisons fund public relations campaigns designed to whip up crime hysteria in order to increase profits?

Campaign Contributions

Campaign contributions refer to the money given to political candidates for the purpose of funding election campaigns. Gill (2005) points out that these contributions are usually given to candidates that the donor already agrees with; however, there is a public perception that campaign contributors often expect certain policy outcomes in return for monetary donations. According to Feinstein (2002), "soft money threatens to overwhelm our system and the public's confidence." Campaign contribution literature reflects how interest groups influence the political process through the donation of money to political parties and/or candidates (Gill 2005; Herndon 1982; Snyder 1993). The National Institute on Money in State Politics (2006, 5) asserts that "[w]hile the companies and their officials were working the halls of state capitols to advocate their policy positions, they also were opening their checkbooks during campaign season." The National Institute on Money in State Politics studied the patterns of political contributions in the southern states during the 2000 election year. Amid declining state correction budgets and the industry's inability to deliver more cost-effective and efficient services than their public counterpart, the private prison industry has sought to influence political actors to maintain their market for service. This influence, in the form of campaign contributions, demonstrates the industry's willingness to ensure that future revenues are certain.

According to Bender (2002, 4), "[p]rivatized corrections companies contributed more than $1,125,588.00 to 830 candidates in 14 Southern states in the 2000 election cycle." The five states whose candidates received the largest donations were Texas, North Carolina, Florida, Louisiana, and Virginia. These states alone account for $881,206.00, or 78 percent of the total contributions given to candidates in the southern states. Likewise, of the 830 recipients of these contributions, these five states account for 64 percent of the recipients of contributions in the southern states. Bender (2002, 5) further explains that "[t]he companies focused their political money largely on legislative races in the 14 states: 775 legislative candidates received 70% of the industry's contributions, with 83% of that going to campaign winners." The private prison industry "concentrated their giving on legislative candidates who, if elected, act on state budgets and sentencing laws. These candidates received almost half of the money given to candidates—slightly more than $1 million" (National Institute on Money in State Politics 2006). In many cases, these legislators sat on committees that governed private prison ventures. For example, in Florida, most of the legislators who received contributions served on committees that made decisions on the use of private prison services and corrections policy (National Institute on Money in State Politics 2006).

The private prison industry achieves its revenue stream from one source: government. Because private prisons are funded entirely in this fashion, these companies must ally themselves with the political establishment. This creates a mutually beneficial relationship between the prison-industrial complex and the political establishment of the United States. Specifically, the prison-industrial complex needs political support to pass pro-privatization legislation and tough-on-crime bills to ensure future revenues, and politicians need financial support to increase campaign funding. Likewise, private prisons have only one customer and must derive all of their revenues from the single buyer. One can argue that because public officials are the only procurer of private prison services and because they use the taxpayers' money, there is the potential to buy support for private prison endeavors. The use of campaign contributions to garner political support for pro–private prison legislation can be easily classified as an excluded harm to society. For example, although there is no definitive link between private prison campaign contributions and pro–private prison legislation, the industry targets the anticipated campaign winners and incumbents (National Institute on Money in State Politics 2006) that have influence over the process. In many cases, these incumbents serve on committees that review and approve private prison contracts. Even under circumstances in which private prisons are in use, the cancellation of contracts because of charges of abuse is often unlikely because of the makeup of these types of committees and the inherent problems that plague the system. As Dolovich (2005, 497) notes, "absent both political pressure to replace abusive or otherwise ill-performing contractors and a willingness to bear the financial cost of such replacement, the state is unlikely to act." Likewise, private prison companies seek to influence committees and budgets to prevent the replacement or rebidding of private prison contracts. With private prisons funding the political campaigns of legislators, it is unlikely that private prisons will be held accountable for poor performance.

Revolving Doors

The concept of revolving doors aptly explains the movement of public officials who serve in a regulatory capacity from the public sector to the private industry that they previously regulated. The benefits received by private companies for hiring former public officials include inside knowledge on the policy/contracting process, established contacts and professional/political relationships, and formal knowledge of legislative loopholes in the system. The principle of revolving doors can be used to offer future employment after public service in exchange for favorable policy decisions. As a tool, the promise of future high-paying, lucrative employment opportunities can be a persuasive tool to sway public officials to make policy decisions in favor of private prison companies.

The board of directors for private prison companies resemble the starting lineup of past administrations and state and federal corrections systems. For example, when he retired after serving 30 years with the federal prison system, 17 years as the director, Norman Carlson assumed a position on the board of the Wackenhut Corporation (which is now the GEO Group). Likewise, Corrections Corporation of America (CCA), GEO Group, and Cornell boast boards that include senior management officials from the federal government, senators, and lobbyists. Private prison organizations will argue that they are merely hiring the most qualified and tenured executive staff. On the opposite end of the spectrum, however, private prison executives have not typically moved to the public sector prison industry. One could argue that the private sector is using the experience built in public prisons; however, the occurrence of revolving doors is almost necessary given that the private prison company emerged in force only 30 years ago. The movement of public prison executives to the private sector is no different from what happens in the military-industrial complex. For example, ranking military officials often take jobs in the private sector in the areas in which they performed their military jobs. The private prison industry can boast that it maintains the mostly highly qualified personnel in key management positions. In most cases, they are correct; however, private prisons are also obtaining inside knowledge of the government processes, influence with politicians, and career experience that can be used to support PAC agendas.

Policy Advisory Councils

Since the mid-1980s, there has been a marked increase in tough-on-crime legislation at both the state and federal levels. According to Sarabi and Bender (2000, 3), "[s]tate and federal legislation has criminalized more and more behaviors, incarcerated offenders for longer stretches of time, and dismantled most rehabilitative and transition services that could help prisoners successfully integrate into society." These legislative initiatives, coupled with increased pro-privatization legislation, have severe implications for the American penal systems. Each of the tough-on-crime initiatives favors the prison-industrial complex by ensuring that future inmates will receive longer sentences, that current inmates will be less costly for private prisons to incarcerate, and that released prisoners will have a strong chance of recidivism. To promote these initiatives alongside the use of campaign contributions, lobbying, and other methods, the private prison industry has focused on the use of PACs, which are important in the policy process because they often contain subject matter experts who are able to provide expertise in drafting and implementing complex policy initiatives; however, they can also influence the process by pushing non-partisan agendas that benefit corporate elites. The ideal PAC would be a group of impartial and objective subject matter experts who provide expert policy advice. In the context of public policy, the PAC should be separate from the policy sponsor and should give input into the policy process for that specific subject area. An effective PAC will provide administrative expertise, often in the form of draft policies and legislation. In the area of private prisons, for the primary PAC, the American Legislative Exchange Council (ALEC), the composition is neither impartial nor objective in the policies it advocates.

To promote privatization initiatives and tough-on-crime legislation, the private prison industry uses ALEC, which was created in 1973 by a group of conservative legislators and policy advocates to be a nonpartisan council to advocate limited government, free markets, and federalism. For the private prison industry, "ALEC claims credit for the widespread adoption of Truth in Sentencing and Three Strikes/Habitual Offender legislation. Through its support of ALEC, [the private prison industry] is helping to create greater demand for its services as a result of changes in state policies that keep more people behind bars for longer periods" (Gainsborough 2003, 5).

ALEC's membership consists of like-minded legislators whose objective is to promote the use of the free market and conservative policy advancements. For corrections policy, ALEC promotes the use of private prisons for the alleged cost savings and efficiencies as well as the tough-on-crime initiatives.

> ALEC's far-reaching national network of state legislators that crosses geographic and political boundaries, and affects all levels of government, is without equal. No other organization in America today can claim as many valuable assets—both people and ideas—that have influence on as many key decision-making centers. (ALEC 2010)

ALEC pushes pro-privatization and tough-on-crime legislation to support industry by forgoing what is inherently treasured by society—fair and just sentencing and an impartial justice system.

Illegal Activity: Bribery

The shift to privatized prisons based on the private industry's efficient business practices also opens the door to other less cherished and illegal strategies for ensuring policy decisions or increasing the population in privately owned prisons. Either rarely detected, or less often used than the other methods of market grooming, illegal activities have and do occur. The case of Luzerne County, Pennsylvania, demonstrates the capabilities of private prison companies to ensure future revenues and provides unique perspectives on how private prison companies have resorted to filling the beds of their facilities. In addition, the case represents how the power elite, those members of society including the wealthy, highly educated, and influential, are capable of perpetrating moral harms on society that create turmoil and distrust.

In the case of Luzerne County, two judges plead guilty for taking more than $2.6 million in kickbacks and bribes for guaranteeing the placement of juvenile offenders in a privately run detention facility. The justices, Michael T. Conahan and Mark A. Ciavarella Jr., in their official capacities, aided PA Child Care, LLC, in the development, construction, and operation of a juvenile detention facility in Luzerne County.

All in all, between 2003 and 2007, the judges successfully closed the county-run juvenile detention center by the removing funding in the county budget for the government-owned facility. The closure sent all convicted juvenile offenders to the privately run facility. Meanwhile, the judges received bribes and kickbacks from the privately run facility for tougher sentencing of juvenile offenders. These sentences significantly contrasted from what juvenile probation officers recommended.

In rejecting the plea agreements of both judges, the Honorable Edwin M. Kosik (2009), who is quoted at the beginning of the chapter, noted a troubling undertone that should be of great concern to society. In the case of Luzerne County, the methods the private prison company used to ensure prison capacity was maintained violates the social norms of society and the sensibility of the courts. Although Luzerne County was a single case of illegal activities used by private prison companies, it has several implications. First, it has been demonstrated that private prisons are willing and capable of using illegal means to satisfy private ends from the public means. Second, the case demonstrates that the elite deviance model aptly describes the methods used by private prison companies and that one case can affect hundreds, if not thousands, of citizens, in this case, juveniles. Third, given the duration of the illegal activities and the unlikelihood that the illegal activities can be detected, the difficulty in determining the frequency of illegal activities proves to be a daunting task. There are questions that cannot be fully answered: How often are illegal activities, such as bribery, used to ensure the desired outcomes of private prisons? How far do these crimes reach?

Conclusion

During the 1980s and 1990s, the war on crime and the war on drugs remanded tens of thousands of criminals to the nation's corrections system. At all levels—local, state, and federal—the massive influx of prisoners quickly overwhelmed the system. Twenty years later, the private prison industry's growth began to stagnate. The emphasis on "build, baby, build!" quickly changed to "fill, baby, fill!" The private prison industry had the vast infrastructure to house offenders but quickly ran out of inmates to fill these facilities. The industry needed a reliable method to ensure that future revenue streams were maintained. These revenue streams are needed to support the expansive industry. Although no different from other large industries and special interest groups, the private prison industry used common market tools (e.g., lobbying, policy advisory councils, and campaign contributions) and even resorted to committing crimes (bribery) to maintain or increase the private prison market.

In most cases, the general public would have overlooked the use of these common business tools. In the case of private prisons, however, these tools are used to groom the market for the benefit of the private company and its stockholders and, thus, represent excluded harms on society. Lobbying for increased sentencing guidelines has resulted in overcrowding and has in many cases increased the likelihood of recidivism. Tough-on-crime sentencing laws, which include mandatory sentences for some offenses, serve the interest of filling private prison beds and not rehabilitation. Like lobbying activities, campaign contributions have targeted candidates who will pass additional tough-on-crime legislation, like the three-strikes laws and truth-in-sentencing guidelines, or will maintain current laws. Campaign contributions have almost always gone to the winning candidates; however, contributions as a whole have been spread equally across party lines. Private prison companies also recruit executive-level staff from the public sector to serve on the private boards.

The revolving door between public and private prisons serves the private prison industry in two ways. First, the private prison companies are able to boast that they have extensive leadership experience that comes from the public sector. These former public sector employees will continue to foster confidence in the system. Second, these former public, now private, executives often sit on PACs that push tough-on-crime legislation. Given their extensive public service background, these executives are able to gather support for private prison initiatives. PACs, such as ALEC, also push pro-privatization agendas and tough-on-crime legislation. In some cases, the legislation dismantles rehabilitative policies that help prisoners reintegrate into society. Intentionally increasing recidivism rates and mandating harsher sentencing guidelines for prisoners detracts from public confidence in the corrections system and further erodes the legitimacy of the judicial system. Although legal in nature, these methods of market grooming represent elite deviance. The power elite, private prison executives, and legislators are exchanging the public means for private ends.

The last and perhaps most troubling aspect of the methods for grooming the private prison market involves what the system seeks to correct—illegal activity. The case of Luzerne County, although a single case, demonstrates the lengths that private prison companies are willing to go to maintain current revenue sources and guarantee future revenue streams. The actions of the private prison company and judges involved negatively affected thousands of juveniles, many of whom were sentenced to the privately owned detention facility against the recommendation of public case workers. The case represents elite deviance at its worst and demonstrates that the methods used by the private prison industry have the potential to swing the prison doors both ways.

References

American Legislative Exchange Council (ALEC). 2010. "ALEC's Most Valuable Assets: People and Ideas." http://www.alec.org/about-alec/history/.

Bender, Edwin. 2002. *A Contributing Influence: The Private Prison Industry and Political Giving in the South.* Helena, MT: National Institute on Money and State Politics.

Cook, Nancy. 2010. "How the Recession Hits Private Prisons." *Newsweek*, June 30.

Culp, Richard F. 2005. "The Rise and Stall of Prison Privatization: An Integration of Policy Analysis Perspectives." *Criminal Justice Policy Review* 16 (4): 412–442.

Dolovich, Sharon. 2005. "State Punishment and Private Prisons." *Duke Law Review* 55 (3): 438–546.

Feinstein, Diane. 2002. "Bipartisan Campaign Reform Act of 2002." *Congressional Record Daily*, March 20, S2153.

Frank, Nancy, and M. Lynch. 1992. *Corporate Crime, Corporate Violence: A Primer.* New York: Harrow and Heston.

Friedrich, David O. 1996. *Trusted Criminals: White Collar Crime in Contemporary Society.* Belmont, CA: Wadsworth-ITP.

Gainsborough, Jenni. 2003. "The Truth about Private Prisons." Alternet. http://www.alternet.org/story/17392/?page=2.

Gilham, S. A. 1984. "The Economics of 'Organized' and 'White-Collar' Crime. " *Review of Policy Research* 3:335–341.

Gill, David. 2005. "Soft Money and Hard Choices: Why Political Parties Might Legislate against Soft Money Donations." *Public Choice* 123 (4): 411–438.

Hagan, Frank E., and David Simon. 1998. "From Inslaw to Iraqgate: Elite Deviance (in the Bush Era)." *Justice Professional* 10:229–248.

Herndon, J. F. 1982. "Access, Record, and Competition as Influences on Interest Group Contributions to Congressional Campaigns." *Journal of Politics* 44 (4): 996–1019.

Johnston, Van R. 1990. "Privatization of Prisons: Management, Productivity, and Governance Concerns." *Public Productivity and Management Review* 14 (2): 189–201.

Kosik, Edwin. 2009. *United States of America v. Michael T. Conahan and Mark A. Ciavarella, Jr.* No. 3:-09-CR-28. http://www.justice.gov/usao/pam/Corruption/Ciavarella_Conahan/Conahan%20%20Ciavarella%20-%20Kosik%20Order%20Rejecting%20Plea.pdf.

Mills, C. Wright. 1956. *The Power Elite*. New York: Oxford University Press.

Mills, C. Wright. 1958. "The Structure of Power in American Society." *British Journal of Sociology* 9 (1): 29–41.

National Institute on Money in State Politics. 2006. "Policy Lock-Down: Prison Interests Court Political Players." http://www.followthemoney.org/press/Reports/200605021.pdf.

Perrone, D., and Travis C. Pratt. 2003. "Comparing the Quality of Confinement and Cost-Effectiveness of Public versus Private Prisons: What We Know, Why We Do Not Know More, and Where to Go from Here?" *Prison Journal* 83 (3): 301–322.

Price, Byron. 2006. *Merchandizing Prisoners: Who Really Pays for Prison Privatization?* Westport, CT: Praeger Publishers.

Reiman, Jeffery. 1996. *The Rich Get Richer and the Poor Get Prison: Ideology, Class, and Criminal Justice*. New York: MacMillan.

Robinson, Mathew. B. 1999. "What You Don't Know Can Hurt You: Perceptions and Misconceptions of Harmful Behaviors among Criminology and Criminal Justice Students." *Western Criminology Review* 2 (1). http://wcr.sonoma.edu/v2n1/robinson.html.

Robinson, Matthew, and Daniel Murphy. 2006. *Greed Is Good: Maximization and Elite Deviance in America*. Lanham, MD: Rowman & Littlefield Publishers.

Rosoff, S., H. Pontell, and R. Tillman. 1998. *Profit without Honor: White-Collar Crime and the Looting of America*. Upper Saddle River, NJ: Prentice-Hall.

Sarabi, Brigette, and Edwin Bender. 2000. *The Prison Payoff: The Role of Politics and Private Prisons in the Incarceration Boom.* Portland, OR: Western States Center and Western Prison Project.

Shelden, Randall G. 2004. "The Imprisonment Crisis in America: Introduction." *Review of Policy Research* 21 (1): 5–12.

Shichor, David. 1995. *Punishment for Profit: Private Prisons/Public Concerns.* London: Sage Publications.

Simon, David. R. 2002. *Elite Deviance.* 7th ed. Boston: Allyn and Bacon.

Snyder, J. M. 1993. "The Market for Campaign Contributions: Evidence for the U.S. Senate 1980–1986." *Economics and Politics* 5 (3): 219–240.

Sutherland, Edwin H. 1949. *White Collar Crime.* New York: Dryden Press.

Volokh, Alexander. 2008. "Privatization and the Law of Economics of Political Advocacy." *Stanford Law Review* 60 (4): 1197–1254.

6

Private Prisons as a Response to the "Second Ghetto"

Brandi Blessett

> *How is it possible that criminal laws ostensibly written to avoid class and color bias would lead to throwing so many (sub)proletarian black men under lock, and not other black men? The class gradient in racialized imprisonment was obtained by targeting one particular place: the remnants of the black ghetto*
>
> — Loic Wacquant (2001, 61–62)

Privatizing services is a very political decision. From trash collection to road maintenance or mail service, an affirmative or opposing argument can be made to justify or deny the utility of privatization. This book series provides a comprehensive outlook on the impact of private prisons from an environmental, financial, and political perspective. Although all are important considerations, politics are a fundamental driver in shaping public perception and ultimately in formulating public policy. In this regard, privatizing prisons can be lauded as a cost-effective way to save taxpayer dollars and protect the citizenry at large. It is often promoted as a win-win situation. However, prison privatization disproportionately advantages the affluent, while poor communities are burdened with the disadvantages.

Urban communities have been socially constructed by politicians, the media, and suburban residents as inferior, depressed, and unsightly jurisdictions. Such negative connotations have led to ill-conceived and even punitive public policy responses to crime, violence, and poverty. Gustafson

(2009) explicitly argued that welfare and criminal justice systems have become bedfellows in the criminalization of poverty whereby politics and government resources are used to stigmatize, monitor, and regulate the poor. The rhetoric of politicians, pundits, and the media characterized minorities and their communities in demeaning ways, creating an unsympathetic response from the broader society. Hence, the social, political, and economic landscape of urban communities was systematically being isolated and alienated from mainstream society.

Over time, urban environments have become financially instable, their residents politically powerless and absent of social capital. Consequently, central cities developed a reputation for accommodating some of America's most paramount social ills. In housing society's most vulnerable populations, urban ghettos have become widely associated with unemployment, drug-related crimes, and single-parent, female-headed households. Such disparaging social characteristics, clustered within a geographic area, have been defined as "concentrated disadvantage" (Sampson and Loeffler 2010, 26). According to Sampson and Loeffler (2010), intense spatial inequality exacerbates existing patterns of criminal justice punishment, whereby these neighborhoods tend to experience high rates of incarceration and, therefore, disproportionately draw ex-prisoners back to them upon their release. The self-fulfilling prophecy of turmoil, decay, and destruction remains steadfast in the public's perception of urban dysfunction.

This chapter seeks to highlight the interplay between various actors and the political landscape that has systematically disadvantaged urban communities. We begin with an overview of the emergence of the second ghetto. Next, the discussion transitions to the actors and the political influence of second-ghetto formation and policy solutions that have evolved to manage urban populations. Third, the chapter looks at the interconnectedness of second-ghetto communities and the rising incarceration rates over time. The chapter concludes with a review of outcomes and potential next steps to halt the intergenerational effects of the prison pipeline.

The Environment

The designation of the "second ghetto" emerged during the early 1980s, when Arnold Hirsch's seminal piece, *Making the Second Ghetto* (1983), was published. This study highlighted the interaction between public administrators, public policies, and public resources as factors that determined the residential patterns of African Americans in urban areas. After the Great Depression, central cities began to experience unprecedented decline. The massive depreciation of land and investment, the financial instability of the urban core, and the out-migration of the middle class and manufacturing hit inner cities hard. By the early 1950s, public and private partnerships had emerged to stem the tide of blight and abandonment. In an effort to remain competitive with the burgeoning suburbs, central city officials initiated discussions and plans that included a major overhaul of infrastructure and means of attracting capital investment. Although the impetus behind urban renewal was to physically remake the inner city, it also served as a tool to carry out the racial preferences of the urban elite by pushing African Americans to the outer fringes of the city (Gotham 2001; Highsmith 2009; Hirsch 1983; Mohl 2003b; Wilson 2007). Hirsch's study focused solely on Chicago, but the patterns and relationships he described were applied to inner-city communities across the country, including Miami (Mohl 2003a, 2003b), Kansas City (Gotham 2001), and Detroit (Sugure 1996).

The second ghetto began to take shape during the 1940s, when the deterioration of central cities greatly affected their ability to remain autonomous and competitive with the burgeoning suburbs. Urban renewal was proposed as a rehabilitative tool that enabled comprehensive development of the central business district, downtown areas, and other valuable land. Urban renewal empowered local administrators to designate neighborhoods as "slums" so that they could be razed and used for revitalization. Unfortunately, African American communities were overwhelmingly the target of the federal bulldozer as they were often the impoverished and destitute areas of the city. Local administrators, business leaders, and politicians—the urban elite—thought African American proximity to redevelopment and the central business district would decrease the area's overall attractiveness to potential investors. Collectively, the urban elite steered African Americans into neighborhoods and communities that would not affect the revitalization efforts of the city. Essentially, they were moved far away from the real estate areas that were prime for current and future redevelopment (Hirsch 1983; Mohl 2003b).

Forcibly displaced from their communities, African Americans were relocated to other areas in the city. Oftentimes these new neighborhoods had inferior accommodations compared with the slums that were being razed. In Baltimore, approximately 80 to 95 percent of those displaced by urban renewal were African American, and most were relocated to neighborhoods that were heavily black and deteriorating (Haeuber 1974; Olson 1976). These actions led to the making of the second ghetto, which became the only residential option for most African American families regardless of financial status. Whereas poor families were subjected to second ghettos because of financial constraint, middle-class African American families were refused mortgages based on explicit racism and discrimination. Homeownership was blatantly denied, so most families had to settle for public housing or substandard rental properties.

Second-ghetto communities quickly became like the slums of old, but in this case, they were concentrated and hidden from mainstream society. These communities were usually cordoned off by highway construction and massive industrial complexes, severely limiting mobility and access to the outside world (Wilson 2007; Wilson 2009). In essence, large swaths of urban communities evolved into second ghettos—whereby poor families transitioned into a perpetual underclass forced to endure the most dysfunctional social ills that plague our society. The prominence of second-ghetto communities across the country can be attributed to the urban and political elite that significantly influenced public perception regarding inner cities and their residents. Second ghettos became the scapegoat for everything that went wrong in American society, and solutions were needed to manage the dysfunction to prevent it from spilling over into mainstream society. Wacquant (2010, 74) argues that "the downsizing of the welfare wing and the upsizing of the criminal justice wing of the American state . . . [has been] fueled by a politics of resentment toward categories deemed undeserving and unruly."

To address urban deterioration, policies have been created and promoted by legislators, influenced by interest groups, implemented by administrators, and disseminated through various media conduits. These groups—urban and political elites—form a very powerful cohort that has the ability to impose its will on unsuspecting and vulnerable populations, particularly inner-city residents. Urban and political elites are effective because they are knowledgeable, resourceful, and extremely organized. Therefore, with urban residents inadequately represented by most, if not all, of these constituent groups, policy decisions have facilitated the making of the second ghetto and the subsequent punitive response by the broader society. In other words, there is a highly stigmatized community and an expensive penal institution ready to capture all of the miscreants that fall out of line. Without social capital and political power, urban residents and their preferences are dictated by the whims of players who do not directly reside in these communities (Massey and Denton 1993).

The Actors

The making of the second ghetto and the broadening spectrum of the criminal justice system has advanced based on the actions of an elite group of actors. Politicians are often elected based on a "tough on crime" rhetoric that is waged against people and spaces (Smith 2004). During the first half of the 20th century, politicians successfully constructed urban communities as deviant places that were worthless and undeserving of public resources and support. The sensationalized portrayals of gangs, mayhem, "poverty pimps," and Reagan's "welfare queens" justified policy changes that would slash social programs and ramp up efforts to fight the war on drugs and the war on crime. These campaigns justified decreasing the size of government and limiting aid to poor urban families, while increasing the budgets for law enforcement agencies and prison construction (Gustafson 2009; Loury 2008, 2010; Wacquant 2001, 2010). The end result was harsher and longer sentences for criminals.

Consequently, the Reagan presidency witnessed a proliferation of private prison companies that sought to ease the pressure of prison overcrowding and budget constraints faced by state and local agencies. During the 1980s and 1990s, privatization rose substantially as local governments in the United States responded to federal aid reductions and assertive responses to fiscal austerity (Ward 2008). Privatization was lauded as more cost-effective and efficient at providing services than the public sector. Therefore, with a burgeoning criminal class due to harsher sentencing, public facilities were incapable of accommodating the massive influx of prisoners, probationers, and detainees. As a result, companies like Wackenhut (now known as the GEO Group) and the Corrections Corporation of America (CCA) emerged to house and detain criminals, youth offenders, and illegal immigrants through a variety of prisons and detention centers. The changes in public policy have made incarceration a very profitable industry. Architectural firms, communication companies, and food and drug-treatment services have become the benefactors of private prison construction as the number of people who pass through the criminal justice system increases.

Although politicians represent larger demographic bodies, interest groups are focused and direct in their pursuit of resources, funding, and political clout. Their influence is far reaching and has the potential to warp spending choices in ways that are economically and distributionally perverse (Donahue 1989). With respect to prison privatization, it has been argued that "the profit motive of private prison companies inherently creates a problematic entanglement between interest in profit and public policy" (Sentencing Project 2004, 4). For example, CCA and Wackenhut are major contributors to the American Legislative Exchange Council (ALEC), a policy organization that helped successfully implement truth-in-sentencing and three-strikes laws (Sentencing Project 2004). These mandatory sentencing requirements ensure that more offenders are detained over a longer period of time. As second-ghetto neighborhoods are disproportionately crime ridden, they are often targeted for surveillance and aggressive police details. In this regard, interest groups have effectively used their power and authority to marginalize urban communities and their residents.

The second ghetto was formed based on the concerted effort of urban and political leaders to revitalize struggling inner cities, which occurred at the expense of poor minority populations. These impoverished communities introduced a stockpile of residents into the criminal justice system and ultimately fueled the prevalence of private prison speculation. As public policies stigmatized people and places, particularly urban neighborhoods and African American and Latino groups, the ability to profit from incarceration and detention proved to be fruitful. According to the Pew Center on the States (2008a), in 2007, approximately $49 billion was spent on corrections. Although the report does not aggregate the amount of money available to private firms, the mounting convictions of offenders has continued to strain an overwhelmed prison population. Therefore, private prisons have been available to siphon prisoners from public rosters and place them into private facilities, ultimately contributing to an environment that seeks punitive not rehabilitative action.

The presence of law enforcement in urban communities is like a double-edged sword. On the one hand, crime rates dictate the need for a strong presence to deter total and complete anarchy in ghetto communities.

However, systemic issues and policy decisions at all levels of government create these socially disorganized neighborhoods in the first place. The disproportionate concentration of African and Latino Americans in urban neighborhoods justifies differences in regards to perception, politics, and punishment compared with their white and suburban counterparts. Where affluent groups enjoy suburban life with such vast amenities as grocery stores, restaurants, excellent school systems, and an abundance of employment opportunities, minority and poor residents are confined to undesirable areas. Pellow and Brulle (2005) characterize "undesirable" based on morbidity and mortality rates, the level of pollution exposure, and the effects of concentrated crime and violence, all of which significantly contribute to social, environmental, and health inequalities. Therefore, the prospects of incarceration are inherently present for the latter group.

Loury (2010, 139) suggests that mass incarceration is a political issue that arises from a distinction between the "locus of control" and the "locus of interest" in the formulation of punishment policies. In this instance, input into the decision-making process is outside the realm of urban residents. Therefore, the affluent population is likely to use prisons as a way to maintain the social hierarchy and ensure their dominant status (Smith 2004). The democracy-in-action hypothesis contradicts the earlier statement because it argues that incarceration is not directed at particular populations but is simply a structural response to public attitudes (Smith 2004). However, politics and the media have proven to be very influential in shaping the perceptions of the public at large. For example, Reagan's welfare queen rhetoric was drastically overstated, but it was effective in shaping public opinions about the poor and justifying the reduction of government programs that targeted poor communities (Gustafson 2009).

The Relationship

Second ghettos offer their residents inadequate educational curriculum, poor employment options, and limited resources for its residents. Thus, inadequate educational and employment opportunities in urban communities lead to idle minds that engage in crime and other illicit behaviors to pass the time. The relationship between incarceration and the second ghetto stems from the concentration of disadvantaged minorities that ultimately end up as prisoners in the U.S. penal system. As a result, drug-related offenses, violent crime, and property offenses feed the prison boom and fuel discussions of stricter penalties for criminals (Pettit and Western 2004). Consequently, policy makers pursue justice with a vengeance. According to Wacquant (2010) prison and jail expenditures in America jumped from $7 billion in 1980 to a dramatic $70 billion in 2007 with corrections being the third largest employer, behind only Manpower, Inc., and Wal-Mart, with a monthly payroll of $2.4 billion. In this regard, there is money to be made with enhanced efforts to be tough on crime.

The pipeline to prison is pervasive in urban ghettos because these environments have become toxic locales perpetuating destruction, decay, and disorder. For-profit prison providers have so much confidence in the prison pipeline that the building of speculative prisons had become a common occurrence. Price (2006) suggests that companies are so certain they will be able to fill prisons that they have built prisons without a corrections department guarantee of prisoners. Although the zenith of speculative prisons has subsided, their permanence is witnessed in rural communities across the country that rallied such efforts under the guise of job creation and economic development (Price 2006). The implications are significant, particularly when one considers that these institutions are only viable to the community if prisoners are using the facility.

In this case, it is no surprise that financial contributions have flowed to think tanks, political parties, and various lawmakers from the private prison lobby (Price 2006; Sentencing Project 2004). In the 2000 election cycle, for example, these donations were used to support conservative legislators who promoted privatization and to incumbents who would be making policy and budget decisions (Bender 2002; Sentencing Project 2004). For clarity, it must be stated that a National Institute on Money in State Politics report revealed that private prison companies contributed almost equally to both the Democratic and Republican campaigns, at 48 percent and 49 percent, respectively, and the remaining balance went to caucus committees (Bender 2002). From 2000 to 2004, the prison lobby, which includes private prison firms, investment and construction companies, food service providers, health care management firms, and counseling services providers, gave $3.3 million to candidates and state political parties across 44 states.

Ultimately, the second ghetto became the lifeblood of law enforcement institutions and correctional agencies in urban American communities across the country. The pipeline to prison started in the inner cities after

World War II, when the prison demographic shifted from 70 percent white before World War II to 70 percent black by 2000 (Loury 2008). The racial transformation of the prison population speaks to the concentrated efforts of political and urban elites to cooperatively disenfranchise poor minorities through punitive means. The interrelationship of poverty, race, and crime highlights a perpetual underclass that is moving from generation to generation. According to a Children's Defense Fund (2007, 16–17) report,

[a] Black boy in 2001 has a 1 in 3 chance of going to prison in his lifetime; a Black girl has a 1 in 17 chance. A Latino boy born in 2001 has a 1 in 6 chance of going to prison in his lifetime; a Latino girl has a 1 in 45 chance. About 580,000 Black males are serving sentences in state or federal prison, while fewer than 40,000 Black males earn a bachelor's degree each year. One in 3 Black men, 20–29 years old, is under correctional supervision or control. . . . Of the 1.5 million children with an incarcerated parent in 1999, Black children were nearly nine times as likely to have an incarcerated parent as White children; Latino children were three times as likely as White children to have an incarcerated parent.

Although staggering, these statistics highlight a quality of life that is becoming all too familiar for young urban residents.

Comparative statistics between whites and African Americans are daunting. African Americans lag behind other races in all social indicators of well-being: education and income, labor force participation and poverty, health outcomes (life expectancy and child mortality), and crime and criminal justice (Gyimah-Brempong 2008). This has led to overwhelming support for the thesis that the poor are perceived as more threatening, and punishment for African Americans is harsher, thus making class and race key factors in prison rates (Gustafson 2009; Loury 2008, 2010; Massey and Denton 1993; Pettit and Western 2004; Wacquant 2001, 2010). Gyimah-Brempong (2008, 177) argues that

[h]igh crime rates have direct negative impacts on the well being of African-Americans. . . . High crime rates have negative effect on job creation, housing values, as well as the provision of social services in African-American neighborhoods. Finally, high crime rates in the African-American community have negative externalities on all

African-Americans. The fact that every African-American is viewed with suspicion when shopping or driving is a direct consequence of the perceived "criminality" of African-Americans, and I believe virtually every African-American experiences such perception no matter his/her status in life.

The Outcome

The rhetoric of crime and punishment is here to stay. As demonstrated in this chapter, public opinion, public policies, and public resources stand firm in support of the conception that more incarceration leads to a safer and secure society. However, even when crime rates decreased, the rate of imprisonment steadily rose (Loury 2010; Sampson and Loeffler 2010; Wacquant 2010). Therefore, offenders are punished for their crimes, but instead of being rehabilitated, they often leave prisons more corrupt than when they entered, particularly as prisons and jails have transitioned from rehabilitative to strictly disciplinary centers (Loury 2008). Additionally, the social multiplier theory of crime suggests that criminals learn from each other through social interaction, which creates more efficient and effective criminals. Whether in jail or in their communities, without positive and constructive programs to engage ex-offenders, the pipeline to prison will continue its perpetual cycle.

Living in an environment that is devoid of access, opportunity, and hope can only lead to destruction and dysfunction. Unfortunately, this is the reality for a large segment of poor and minority populations across this country. These second-ghetto communities are made by the American urban and political elite. They developed the policies and supplied the rhetoric that justified the disciplinary approach to crime and violence in society. The ineffective war that has been raged on crime and drugs has not improved the lives of the people most affected by these disparaging issues. In fact, the life trajectory of urban youth is more dim and dismal than it has ever been in recent history. The biological and psychological stress that accompanies growing up in such destitute environments is likely to restrict emotional and behavioral development. Children who grow up in traumatized environments (e.g., high incidences of crime, single-parent households, and victims of abuse or neglect) are at great risk for committing violent crimes or being the victims of violent crime (Children's Defense Fund 2007). In effect, the cycle will continue to perpetuate itself generation after generation if proactive steps are not taken to modify such outcomes.

Urban and political elites have greatly profited from the misery inflicted on the poor as public–private partnerships have thrived under the guise of protecting society and the American way of life. On the other hand, families and communities are being destroyed by biased mandatory minimum sentencing laws that specifically target nonviolent offenses (Arditti, Lambert-Shute, and Joest 2003; Marbley and Ferguson 2005). If a crime is committed, violent or otherwise, people need to be held responsible for their actions. However, this research is advocating more proactive means to support urban residents before a life of crime and violence becomes an option. Inexplicably, urban residents live in environments where infrastructure is lacking, social programs are nonexistent, recreational facilities are scarce, and urban education systems are grossly underfunded (Massey and Denton 1993; Sentencing Project 2004; Wacquant 2001; Wilson 2007; Wilson 1987). In such an environment, children and adults are socialized to fail.

Consider recidivism rates, whereby offenders who are released from prison reenter the same communities that have little to offer in terms of recreation, employment, or education. A criminal background denies the ex-offender access to the ballot, federal loans to pursue higher education, and subsidized housing—all factors that help empower citizens to lead productive lives. Consequently, the likelihood that ex-offenders will become repeat offenders is greater when these conditions are the only option (Sampson and Loeffler 2010). Despite having paid their debt to society, ex-offenders are still stripped of their rights and forced to exist in a society that has deemed them inadequate. Under such circumstances, it is no surprise that within three to five years of their release, a majority of inmates return to prison (Marbley and Ferguson 2005).

So what's next? If crime rates have dropped but incarceration rates are stable or even increasing and the public sentiment about crime is unchanged, what can be said about the war waged on crime? Billions of dollars have been injected into the system but nothing has improved; in fact, it can be argued that things have gotten worse. The amount of money spent on incarceration is outpacing the amount of state budget funding for pre-kindergarten and higher education. For example, from 1987 to 2007, inflation-adjusted spending for education increased by 21 percent, whereas funding for corrections rose 127 percent (Pew Center on the States 2008a). As a country, the United

States has placed more value on punishment than education. Collectively, these actions will exacerbate the existing racial and class disparities, formalizing the social hierarchy in American society between the haves and have-nots.

The second ghetto and incarceration are closely related. In both public and private prison institutions, the greatest proportion of inmates are poor and minority, most often originating from urban centers around the country. Albert Einstein supposedly defined insanity as doing the same thing over and over again and expecting a different result. Well, if the discourse and public policy actions surrounding crime and punishment do not change, then we will soon become a grossly incarcerated society—insanity manifested.

References

Arditti, Joyce A., Jennifer Lambert-Shute, and Karen Joest. 2003. "Saturday Morning at the Jail: Implications of Incarceration for Families and Children." *Family Relations* 52:195–204.

Bender, Edwin. 2002. *A Contributing Influence: The Private Prison Industry and Political Giving in the South.* Helena, MT: National Institute on Money in State Politics.

Children's Defense Fund. 2007. *America's Cradle to Prison Pipeline.* Washington, DC: Children's Defense Fund.

Donahue, John D. 1989. *The Privatization Decision.* New York: Basic Books.

Gotham, Kevin Fox. 2001. "A City without Slums: Urban Renewal, Public Housing, and Downtown Revitalization in Kansas City, Missouri." *American Journal of Economics and Sociology* 60 (1): 285–315.

Gustafson, Kaaryn. 2009. "The Criminalization of Poverty." *Journal of Criminal Law & Criminology* 99 (3): 643–716.

Gyimah-Brempong, Kwabena. 2008. "Crime and Race: A Plea for New Ideas." *Review of Black Political Economy* 34:173–185.

Haeuber, Douglas H. 1974. *The Baltimore Expressway Controversy: A Study of the Political Decision-Making Process.* Baltimore, MD: Johns Hopkins University Center for Metropolitan Planning and Research.

Highsmith, Andrew R. 2009. "Demolition Means Progress: Urban Renewal, Local Politics, and State-Sanctioned Ghetto Formation in Flint, Michigan." *Journal of Urban History* 35:348–368.

Hirsch, Arnold R. 1983. *Making the Second Ghetto: Race and Housing in Chicago, 1940–1960*. Cambridge: Cambridge University Press.

Loury, Glenn C. 2008. *Race, Incarceration, and American Values, Tanner Lectures on Human Values at Stanford*. Cambridge, MA: MIT Press.

Loury, Glenn C. 2010. "Crime, Inequality, and Social Justice." *Daedalus* 139 (3): 134–140.

Marbley, Aretha Faye, and Ralph Ferguson. 2005. "Responding to Prisoner Reentry, Recidivism, and Incarceration of Inmates of Color: A Call to the Communities." *Journal of Black Studies* 35 (5): 633–649.

Massey, Douglas S., and Nancy A. Denton. 1993. *American Apartheid*. Cambridge, MA: Harvard University Press.

Mohl, Raymond A. 2003a. "Ike and the Interstates: Creeping Toward Comprehensive Planning." *Journal of Planning History* 2:237–262.

Mohl, Raymond A. 2003b. "The Second Ghetto Thesis and the Power of History." *Journal of Urban History* 29:243–256.

Olson, Sherry. 1976. *Baltimore*. Pensacola, FL: Ballinger Publishing Company.

Pellow, David Naguib, and Robert J. Brulle. 2005. "Power, Justice, and the Environment: Toward Critical Environmental Justice Studies." In *Power, Justice, and the Environment*, edited by D. N. Pellow and R. J. Brulle, 1–19. Cambridge, MA: MIT Press Books.

Pettit, Becky, and Bruce Western. 2004. "Mass Imprisonment and the Life Course: Race and Class Inequality in U.S. Incarceration." *American Sociological Review* 69 (2): 151–169.

Pew Center on the States. 2008a. *One in 100: Behind Bars in America 2008*. Washington, DC: Pew Charitable Trusts.

Pew Center on the States. 2008b. "Pew Report Finds More Than One in 100 Adults Are Behind Bars." Press release. http://www.pewcenter onthestates.org/news_room_detail.aspx?id=35912.

Price, Byron E. 2006. *Merchandizing Prisoners*. Westport, CT: Praeger.

Sampson, Robert J., and Charles Loeffler. 2010. "Punishment's Place: The Local Concentration of Mass Incarceration." *Daedalus* 139 (3): 20–31.

Sentencing Project. 2004. *Prison Privatization and the Use of Incarceration*. Washington, DC: Sentencing Project.

Smith, Kevin B. 2004. "The Politics of Punishment: Evaluating Political Explanations of Incarceration Rates." *Journal of Politics* 66 (3): 925–938.

Sugure, Thomas J. 1996. *The Origins of the Urban Crisis*. Princeton, NJ: Princeton University Press.

Wacquant, Loic. 2001. "Deadly Symbiosis." *Punishment & Society* 3 (1): 61–62.

Wacquant, Loic. 2010. "Class, Race and Hyperincarceration in Revanchist America." *Daedalus* 139 (3): 74–89.

Ward, James D. 2008. "Privatization and Social Equity: A Research Note." *Journal of Public Affairs Education* 14 (1): 111–114.

Wilson, David. 2007. *Cities and Race: America's New Black Ghetto*. New York: Routledge.

Wilson, William Julius. 1987. *The Truly Disadvantaged: The Inner City, the Underclass, and Public Policy*. Chicago: University of Chicago Press.

Wilson, William Julius. 2009. *More Than Just Race*. New York: W. W. Norton & Company.

7

Grassroots Efforts against Private Prisons[1]

Carol F. Black

The focus of this chapter is on highlighting efforts of grassroots groups that are working against the privatization of prisons. Grassroots groups in this case refers to groups of citizens that come together to speak with a collective voice and take action on some social or political issue affecting their lives or the lives of those in their own communities. Privatization of prisons refers to the state and federal governments' practice of selling the management of their prisons to a private company or corporation.

One of the main arguments against privatization of prisons is that corporations are in the business of profit. Their first responsibility is to their shareholders, who have made an investment in the success of that company as measured in terms of profit. They have a monetary interest in the continuation of that company and the growth of their profit margins. They have a vested interest in people continuing to commit crimes and inmates serving longer sentences. To put it simply, the more prisoners their facilities hold, the more profit they make.

When prisons are run for profit, they stand in the way of any reduction in our prison population. Creative and alternative programs to incarceration, such as those involving treatment for drug addiction combined with mental health therapy and work in the community, are contrary to the incentives of corporations because they reduce profit margins. Should the government be in the business of keeping people, many of whom did not commit violent crimes, in prison for profit? Many grassroots groups are coming together to advocate against this practice.

The get-tough-on-crime political trend in America from the 1970s to the 1980s resulted in many changes to sentencing laws, which increased the length of time served for various crimes. Truth-in-sentencing laws, for example, mandated that 85 percent of any sentence given should be served behind bars. States adopting these practices were given federal grants. Changes in drug laws also increased the prison population by putting those convicted of drug crimes, especially those involving crack cocaine, behind bars for a determined sentence, rather than in treatment programs. All of these changes increased the prison population, making prisons the over-crowded, violence-filled environments they are today. Current downward economic trends have state governments looking for ways to decrease prison costs. Private prisons promote themselves as one way to decrease costs. However, groups opposed to privatization argue that the proposed savings are lost over the long term in the form of corporate profits. In addition, lessened public safety, more violence within the prisons, and more prisoner escapes are consequences of private prisons. Privately run prisons tend to have fewer employees than prisons operated by the state, and those employees work for less pay and receive fewer benefits (*Edinburgh Evening News* 2010; *Santa Fe New Mexican* 2008). The turnover rate is higher for private prison personnel, so private prisons tend to have employees with less experience. Employees with less experience tend to react with less tact and wisdom in difficult situations, resulting in more retributive behavior.

Because of such reasons as these, grassroots groups against private prisons are arising on many fronts; they are becoming organized and are leading community efforts against building more private facilities in their communities. In some cases, they have led successful lawsuits against abuses that have occurred inside private prisons, some resulting in death (*Palm Beach Post* 2010; *Philadelphia Inquirer* 2009; Shahshahani 2009). Many of their efforts will be highlighted in this chapter, which is not meant to be comprehensive and all-inclusive, but, instead, representative of the many efforts taking place across the country. Some of the groups are established on the Internet and have their own publicly available newsletters documenting their projects. I have collected information from their websites and have interviewed some of those most actively involved in organizing such efforts around the country. Additionally, a nationwide news search identified more than 50 articles on privatization of prisons in just the past two years. These news articles provided ample background material for the lively debate occurring on whether or not to use private facilities.

Grassroots Groups for General Prison Reform

One of the unintended consequences of the growth in the prison population over the past 30 years, from 200,000 incarcerated in 1970 to two million in 2000 (Mauer 2001), is the growth of grassroots citizens' groups working on prison reforms. They exist in a wide variety of types and focus on a multitude of issues, but are all dedicated to reforming the prison system in some way to make it more rehabilitative and humane. They are organized in every region and nearly every state of the United States.

Many members of these groups are women with a loved one who is incarcerated. Because most of the current prison population is male, the loved one behind bars is oftentimes a son, brother, husband, or boyfriend and is oftentimes incarcerated for a nonviolent crime. Before coming into direct contact with the prison system, they likely believed the American criminal justice system is the best justice system in the world. They likely believed their loved one, even if guilty, would be treated fairly and humanely. They were unaware that more than 90 percent of all criminal cases never go to trial because a plea bargain deal is struck (Mauer 2001), thus taking away the American ideal of innocent until proven guilty. They were not prepared for the reality of overcrowded, unhealthy, violence-ridden state and federal prison environments, and they never considered that they would be fighting for their loved one's very survival while he served his time behind bars. Their shock at the reality of prison life led many to seek more information and to find others in the same position as themselves. Many go to the Internet to educate themselves on prison issues and find, to their surprise, organized groups already working on various prison reforms (Black 2010). They learn from these groups how to best interact with prison personnel on their incarcerated loved one's behalf. They become skilled advocates for their loved ones, aware of the various levels of prison personnel and administration that make policies related to prisoners—from correctional officers to wardens and on up to the level of state governors or the United States Congress. They become better informed on their rights as

U.S. citizens and educated on legislative and legal matters related to prisoners. They decide to stay involved in educating other families and the general public about the realities of U.S. prisons. They attend meetings, take collective action on bills coming before their state legislatures, write letters to editors of their local papers, hold rallies, advocate for or against persons to be appointed to parole boards, testify before state representatives or Congress, or in other ways advocate for a better functioning, more just prison system.

Not all of the members of prison reform groups are women with loved ones who are incarcerated. Some are women or men who became involved in prison ministry or life education workshops for prisoners. Some come from programs that set up pen pals for prisoners. Some are husbands, fathers, uncles, and brothers of male and female inmates, but for the most part, they are not visible in many of these groups. Gender roles, as played out in our society, place women in the position of nurturers and caregivers. They tend to be the ones who show up at meetings and advocate for their loved ones who are incarcerated.

However, there is one group of men who are more visible in prison reform groups: men who were formerly incarcerated. Their involvement stems from their own experience behind bars. Some contacted advocacy groups while incarcerated, and those groups helped them survive a situation of abuse from corrections officers or other inmates. Some were assisted by prison reform groups in getting medication they desperately needed or in being placed in a transitional program to help them adjust to life on the outside. Once released, they made a commitment to join the group and advocate for those who are still incarcerated. For many of them, leaving prison meant leaving good friends behind, friends who had become like brothers while on the inside. Once outside, newly released inmates are not allowed to visit a prisoner until they finish their parole, which can take many months. For various reasons, some men who finish their prison terms and are released decide to give back to their brothers and sisters who are still incarcerated and become advocates for prison reform.

And finally, some members of prison reform groups become involved as college students or political activists because of their concern about the focus on punishment rather than rehabilitation or about prison conditions. They learn of our deplorable recidivism rate, which points toward our prisons actually fostering criminality, rather than diminishing it. One report from the Bureau of Justice Statistics states that two-thirds of all inmates released from state prisons commit a new serious crime within three years of their release (Langan and Levin 2002).

Grassroots Efforts against Private Prisons

When I began to research grassroots efforts against private prisons, I expected to find groups similar to those that were working on various prison reforms in general. I expected to find groups of citizens, many of them with loved ones incarcerated, and with most of the membership being women. Instead, I found great differences in composition of membership and the way these groups functioned compared with general prison reform groups. The first striking difference was that most of those who were active in grassroots groups against private prisons were men. They were also very different in the way they went about fighting private prisons. These men tend to travel and follow private prison contractors from state to state. Rather than focusing on the correctional system of one state or another, they are in a fight against privatization of prisons nationwide. They understand who they are fighting, they have developed standard tactics, and they are prepared to travel wherever they need to do battle. Some engage in this battle as a full-time job. Supported by grassroots lobby groups, they have dedicated their work lives to this cause.[2]

Increase in Privatization of Prison Services

Some activist groups have noticed an increase in the private sector's role in the delivery of prison services, even when the prisons are state operated. A source in Pennsylvania reported recent privatization of prisoner medical care, the commissary, and vendors that operate money machines where family members of an inmate can deposit money for a prisoner. Before September 2010, family members were able to send a money order through the mail to the prison. Now, they have to make a transaction through a private company, JPay, which charges a transaction fee of $5 per every $100 deposited to the inmate's account (e-mail to the author, October 6, 2010). They need money because, increasingly, inmates are charged for every needed item they use, including clothes, shoes, or toothpaste. In some cases, inmates are now being charged room and board. The reason prisons have a commissary store is that meals have been watered down and the portions cut down; the nutritional content of the diet is so low that many medical problems develop. To supplement their diets, inmates are permitted to buy food at the commissary store at inflated prices. As inmates, they cannot afford these fees, so their family members, who have not committed any crime, pay them (Black 2010).

The Southern Center for Human Rights is fighting unfair fees charged by privatization of probation companies to those with the least income. An article from the *Augusta Chronicle* explains how traffic court fines in Richmond County, Georgia, can lead to jail time (Hodson 2009). People who can pay their fines walk out of court free. Those who cannot pay the fines are usually allowed to make payments. However, the private probation company collecting the fines can keep half the money paid if the monthly fees are not paid in full each month. Hodson (2009) gives the example of a 63-year-old assistant minister who lived on Social Security and was placed on probation after agreeing to make monthly payments on her traffic fine of $140. Her monthly payments now included a probation fee and victims' fund fee of $39 per month, in addition to her traffic fine amount. She was eventually threatened with jail time, and that is when the Southern Center for Human Rights intervened on her behalf. The court and probation system thus traps those who have the least to begin with, while private companies that have a vested interest in the system's continuation reap the profits (Hodson 2009).

Groups Issuing Position Statements against Private Prisons

Many religious groups are taking a stand against private prisons on moral grounds. The American Friends Service Committee, which is connected to the Quakers, long-time activists in the area of human rights, held a series of public forums on private prisons in Tucson. Prompted to address the issue after the highly publicized recent escape of inmates from a private facility in Kingman, Arizona, the group gathered a broad array of speakers and listeners to attend the event, "in the interest of government accountability, integrity of our corrections system, and public safety" (AFSC 2010). Speakers included people on all sides of the controversy, including prison staff, the Arizona Department of Corrections, an Arizona state representative, a Tucson city council member, and experts on the financial and social impacts of prison privatization. The event was attended by 150 people. Subsequently, the State of Arizona rescinded its request for 5,000 new private prison beds and issued a new request for 2,000 beds, which remained pending at the time of writing. The AFSC unsuccessfully sued to try to stop the first bidding process (AFSC 2012). Activist Frank Smith, interviewed in this chapter, believes CCA will get the bid for 2,000 new beds, but this will not require the building of a new prison (Frank Smith, personal communication, April 28, 2012).

Other religious groups that have issued public statements against private prisons on moral grounds alone are the United Methodist Church, the Presbyterian Church USA, the Southern Catholic bishops, and the Episcopal Diocese of Newark (Private Corrections Working Group 2010a). To quote one of these statements: "Since the goal of for-profit private prisons is earning a profit for their shareholders, there is a basic and fundamental conflict with the concept of rehabilitation as the ultimate goal of the prison system" (Private Corrections Working Group 2010a).

Additionally, some prison reform groups not specifically involved in organized efforts against private prisons have issued a position statement against them. Citizens United for the Rehabilitation of Errants (CURE) is a nationally organized prison reform activist group with chapters in most of the 50 states. CURE considers itself a watchdog for abuses against inmates and fights for humane and rehabilitative treatment of prisoners. Among the official position papers CURE has issued is one that addresses its opposition to private prisons, in which the organization states that all prison facilities should meet the following criteria:

1. Operate the detention facility in a way that ensures humane treatment and respect for the dignity of the detained individual.
2. Establish procedures that clearly state how long the individual will be detained and/or what must be done to earn release.
3. Provide treatment, rehabilitation, and educational programming that address the problems that led to the detention.
4. Operate the facility in a way that does not exploit the detainee and/or his or her loved ones. (CURE 2010)

CURE believes detention facilities should be state operated but asks that private facilities be held to these criteria, be monitored periodically, and have clear penalties in existence for failure to comply.

Intensive Efforts of Groups against Private Prisons

The following groups have involvement that is so extensive they could be the subject of an entire book. Some of their main success stories, and those involved in making them happen, will be shared in this section.

Prison Legal News

Prison Legal News (PLN) is a nonprofit organization founded in 1990 that produces a monthly publication covering a broad range of criminal justice–related issues. Based in Vermont, the group says it is dedicated to protecting human rights in detention facilities. It has reported extensively on the private prison industry and has pursued successful litigation against two of the largest private prison companies, GEO Group and the Corrections Corporation of America (CCA).

In August 2009, PLN successfully intervened to compel records of a settlement between CCA and some of their employees to be made public. The case, *Barnwell et al. v. Corrections Corp. of America*, included a $7 million maximum gross amount payable by CCA in the settlement, depending on how many CCA employees opted to be part of the lawsuit. The suit successfully alleged that CCA employees were obliged to work hours off the clock, or to otherwise inaccurately report their work hours. The part PLN played was to file a motion to unseal the documents and make them available to the public (Prison Legal News 2009).

In March 2010, after the State Supreme Court of Tennessee declined to hear a final appeal by CCA, PLN won a case to have records opened that revealed lawsuits against CCA, the largest private prison facility in the nation, as well as reports or audits that found contract violations by CCA. Alex Friedmann (read more about him in the section on PCI), long-time activist against prison privatization and associate editor of PLN, is quoted as saying, "Allowing a private company to incarcerate people, and generate profit from their incarceration, is morally wrong and a social injustice" (Prison Legal News 2010a). CCA argued that it is a private corporation and not bound by the Public Records Act, as are government institutions. The Court of Appeals rejected that argument, stating, "With all due respect to CCA, this Court is at a loss as to how operating a prison could be considered anything less than a government function" (Prison Legal News 2010a).

In June 2010, PLN won another case against CCA regarding a facility in Arizona that was restricting inmate access to books, allowing only books from Amazon and Barnes and Noble book companies to be received by inmates. PLN successfully argued that this was a violation of First Amendment rights and the Arizona Constitution. Books on their list of banned publications included many self-help books, dictionaries, and other educational materials. PLN was awarded $70,000 in damages and attorney's fees because of the prison's previous refusal to allow PLN books in the prisons of Arizona (Friedmann 2010).

In 2005, PLN used Florida's public record law to initiate a case against the second-largest private prison company in the nation, the GEO Group. This case, like many of PLN's cases against private prison companies, had the goal of making the company's records as public as those of any state institution. The GEO Group may be a private company, but it is in the business of managing a state institution responsible for the care and welfare of those within its walls. The case dragged on for five years, while the GEO Group refused to turn over files documenting contractual violations and litigation against them resulting in settlements or verdicts, even while four motions were filed in circuit courts ordering the GEO to produce the documents. In the end, the GEO Group had to pay $40,000 in attorney fees to PLN and had to produce a spreadsheet that detailed litigation, complaints, and settlements from 10 lawsuits. The case was settled May 10, 2010 (Prison Legal News 2010b).

Clearly, PLN is a relentless foe of private prison corporations, choosing the courtroom for a battlefield. PLN is one of the few prison reform groups that deals directly with the legal system, taking part in lawsuits and working with attorneys and the American Civil Liberties Union (ACLU) to win its cases. Most prison reform groups do not get involved in legal cases or legal counsel on individual inmate's cases, but rather, they work in an educational capacity, as advocates against abuses, or as organizers on other prisoner-related issues.

Private Corrections Working Group

One of the groups working on educative efforts is the Private Corrections Working Group (PCWG), which has a mission to "provide information and assistance to citizens, policy makers, and journalists concerning the dangers and pitfalls of privatization of correctional institutions and services in order to reverse and stop this social injustice" (Private Corrections Working Group 2010b). The PCWG website lists numerous nationwide Associated Press news releases, many of them authored by PCWG members and indicating their involvement in spreading knowledge about lawsuits against private prisons. PCWG publishes salaries of chief executive officers in many companies managing prisons for profit, including bonuses and stock options. "Rap sheets" for private companies contracting various prison services, such as food services, testify to the problems appearing in many of these companies' services. PCWG's director is Ken Kopczynski, whose book *Private Capitol Punishment: The Florida Model* (2004) tells the story of prison privatization and corruption in Florida. Included is the story of Professor Charles Thomas, who wrote his praises of private prisons while investing in private prisons stock and receiving payments from private prison companies.

Private Corrections Institute

A nonprofit subsidiary group within PCWG is the Private Corrections Institute (PCI), which, in addition to publishing a wealth of informative reports on the Internet, works with people at the grassroots level who oppose construction of a private prison in their communities. Alex Friedmann, president of PCI, spent seven years behind bars, where he formed his impressions of state-run versus privately run prison facilities. He noticed in the privately run facility that the constant emphasis on profit resulted in a lack of necessary everyday items, such as toilet paper, blankets, and soap, being given to inmates. For men dealing with the realities of prison life, "an added lack of these kinds of items can result in a riot," states Friedmann (personal communication, October 15, 2010). He also noticed that correctional officers in the private facility, which was very much like the state facility in size and design, lacked experience and expertise, so they were quick to respond with unnecessarily harsh retaliation to any infractionary behavior from an inmate.

Friedmann became involved in prison reform while still an inmate, publishing a small monthly newsletter, the *Private Corrections Industry News Bulletin*, which reported on news and developments related to the private prison industry. This publication was sent to a friend who distributed it to a small number of people working in prison reform. Friedmann filed suit against CCA and its employees in federal court, alleging First Amendment retaliation and due process claims, but he lost this case at trial (Alex Friedmann, personal communication, October 15, 2010).

Friedmann joined PCI after finishing his sentence 11 years ago, and he remains an active and informed advocate in the fight against private prisons. He provided information and fact sheets to, and worked with, community groups that successfully opposed CCA's proposed takeover of Tennessee's prison system in 1997–1998, including religious groups and the Tennessee State Employees Association. He has spoken in opposition to private prisons on radio and television and to a congressional Correctional Officers Caucus meeting in Washington, D.C., sponsored by the American Federation of State, Municipal and Court Employees. He is often called upon to speak at rallies, conferences, and other events related to prison privatization. In October 2007, he spoke in opposition to prison privatization before the Pennsylvania state legislature at a joint hearing of the labor and justice committees.

Since joining the staff of PLN as associate editor in 2005, Friedmann has conducted research and written many articles for PLN's monthly publication on a variety of criminal justice topics. Friedmann organized and coordinated a successful year-long campaign opposing the federal judicial nomination of Gus Puryear, CCA's general counsel, which resulted in extensive media coverage and Puryear's withdrawal from judicial nomination ("Tennesseans Against Puryear" 2009; Wright 2009; Alex Friedmann, personal communication, October 14, 2010). Along with PLN editor Paul Wright, Friedmann provided information to the production staff of Michael Moore, who included a segment on prison privatization in his film *Capitalism: A Love Story*, and their names were listed in the credits. For the television show *Boston Legal*, Friedmann provided counsel for an episode on private prisons.

One of the most creative actions Friedmann took against private prisons was to buy one share of CCA stock in 2005 in order to be allowed entrance into CCA annual shareholder meetings and ask questions of CCA's board. He then purchased another 190 shares, so that he would be able to introduce shareholder resolutions in the future.

PCI Man in the Field: Frank Smith

The name that stood out over and over again in research on grassroots efforts against private prisons is Frank Smith, the person PCI sends to survey communities that are asking for help in preventing construction of a new private prison facility in their locality. Smith says he does not have any set method, but he goes to each locality and finds possible groups to work with. Each place is different, so he needs to go there to judge how to best create an action plan in that location. His activism began in Alaska, where he happened to be working as a prison counselor when the corrections department contemplated sending some of their prisoners to Texas. Smith circulated research on the effect visitation has on recidivism. A number of authors have expressed the view that bonds and ties to family create a better possibility that the inmate will be motivated toward a life that is less tied to criminal activity, yet the prison system frequently moves inmates from one facility to another, even from one state to another, which breaks down family ties, making it more difficult for them to visit (Black 2010; Fishman 1990; Girschick 1996).

A collaboration of efforts and effects stopped the construction of private prisons in the state of Alaska. Frank Smith and his colleague Dee Hubbard were primary protagonists in the effort to rally the public against the building of private prisons in their state. Their efforts were helped when they uncovered greed and corruption among some high-level politicians and contractors, who were eventually convicted of bribery on many counts and served time in federal prison.

During the 1990s, a campaign to build private prisons in Alaska was begun by a few key players. One was Bill Weimar, a businessman who already owned a number of halfway houses connected to the state corrections system and was the principal spokesperson for the idea to build the first two private prisons in Alaska. One of the appeals made for private prisons to be built in this state was to return native prisoners to Alaska. More than 800 native prisoners had already been shipped to prisons in the lower 48 states because Alaskan prisons were crowded beyond their capacity (Kizzia 2008). Additionally, the usual appeals were made that private prisons are cheaper to operate and would save the state money. Two prisons deals were already approved and others were headed into the state legislature when local opposition formed a strong alliance to stopping them. Who stood to lose money if these prisons were not built? VECO Corrections Group North, a construction firm that had a 25-year prison deal worth $1 billion; Cornell Corrections, a private prison company based in Texas, which had ties to Halliburton; and Bill Weimar's own company, Allvest (Fitts, 2006; Kizzia 2008). The first private prison was to be built on VECO-owned land. The wife of the House finance chairman, Republican representative Eldon Mulder, worked for Cornell lobbyist Joe Hayes. Former state senator Jerry Ward had ties to a Cornell partner, the Kenai Natives Association. Too many obvious ties of state politicians and construction executives made their motives transparent enough to be easily toppled. Representative Eric Croft, a Democrat, complained, "What I see over and over is repeated sole-source, pre-arranged, heavy money deals that go to specific contractors...it's never been a clean, competitive proposal" (Kizzia 2008).

Resistance came from local guard unions, who stood to lose income with the influx of private prisons and their lower wages; Native groups; and many other community and civic organizations brought together through the efforts of Frank Smith and Dee Hubbard. They eventually brought about the downfall of the private prison proposal in Anchorage. When a city-wide vote was placed on a public ballot, Anchorage voters rejected the building of a private prison in their city by a 2-1 margin.

Those wanting to push private prisons into Alaska did not stop there. They moved on to other cities and proposed similar projects. The battle went from Anchorage to Fort Greely near Delta Junction. When Weimar brought Cornell Corrections into the plan for Delta Junction, public sentiment changed and the contract was broken. Cornell Corrections sued Delta Junction and won a settlement of $1.1 million. The last stand was made at Kenai Peninsula Borough, where a contract was given to Corrections Group North but then cancelled after a rising wave of public opinion against construction of the private prison. The Borough Assembly decided to ask for public approval in a popular vote, and the prison proposal lost by a 3-1 ratio (Kizzia 2008; Frank Smith, personal communication, October 15, 2010).

Frank Smith made this work his temporary life mission, following the contractors throughout the state, organizing human rights groups, and educating the public about private prisons and their possible repercussions on their communities. Dee Hubbard, a friend and collaborator, was a central, behind-the-scenes informant throughout this process. She worked with Smith on all fronts, whether in person or by researching information for him and others who were working to stop the private prison initiative in Alaska. Hubbard, who worked for the state legislature as a grant writer, first heard of the private prison proposal in 2002. She told her husband,

> There goes our state again.... They're going to build a private prison, guarantee this prison that it'll have a contract for years, and after so many years they're going to give the prison to the state.... I want to build a store, have the state give me a contract that they'll buy from me for so many years, I'll run the store ... and then the state can just give me the store. (Mauer 2009b)

In her position within the state legislature, Hubbard was able to discover corruption within it—which contractors were making deals with what legislators and what was planned next. What actually emerged was a story even bigger than the prison industry, which encompassed bribery and corruption in the state legislature related to oil-tax and pipeline measures and prison matters (Mauer 2009a). Hubbard became an FBI informant in this investigation.

The fight regarding private prisons in Alaska ended with a last stand in Whittier. Bill Weimar made illegal payments to a legislative candidate in return for his support of the private prison project. The effort failed. By 2005, Whittier said it was done with the prison proposal, and Cornell said it would no longer pursue private prisons in Alaska, though the company was still active in building halfway houses (Kizzia 2008). The federal corruption investigation culminated in a number of convictions and prison terms for bribery and other white-collar crimes. The FBI investigation, termed Operation Polar Pen, originally investigated corruption linked to the private prison industry. From there, the investigation led to further corruption charges linking the state legislature to bribery within the oil industry and pipeline measures (Kizzia 2008; Mauer 2009a, 2009b). Those indicted for taking or giving bribes included Bill Weimar, lobbyist Bill Bobrick, former representative Tom Anderson, former representation Vic Kohring, former state corrections commissioner Frank Prewitt, and VECO Corporation chief executive Bill Allen. After winning the fight in Alaska, Smith moved on to private prison industry battles in other states.

In Oklahoma, a proposal collapsed in the face of a planned picket of two upcoming weekend concerts at an Indian reservation casino, after resident leaders consulted with Smith about mediation. He counseled homeowners to reject it. The project was stopped but there was some talk of moving it elsewhere, and the issue is not yet resolved. Some of Smith's most recent efforts and success stories have been in the state of Arizona. His final advice in organizing efforts against privatization is:

> Resist the proposals as soon and as vigorously as possible after they're announced or discovered. It may be intense, but it's time very well spent, as one could fritter away years and a lot of money on a drawn-out battle. And what I tell organizers all over the country . . . is that they need to build a relationship with the media years before they actually have need of it. (Frank Smith, personal communication, October 15, 2010)

Smith uses a fairly simple plan of action wherever he goes. He assesses a community where privatization is being talked about; contacts the media, including radio and television; writes letters to the editor in the local paper; and asks that information on contracts be made public through the Freedom of Information and Open Records Acts. Private companies do not like to give out this information, but by law, they must. Many civic, labor, civil rights, and religious groups will lend their support to a situation they conceive to be morally unjust and detrimental to the labor force of their own community. All of this amounts to a massive amount of organized coalition building, and these coalitions, when united in a cause and covered by the media, make for a formidable force toward changing plans to build a private prison. What helps bring success to their efforts are that "for-profit operations have a dismal record, they're dangerous and they've been demonstrated to actually damage local economies," says Smith (personal communication, October 15, 2010). He adds that they have very good research to back up their claims. Challenges to successful coalition building include corruption of local officials and plans for privatization being secretive and set in place for a long time before their arrival.

Grassroots Leadership

Grassroots Leadership, based in Texas, is another nonprofit group that opposes private prisons. Their website states, "We believe that no one should profit from the incarceration of human beings. We work with communities across this nation, to abolish for-profit prisons, jails, and detention centers" (Grassroots Leadership 2010). The group promotes itself as a southern-based multiracial team of organizers who work within local labor, campus, and faith organizations to promote thinking critically and achieving justice and equity. The group originally formed 30 years ago as a multiracial coalition united in concern that privatization in many social service areas was eroding the gains made during the civil rights movement. Privatization of hospitals, schools, and now prisons puts private companies in the place of governments bound to policy changes made in the area of civil rights.

Though the home office of Grassroots Leadership is in Charlotte, North Carolina, a lot of the efforts against private prisons are now focused in Texas. An interactive map on their website points to at least 70 privately run prisons and detention centers in the state of Texas.

Bob Libal now works full time for Grassroots Leadership. As a graduate student at the University of Texas, Libal became involved in the "Not With Our Money" campaign, which, under the direction of Kevin Pranis from 1999 to 2001, waged a successful effort through organizing college/university students to force Sodexho-Marriott to divest its stock holdings in CCA, and it later targeted institutions that finance the private prison industry, such as Lehman Brothers (Bob Libal, personal communication, October 15, 2010). At Yale, a graduate student organization worked with Grassroots Leadership against the university's investing a large endowment in private prisons through Farralon Capital Management, a hedge fund, and eventually forced divestment from CCA stock. Student groups around the country protested Sodexho, a company that often runs campus dining halls, and were successful in forcing Sodexho to divest its stocks in CCA (Bob Libal, personal communication, October 14, 2010).

Another very successful campaign was conducted in Tennessee, where privatization of the entire state prison system was being planned. Grassroots Leadership worked with the American Federation of State, County and Municipal Employees (AFSCME) 1733, the union formed under the direction of Dr. Martin Luther King Jr. Grassroots Leadership formed a huge coalition of groups, including many churches, the Rainbow Coalition, the Mid-South Peace and Justice Center, the AFSCME 1733 union, and even correctional officers who spoke at meetings against further incarceration instead of teaching skills to inmates so they don't want to return to prison (Bob Libal, personal communication, October 14, 2010).

Grassroots Leadership got media coverage when a Catholic priest who was on their staff part-time spoke in front of the Black Baptist Convention, and their effort was successful in stopping privatization of the Tennessee state prison system.

Federal Immigration Family Detention Centers

One of the most successful campaigns Grassroots Leadership and many other groups were involved in was the closing of the T. Don Hutto federal detention facility in Texas. Run by CCA, this facility, like many other federal facilities today, was in the business of not only incarcerating adults who were caught crossing the border illegally but their children as well. Stocks in private prison companies were not doing well in the 1990s. The federal government, under the leadership of George W. Bush, came up with a new plan for their success (*New York Times* 2009; *Register-Guard* 2009). Rather than working illegal aliens through civil proceedings and deporting them back to their home countries, the federal government began incarcerating them for months at a time in facilities managed by private companies. Family detention centers were created where children were incarcerated with their parents behind barbed wire, dressed in prison uniforms, and given one hour of recreation and one hour of school instruction per day. The rest of the time, children were held inside an 8-foot-by 12-foot prison cell with their mother. The children have testified that they were threatened with separation from their mothers (Gossage and Keber 2007). Under the George W. Bush administration, Operation Streamline mandated the criminal prosecution of border crossers in certain areas. These family detention centers now exist around the country and are a growing, for-profit business.

One person who became appalled at the T. Don Hutto family detention center was Jay Johnson-Castro, who decided to do a symbolic walk for a few hundred miles along the border wall. Along the way, he learned the horrific story of the T. Don Hutto detention facility and decided to become more involved in the effort to close it (Johnson-Castro 2009). A large number of groups came together to form a coalition in this effort, including the University of Texas Law Clinic, the ACLU, Grassroots Leadership, and many other human rights groups. They held frequent vigils at the facility, sometimes by candlelight, and gathered to wave flags and sing songs. They gained media attention, attracting people from larger cities to this small rural facility, outside of town, behind railroad tracks, a place many of the local townspeople did not even know existed (Jay Johnson-Castro, personal communication, October 15, 2010). At the Christmas holiday, they came bringing gifts for the incarcerated children, which were refused by facility officials. The second year, they came again, and again their gifts were not taken inside the prison. The third year, the group decided to sing and walk their way defiantly all the way into the reception area of the prison, where they left their gifts of toys for the children peacefully and without incident. They printed T-shirts and, through networking efforts, eventually got one sent to President Barack Obama. After many years with dozens of vigils and intense effort by many groups, President Obama ordered this facility closed to any further family detention. However, other family detention facilities still exist, and the fight has only begun against this practice. Johnson-Castro continues his walks, most recently in Arizona, to protest children being held for profit behind barbed wire within the boundaries of our nation. Meanwhile, the T. Don Hutto facility is still open. Though no children are behind its walls, female border crossers are still detained there. The federal government found a way to resurrect the private prison industry in the form of federal prosecution of illegal border crossers.

Conclusion

In this chapter, I have described a few of the prominent groups working at the grassroots level to stop privatization of the prison industry. Their efforts reveal many legal victories, and occasionally the stopping altogether of the building or management of state or federal prisons by private companies. Their formidable foe is greed, and the profit being made by all those holding shares of stock in these companies, which include a number of the most powerful politicians of both major political parties. The groups share a goal that no one should profit from the incarceration of human beings. Their success rests on the shoulders of each and every voter and supporter of human rights. The only way to shift the focus from incarceration to rehabilitation in our society is to allow creative, alternative solutions to flourish. This cannot be done when money is being made from the continuation of our current rates of incarceration.

Success stories of grassroots efforts against the building of private prisons are stories of individual battles won. Powerful corporations and political leaders are fighting to cash in on a very profitable enterprise with a global reach. Still, there are successes to be celebrated. Privatization of prisons has disappeared from Alaska and has been stopped in Tennessee. Children have been removed from the T. Don Hutto facility in Texas, all through grassroots efforts of citizens who came together for a purpose and refused to give in to corporate pressure. Political rhetoric is beginning to sway toward alternatives to incarceration. With the current economic crisis comes local community resistance toward building more prisons. Grassroots groups against private prisons, as well as prison reform groups in all their diversity, continue to appear and grow.

Within each grassroots organization, there are key people who organize, putting out a tremendous amount of time and energy with very little in return. The loss of any one of these key people deals a mighty blow to the fledgling efforts of grassroots resistance. Dee Hubbard was one of those individuals. She passed away in 2009, at the age of 62. Her husband said about her, "When she thought something was unjust, she was not going to sit around and wait for someone to do something—she felt *she was* the someone" (Mauer 2009b). Success comes in the form of persons like Dee who see themselves as the one to do something and make a difference. They decide not to take the path of least resistance. From their efforts, others gain strength, and a broader level of change is born. Each success is one to be celebrated. From many different efforts of groups at various levels comes collective transformation.

Notes

1. Dedicated to the memory of Dee Hubbard.
2. Social science researchers are bound by a code of ethics that guarantees anonymity to all interviewees who desire it. For most of the organizations described here, their presence is publicly available on the Internet, along with real names. Many of these activists write articles in their own newsletters. No one has to join their organization to have access to those newsletters or messages. They are viewable by anyone accessing the Internet. Nevertheless, I have only included real names of those who wished to be identified by name

and gave me written consent to do so. The more publicity their organization receives, the better their cause will be known, and the more likely their goals will be won. They also get calls from other media and press, if their real names are used. They consider it a disservice not to publish their names.

References

American Friends Service Committee (AFSC). 2010. "Public Hearing on Prison Privatization in Arizona." http://afsc.org/event/public-hearing -prison-privatization-arizona.

American Friends Service Committee (AFSC). 2012. "Arizona Judge Rejects Temporary Halt to For-Profit Prison Contracts." http://afsc.org/ story/arizona-judge-rejects-temporary-halt-profit-prison-contracts.

Black, Carol. 2010. *Working for Justice: Families and Prison Reform.* Cologne, Germany: Lambert Academic Publishing.

Citizens United for the Rehabilitation of Errants (CURE). 2010. *Privatization of Prisons.* CURE position paper. http://www.curenational.org/ privacy.html.

Edinburgh Evening News. 2010. "Addiewell: After Riots Leave Two Guards Injured, Critics Warn of Cash Constraints in Private Prisons." January 28. http://ezproxy.newberry.edu:2074/gtx/start.do?prodId=SPN .SP00&userGroupName=wessels.

Fishman, Laura. 1990. *Women at the Wall: A Study of Prisoners' Wives Doing Time on the Outside.* New York: State University of New York Press.

Fitts, Catherine Austin. 2006. "Cornell Corrections." In *Dillon Read & Co., Inc., and the Aristocracy of Stock Profits.* http://dunwalke.com/9_ Cornell_Corrections.htm.

Friedmann, Alex. 2010. "CCA Pays $70,000 in Damages, Attorney Fees to Settle PLN Censorship Suit in Arizona 2010." June 7. https://www .prisonlegalnews.org/22558_displayArticle.aspx.

Girshick, Lori. 1996. *Soledad Women: Wives of Prisoners Speak Out.* Westport, CT: Praeger Publishers.

Gossage, Matthew, and Lily Keber. 2007. "America's Family Prison." Video. T. Don Hutto website. http://tdonhutto.blogspot.com.

Grassroots Leadership. 2010. www.grassrootsleadership.org.

Hodson, Sandy. 2009. "Critics Say Private Probation Punishes Poor Unfairly." *Augusta (GA) Chronicle*. November 15. http://www.schr.org/action/resources/critics_say_private_probation_punishes_poor_unfairly.

Johnson-Castro, Jay. 2009. "Our Hero Jay Johnson-Castro Walks Again." *Texas Civil Rights Review*. http://texascivilrightsreview.org/phpnuke/modules.php?name=News&file=article&sid=683.

Kizzia, Tom. 2008. "Push for Private Prison Was Weimar's Downfall: Guilty Plea: Ex-Halfway House Official Was Accused in Conspiracy Scheme." *Anchorage Daily News*, August 12. http://www.adn.com/2008/08/12/490975/push-for-private-prison-was-downfall.html.

Kopczynski, Ken. 2004. *Private Capitol Punishment: The Florida Model*. Bloomington, IN: Authorhouse.

Langan, Patrick, and David Levin. 2002. *Recidivism in Prisoners Released in 1994*. Washington, DC: Bureau of Justice Statistics.

Mauer, Marc. 2001. "The Causes and Consequences of Prison Growth in the United States." *Punishment & Society* 3:9–20.

Mauer, Richard. 2009a. "Despite His Lockup, Kohring Still Supports Private Prisons: Reform: If the Freed Ex-Legislator Ever Gets Re-elected, He Says He Would Work to Improve Conditions." *Anchorage Daily News*, June 14. http://ezproxy.newberry.edu:2074/gtx/start.do?prodId=SPN.SP00&userGroupName=wessels.

Mauer, Richard. 2009b. "Low-key Anti-corruption Campaigner Is Dead at 62: Dee Hubbard: Activist Assisted FBI Investigating Private Prisons Syndicate." *Anchorage Daily News*, September 2. http://ezproxy.newberry.edu:2074/gtx/start.do?prodId=SPN.SP00&userGroupName=wessels.

New York Times. 2009. "Detained and Abused." August 1, A16. http://ezproxy.newberry.edu:2074/gtx/start.do?prodId=SPN.SP00&userGroupName=wessels.

Palm Beach Post. 2010. "In Sansom's Sneaky Footsteps." March 31, 14A. http://ezproxy.newberry.edu:2074/gtx/start.do?prodId=SPN.SP00&userGroupName=wessels.

Philadelphia Inquirer. 2009. "Cheaper Isn't Always Better." October 29. http://find.galegroup.com/gtx/start.do?prodId=SPN.SP00&userGroupName=wessels.

Prison Legal News. 2009. "PLN Prevails in Motion to Unseal Settlement in CCA Class Action Suit FLSA Case." August 28. https://www.prisonlegalnews.org/21803_displayArticle.aspx.

Prison Legal News. 2010a. "CCA Required to Produce Records after TN Supreme Court Denies Appeal in PLN Suit." March 4. www.prisonle galnews.org/296_displayNews.aspx.

Prison Legal News. 2010b. "PLN Wins Florida Public Records Suit Against GEO Group." May 13. www.prisonlegalnews.org/310_display News.aspx.

Private Corrections Working Group. 2010a. "Religious Statements." http://www.privateci.org/religion.html.

Private Corrections Working Group. 2010b. "Who We Are." http:// www.privateci.org/who.html.

Register-Guard (Eugene, OR). 2009. "Reforming Detention." August 12, A10. http://ezproxy.newberry.edu:2074/gtx/start.do?prodId=SPN.SP00 &userGroupName=wessels.

Santa Fe New Mexican. 2008. "Cost Debate: State Figures Show Private Prisons Cheaper to Run, but N.M. Pays More than Others." July 13. http://ezproxy.newberry.edu:2074/gtx/start.do?prodId=SPN.SP00&user GroupName=wessels.

Shahshahani, A. 2009. "Private Prisons for Immigrants Lack Accountability, Oversight." *Atlanta Journal-Constitution*, June 11, A15. http:// ezproxy.newberry.edu:2074/gtx/start.do?prodId=SPN.SP00&userGroup Name=wessels.

"Tennesseans against Puryear." 2009. Press release. www.againstpur year.org.

Wright, Paul. 2009. "Deconstructing Gus." *CounterPunch: America's Best Political Newsletter*, June 8. http://www.counterpunch.org/wright 06082009.html.

8

Constitutional Implications of Private Prisons

H. Jessica Hargis

As a whole, the study of public administration strives to enhance academe by studying ways to make government more efficient, effective, and democratic (Beckett and Koenig 2005; Cooper 2007; Cooper 1991; Terry 1998, 2005; Waldo 2007, among others). The public administration literature reflects a mounting need for managerial leaders who are responsible for directing and controlling work, acquiring and distributing knowledge, and coordinating agency functions to achieve organizational purpose. Complexity, conflict, change, and uniqueness are all issues that leaders must deal with in order to perform these duties. Public agencies, affected by political, social, and global circumstances and events, create environments that require essential skills to understand and safeguard public values and interests. As privatization and outsourcing of public services becomes a standard pattern of behavior in local, state, and federal government, there is an additional need to understand the constitutional implications of allowing nongovernment entities to administer government functions.

Although private and nonprofit entities provide various public services, such as health care, refuse collection, and various administrative services, this chapter focuses on the government's use of private prisons. The growth of private prisons began in the 1980s, as the culmination of three important factors: calls for a reduction in the size of government through the outsourcing of public services (Durant 1987; Henig 1989–1990; Hill and Hupe 2002; McFarland, McGowan, and O'Toole 2002; Shichor 1995), prison overcrowding (Austin and Coventry 2001; Chang and Thompkins 2002; McDonald 1992; McFarland, McGowan, and O'Toole 2002; Shichor 1995, 1996), and a poorly functioning penal system (Austin and Coventry 2001; DiIulio 1990; Lynch and Sabol 1997; McDonald 1992; Shichor 1995, 1996). Although public prisons used private services early on for various services such as education, medical care, maintenance, and food (Austin and Coventry 2001; Freeman 2000; Shichor 1996), the complete administration of a prison by a private corporations is a modern endeavor (Austin and Coventry 2001; McFarland, McGowan, and O'Toole 2002; Shichor 1995, 1996).

According to the Bureau of Justice Statistics, correctional populations in the United States grew from just under 2 million in 1980 to 7.3 million in 2008 (Glaze, Minton, and West 2009).[1] Additionally, the size of the incarcerated population was more than 1,613,000 under the authority of state or federal correctional jurisdiction and 767,620 under local jurisdiction in 2009.[2] Privately managed and run prisons promised government a more cost-effective solution to housing and caring for inmates (Austin and Coventry 2001; DiIulio 1990; Hart, Shleifer, and Vishny 1997; McDonald 1992; McFarland, McGowan, and O'Toole 2002; Shichor 1996). The literature on prison privatization explores the effect of using private prisons to lower costs (Austin and Coventry 2001; General Accounting Office 1996; Government Accountability Office 2007; Hart, Shleifer, and Vishny 1997), provide better quality of service (Dunham 1986; Hart, Shleifer, and Vishny 1997; McDonald 1992; Metzger 2003), and take legal responsibility for service delivery (Dunham 1986; Freeman 2000; Levinson 2000; Metzger 2003). Assessment of this literature suggests that there are three main constitutional implications to privatizing prison operations. First, can the government legally hand over prison functions to private actors? Second, how does private management of prisons affect the constitutional rights of inmates? Finally, who accepts liability, or can be held accountable, for state action when a private company provides state functions?

This chapter draws on the public administration literature, specifically work related to privatization and prison management, as well as congressional legislation and final, written Circuit Court and Supreme Court decisions (majority, concurring, and dissenting opinions) to understand the constitutional implications of private prisons.[3] As such, the next section examines the implication of delegating public functions to private actors.

This is followed by a section that analyzes the constitutional implications private prisons have on the rights of inmates. Finally, the last section assesses the consequences of prison privatization as it relates to liability and accountability for private prison employee actions.

Delegating Public Functions to Private Actors

Within the study of privatization, three main theories emerge as to why the public sphere turns to privatization as a means of delivering government services (Brown, Potoski, and Van Slyke 2006; Cohen 2001; Cooper 2006; Kettl 1993; Poole and Fixler 1987; Shichor 1995). First, companies working in the private sector are believed to be more efficient because of their clear for-profit motive (Cohen 2001; Cooper 2006; Freeman 2000; McDonald 1992; McFarland, McGowan, and O'Toole 2002). Second, for-profit organizations thrive in a competitive marketplace, providing the impression of providing more effective and efficient delivery of services (Cohen 2001; Cooper 2006; Freeman 2000; Kettl 1993; McFarland, McGowan, and O'Toole 2002). Finally, privatization provides the government with alternative avenues to deliver public services (Brown, Potoski, and Van Slyke 2006; Cohen 2001; Cooper 2006; Hart, Shleifer, and Vishny 1997; Ostrom 1974). Entwined in these three theories is the basic worry that government delivery of services is ineffective because of public organizational inefficiency, an inability to overcome bureaucratic red tape, the influence of politics on operations, and the fear of financial losses.

By providing options, privatization makes available choices when government managers examine how to ensure effective, efficient, and democratic delivery of a public service. Vincent Ostrom (1974), in his book *The Intellectual Crisis in American Public Administration*, supports the availability of choice in the delivery of public services. Ostrom's main argument is that a democratic nation should not limit individual ability to choose from a basket of public services. Ostrom does not discuss which public services should be outsourced, alluding to the notion that all public services can be provided by private entities. Ronald Moe (1987) disagrees with Ostrom in his article "Exploring the Limits of Privatization." Taking into consideration security, constitutional rights, and public safety, Moe questions whether organizations independent from government regulation should provide inherently public services. What constitutes inherently public services, however, has yet to be defined (Goodnow 2004; Savas 2000[4]).

Case Law

The implication of delegating public functions to private actors can be seen in two competing judicial decisions in the Circuit Court of Appeals. The decisions by the Fourth and Ninth Circuits in *Holly v. Scott* (434 F.3d 287, 2006) and *Pollard v. GEO Group, Inc.* (629 F.3d 843, 2010), respectively, provide prime examples of the importance of defining what are inherently public functions. In addition, these cases question whether public functions delegated to private actors constitute state action.

The Fourth Circuit case of *Holly v. Scott* (434 F.3d 287, 2006) involves Ricky Lee Holly, an inmate with diabetes who was incarcerated in a GEO Group privately run prison. Holly claimed that he receive poor medical treatment from GEO Group's staff physician and, therefore, filed a legal claim for damages under *Bivens v. Six Unknown Agents of Federal Bureau of Narcotics* (403 U.S. 388, 1971)[5] against the prison's warden and physician. The basis of Holly's claim was that GEO Group, in managing the prison, acts under the color of state as required under Title 42 U.S.C. section 1983[6] claims. The question before the Fourth Court of Appeals was whether *Bivens* should extend to private prisons. The court said no. Deferring to the legislative branch, the court claimed that without a specific allowance in the Constitution for monetary restitution for constitutional rights violations, Congress would need to pass a law outlining compensation for such a loss, damage, or injury.

The importance of the *Holly* case to the constitutional implication of private prisons is the Court of Appeals' assessment that delegation by public entities to private actors does not constitute action under the state law doctrine. "Under this doctrine, we 'insist' as a prerequisite to liability 'that the conduct allegedly causing the deprivation of a federal right be fairly attributable to the State'" (*Holly v. Scott*, 434 F.3d 307, 2006). The Court of Appeals relies on the "Bill of Rights as a shield that protects private citizens from the excesses of government, rather than a sword that they may use to impose liability upon one another" (434 F.3d 307, 2006).

Furthermore, the Fourth Circuit Court of Appeals argues that because of the precedent set by the Supreme Court in *Richardson v. McKnight*

(521 U.S. 399, 1997),[7] the "public function theory"[8] does not apply to Holly. According to *Richardson*, there is no basis, either historically or legally, to treat private companies who manage prisons as state actors. The Circuit Court agrees with the High Court that prison management is not an exclusively state function. Finally, the court claims that publicly run prisons have different, even greater, responsibilities than privately run prisons. The court does not expand on this claim, leaving open the question as to why a distinction was made between private and public facilities.

In 2010, the Ninth Circuit Court of Appeals ruled in direct opposition of *Holly* in *Pollard v. GEO Group, Inc.* (629 F.3d 843, 2010). In *Pollard*, a federal prisoner, Richard Lee Pollard, claimed that his Eighth Amendment rights had been violated by employees of GEO Group. Like *Holly*, Pollard sought monetary damages against seven GEO Group employees under *Bivens*. Unlike the Fourth Circuit, the Ninth Circuit Court of Appeals found that Pollard had a right to a *Bivens* claim.

The Ninth Circuit Court relied on the public function theory to determine whether GEO Group employees acted on behalf of the state while performing their duties as prison guards. In the majority opinion, the court argued that incarceration of prisoners is, traditionally, "the State's *'exclusive* prerogative'" (*Pollard v. GEO Group, Inc.*, 629 F.3d 859, 2010). Using case law from other circuit courts,[9] the Ninth Circuit argued "imprisonment is a fundamentally public function, regardless of the entity managing the prison" (629 F.3d 859, 2010). In the end, based on their examination, the court found that "GEO employees act 'under color of federal law'" in their treatment of Pollard during his incarceration (629 F.3d 878, 2010).

The Ninth Circuit's decision is consistent with the dissenting opinion authored by Justice Scalia in *Richardson v. McKnight* (521 U.S. 399, 1997), wherein Scalia argues that "private prison management firms, who perform the same duties as state-employed correctional officials, . . . exercise the most palpable form of state police power" (521 U.S. 414, 1997). Based on the complexity of the issue, and the differing decisions within the Circuit Courts, the case will invariably go to the United States Supreme Court to rule. Ultimately, it will be left to the High Court to reconcile the differing opinions between the various Circuit Courts. The difference between *Holly* and *Pollard* is vitally important with regard to the constitutional implication of private prisons. In essence, whether delegation by public entities to private actors constitutes action under the state law doctrine or not depends on which position, *Holly* or *Pollard*, the High Court sides with.

Constitutional Rights of Inmates

Gillian Metzger's (2003) article "Privatization as Delegation" argues that "[a] foundational premise of our constitutional order is that public and private are distinct spheres, with public agencies and employees being subject to constitutional constraints while private entities and individuals are not" (1369–1370). Regardless of their distinctions, Metzger makes a strong case that privatization of government services is a delegation of government authority to private and nonprofit corporations that step in to provide government functions.[10] As such, privatization bridges the gap between public and private spheres. In doing so, privatization does not relieve the government of responsibility or accountability; rather, it involves sharing control and decision making with an outside agent.

In the privatization of prison management, the relationship between government and private prisons becomes one of principal and agent. The principal, that is, the government, hires an agent, that is, a private company, to manage all aspects of a prison. In this scenario, the government seeks to save money by hiring a private company to operate a prison efficiently (Cohen 2001; Dunham 1986; Hart, Shleifer, and Vishny 1997; McDonald 1992), whereas the private company agrees to operate a prison in order to make money (Dunham 1986; Metzger 2003). Inherent in this relationship is what Savas (2000) calls the principal–agent problem. According to Savas, the task of any agent is to fulfill the objectives set forth by their principal. Power and authority held by agents, then, are a direct result of the task they must complete. In the contractual relationship between principal and agent, the principal is the ultimate authority in any decision—either directly or indirectly (Singer 2003). The principal–agent problem, Savas explains, is when the agent does not act in the principal's best interest.

The principal–agent problem inherent in prison privatization is whether the private prison focuses on the principal's main concern, cost savings, while ignoring other important aspects associated with government functions (Austin and Coventry 2001; General Accounting Office 1996; Metzger 2003; Shichor 1995). Other important aspects intrinsic in incarceration of inmates include upholding the democratic values of life and liberty.[11]

This section examines the constitutional implications of private prisons to democratic values, especially when employees of said prisons have no constitutional obligation for due process or equality of services (Metzger 2003; Shichor 1995).

Due Process and Equality

In writing the Declaration of Independence and developing the Constitution, the Founding Fathers recognized that the role of government was to uphold the rule of law. The fear of tyranny played heavily in the decision to ensure that no person or institution would be above the law (Lundmark 2008; Rohr 1986; Rosenbloom, Carroll, and Carroll 2004; Wiecek 1988). On the principle of sovereignty,[12] the framers declared clearly in the Declaration of Independence that "governments are instituted" to protect the fundamental rights of man and that the power of government derives its "just powers from the consent of the governed."

To negotiate its role, local, state, and federal governments must adhere to the fundamental principle of due process, which prescribes a citizen's right to fair and equal treatment under the law. The United States Constitution established specific limitations on the federal government's ability to intrude on a person's right to "life, liberty or property, without due process of law" in the Fifth Amendment, pledging fairness under the law and preventing government usurpation of individual rights. Constitutional restraints on states' rights came with the ratification of the Civil War Amendments, specifically the Fourteenth Amendment. After the Civil War, the government extended protections of the Bill of Rights to state actions as well. According to the first section of the Fourteenth Amendment, "No State shall make or enforce any law which shall abridge the privileges or immunities of citizens of the United States; nor shall any State deprive any person of life, liberty, or property, without due process of law; nor deny to any person within its jurisdiction the equal protection of the laws."

Congress attempted to expand the scope of due process protection to encompass harm by private entities with the passage of the Civil Rights Act of 1875. Section one of the act states:

That all persons within the jurisdiction of the United States shall be entitled to the full and equal enjoyment of the accommodations, advantages, facilities, and privileges of inns, public conveyances on land or water, theatres, and other places of public amusement, subject only to the conditions and limitations established by law and applicable alike to citizens of every race and color, regardless of any previous condition of servitude.

The Supreme Court denounced congressional authority to regulate discrimination by private entities in the *Civil Rights Cases of 1883* (109 U.S. 3, 1883). "It is State action," the majority's opinion read, "of a particular character that is prohibited. Individual invasion of individual rights is not the subject matter of the [Fourteenth] amendment" (109 U.S. 11, 1883). Although Congress had the power to enforce the Amendment through legislation, it did not have the "power to legislate upon subjects which are within the domain of State legislation" (109 U.S. 11, 1883). In his dissent, Justice Harlan argued that private entities, which provide public services, are under congressional jurisdiction. Unlike the majority's overriding decision on the matter, Harlan argued that Congress did have authority to require "full and equal enjoyment" of public and private facilities. In addition, Harlan argued a principle of fundamental values, stating that "[i]t is fundamental in American citizenship that, in respect of such rights, there shall be no discrimination by the State, or its officers, or by individuals or corporations exercising public functions or authority, against any citizen" (109 U.S. 48, 1883).

It was not until the Civil Rights Act of 1964 that Congress reasserted its authority to enforce due process and equality for both public and private actors (Hargis 2009; Kelly, Harbison, and Belz 1991; Rosen 2006; Whittington 2007; Wiecek 1988). The act outlined guidelines:

To enforce the constitutional right to vote, to confer jurisdiction upon the district courts of the United States to provide injunctive relief against discrimination in public accommodations, to authorize the Attorney General to institute suits to protect constitutional rights in public facilities and public education, to extend the Commission on Civil Rights, to prevent discrimination in federally assisted programs, to establish a Commission on Equal Employment Opportunity, and for other purposes. (Civil Rights Act of 1964, Public Law 88-352)

In ten separate sections, the act outlined government support for eliminating discrimination in the areas of voting, public amenities, private business, public schools, and public and private employment. Finally, Title XI identified civil and criminal liabilities for failure to comply with the act.

The court embraced the Civil Rights Act in such cases as *Katzenbach v. McClung* (1964), *Daniel v. Paul* (1969), and *Tillman v. Wheaton-Haven Recreation Association* (1973) by prohibiting discrimination in private restaurants, recreation facilities, and community pools, respectively (Hargis 2009; Kelly, Harbison, and Belz 1991; Rosen 2006). These and other constitutionally "liberal" court interpretations of civil rights legislation provided clear guidelines to ensure due process and equal protection by the government against private discrimination.

Case Law

The 2001 case of *Correctional Services Corporation v. Malesko* (534 U.S. 61, 2001) demonstrates jurisprudential discrepancies of due process and equal protection claims with regard to private prisons. In *Correctional Services Corporation*, the Court determined that companies managing private prisons do not have section 1983 liability and, therefore, cannot be sued under *Bivens* for monetary compensation for constitutional violations. The majority explained its determination in that *Bivens* allowed monetary recovery against federal officers, not the government as a whole. As such, the question in *Correctional Services Corporation* as to whether an inmate can sue the private corporation rather than the individual prison employee for monetary damages of constitutional violations asks the court to expand *Bivens* beyond judicial capacity. Doing so, the court majority argued, would "impose asymmetrical liability costs on private prison facilities alone" (534 U.S. 62, 2001) and "would not advanced Bivens' core purpose of deterring individual officers from engaging in unconstitutional wrongdoing" (534 U.S. 74, 2001).

In addition to its decision on expanding *Bivens*, the Court pointed out that private and public prisons provide different remedies for prisoners alleging violations of rights. Private prisoners, the Court pointed out, "enjoy a parallel tort remedy that is unavailable to prisoners housed in government facilities" (534 U.S. 72–73, 2001). This position clearly demonstrates that prisoners in private and public facilities have different protections (Segal 2002) and is addressed in the dissenting opinion by Justice Stevens, and joined by Justices Souter, Ginsburg and Breyer. Specifically, Justice Stevens points out that failure to permit liability in *Correctional Services Corporation* creates inequality between public and private prison facilities. The dissenters argue that "[p]ermitting liability in the present case ... would produce symmetry: both private and public prisoners would be unable to sue the principal (i.e., the Government), but would be able to sue the primary federal agent (i.e., the Government official or the corporation)" (534 U.S. 81–82, 2001).

Cruel and Unusual Punishment

The Eighth Amendment's prohibition of "cruel and unusual punishments" serves as a basis for a large number of litigious actions, with varied claims, made by prison inmates and their families (Dunham 1986). These claims vary from confinement issues (*Hutto v. Finney*, 437 U.S. 678, 1978) to denial of medical treatment (*Estelle v. Gamble*, 429 U.S. 97, 1976) to failed executions (*Louisiana ex rel. Francis v. Resweber*, 329 U.S. 459, 1947) and everything in between. In determining when prison actions constitute unconstitutionally cruel and unusual punishment, the Court examines whether there is a "wanton and unnecessary infliction of pain" that is "grossly disproportionate to the severity of the crime warranting imprisonment" (*Rhodes v. Chapman*, 452 U.S. 347, 1981).

In 1979, the Supreme Court recognized that, although "convicted prisoners do not forfeit all constitutional protections by reason of their conviction and confinement in prison," they are subject to "restrictions and limitations" (*Bell v. Wolfish*, 441 U.S. 545, 1979). By the very nature of their confinement, inmates rely on prison management to provide all basic needs,[13] such as health care, safety, and food services (Austin and Coventry 2001; Dunham 1986; General Accounting Office 1996; McDonald and Carlson 2005). In *Estelle v. Gamble*, the Court held that "it is but just that the public be required to care for the prisoner, who cannot, by reason of the deprivation of his liberty, care for himself" (429 U.S. 104, 1976).

To ensure protection of democratic values when dealing with basic needs, public managers must include standards of decency for prison management in their contracts (Dunham 1986; Hart, Shleifer, and Vishny 1997; Logan 1992; Metzger 2003). The Supreme Court recognizes that the standard of decency used to evaluate what is and is not "repugnant to the Eighth

Amendment punishments...mark the progress of a maturing society" (*Estelle v. Gamble*, 429 U.S. 102, 1976). Although it does not identify what the standard of decency is, the Court does recognize that "[t]he [Eighth] Amendment embodies 'broad and idealistic concepts of dignity, civilized standards, humanity, and decency'" (*Estelle v. Gamble*, 429 U.S. 102, 1976). Prohibition of cruel and unusual punishment is particularly important because order and obedience are often obtained through inmate punishment (Dunham 1986, Logan 1992, McDonald et al. 1998).[14]

The courts have consistently held that prison management "has a right to...maintain order and discipline in its prisons" (*Holt v. Sarver*, 300 F. Supp. 833, 1969). The Supreme Court recognizes that "[l]oss of freedom of choice and privacy are inherent incidents of confinement in" prison facilities (*Bell v. Wolfish*, 441 U.S. 537, 1979). In addition, the Court acknowledges that some conditions "are restrictive and even harsh" because "they are part of the penalty that criminals pay for their offenses against society" (*Rhodes v. Chapman*, 452 U.S. 347, 1981). Regardless, judicial temperament over the years found that there are "limits to the rigor and discomfort of close confinement which a State may not constitutionally exceed" (*Holt v. Sarver*, 300 F. Supp. 833, 1969).

Although the Supreme Court has not specifically addressed Eighth Amendment limitations placed on private corporations managing prisons, it has repeatedly noted that the Eighth Amendment applies limits on those responsible for managing and administering prisons. An example is the acknowledgement in *Whitley v. Alberts* that Eighth Amendment language warning that "cruel and unusual punishment [shall not be] inflicted, 'manifests' an intention to limit the powers of those entrusted with the criminal law function of government" (475 U.S. 318, 1986). When a private prison acts on behalf of the state to manage a prison, Eighth Amendment restrictions of cruel and unusual punishment apply to their treatment of prisoners same as public facilities.

Case Law

The case law interwoven in the previous discussion emphasizes an important aspect of the constitutional implications of private prisons to Eighth Amendment claims. The judiciary affords great deference not only to federal and state legislation specific to prisoner treatment but also to prison officials. The Court discusses its deference in *Procunier v. Martinez* (416 U.S. 396, 1974). In a unanimous decision, the Court found that:

Traditionally, federal courts have adopted a broad hands-off attitude toward problems of prison administration. In part, this policy is the product of various limitations on the scope of federal review of conditions in state penal institutions. More fundamentally, this attitude springs from complementary perceptions about the nature of the problems and the efficacy of judicial intervention. Prison administrators are responsible for maintaining internal order and discipline, for securing their institutions against unauthorized access or escape, and for rehabilitating, to the extent that human nature and inadequate resources allow, the inmates placed in their custody. The Herculean obstacles to effective discharge of these duties are too apparent to warrant explication. Suffice it to say that the problems of prisons in America are complex and intractable, and, more to the point, they are not readily susceptible of resolution by decree. Most require expertise, comprehensive planning, and the commitment of resources, all of which are peculiarly within the province of the legislative and executive branches of government. For all of those reasons, courts are ill-equipped to deal with the increasingly urgent problems of prison administration and reform. Judicial recognition of that fact reflects no more than a healthy sense of realism. Moreover, where state penal institutions are involved, federal courts have a further reason for deference to the appropriate prison authorities. But a policy of judicial restraint cannot encompass any failure to take cognizance of valid constitutional claims whether arising in a federal or state institution. When a prison regulation or practice offends a fundamental constitutional guarantee, federal courts will discharge their duty to protect constitutional rights (*Procunier v. Martinez*, 416 U.S. 404–406, 1974; footnotes omitted).

The Court's determination in this and other prison-related cases implies that private prisons, in delivering correctional services, are accountable for constitutional rights and must accept liability for wrongdoing.

Liability and Accountability

In the arena of governments' correctional function, the question is whether government benefits from using private prisons. Theoretically, accepting outsourcing and partnerships with private entities requires a change in administrative culture, specifically with the way of thinking, valuing, and perceiving administrative reality (Brown and Potoski 2003; Cooper 2006; DiIulio 1990; Ewoh 1999; Fernandez, Rainey, and Lowman 2006; Fernandez and Smith 2006; Hargis 2009; Kettl 2002; Ostrom 1974; Savas 2000). First, treating service recipients as customers is a major tenet of outsourcing.[15] By serving customers based on what the citizenry wants rather than by controlling options, perceptions of government will change. Second, public organizations and the networks in which they participate are more likely to succeed in the long run if they are operated through a process of collaboration and shared leadership based on public interest. Finally, public managers will need to be attentive to the market and accountable to citizenry. This includes knowledge of statutory and constitutional law, community values, political norms, and professional standards. This final issue raises questions of accountability and immunity for private prison employees.

Supporters of privatization agree that utilization of private and nonprofit organizations provides higher-quality services, encourages effective delivery of services, removes inconsistencies and abuses, and provides services otherwise not available (Cooper 2006; DiIulio 1990; Goodnow 2004; Salamon 2003). Critics of privatization argue that innovation often fails to recognize inherent differences between public and private organizations and blurs the lines of accountability and management (Brown and Potowski 2003; Crawford and Krahn 1998; DiIulio 1990; Metzger 2003; Moe 1994).[16] Regardless of one's position regarding privatization in general, private prisons should be examined in more detail. The argument for government to be more like business and interact in the market system is not necessarily a good thing with correctional services as there is no clear customer.

When creating a contract with private prisons, public managers must create a relationship with the prison provider that supports public values while ensuring inmate rights. It is unlikely that citizens care whether the government outsources prison management unless they are directly affected.[17] In addition, public values are often contradictory, demanding efficiency at the lowest cost while advocating both punitive and rehabilitative functions (DiIulio 1990). As for navigating through the market system, public managers must be aware that their choices are limited. According to the Bureau of Justice Statistics, there are 1,821 state and federal correctional facilities—151 of which are privately operated.[18] Without the option to pit two or more prison providers against each other, public managers lose the ability to obtain the monetary advantage private prisons claim to provide.[19]

Prisoners use prison facilities when they are serving a sentence or waiting for their day in court. The choice of incarceration in a private versus a public prison is not for the inmate to make, and therefore, only their basic constitutional needs come into consideration. According to a General Accounting Office (1996) report on prisons, confinement "carries with it an obligation to meet the basic needs of prisoners at a reasonable standard of decency" (27). Along with standards for security, safety, health care, and hygiene, the General Accounting Office indicates a need for "constitutional standards to ensure due process and fairness" (27).

Constitutional standards require prison officials to be accountable for their actions and accept liability for their failures. Suits against prison officials for constitutional violations often come under Title 42 U.S.C. section 1983, which states that "[e]very person who, under color of" state action deprives someone of "any rights, privileges, or immunities secured by the Constitution and laws, shall be liable to the party injured." Over the course of its history, the Supreme Court has held various executive, legislative, and judicial officials immune from prosecution under section 1983.[20] There are two main steps in determining accountability and immunity.

First, determining accountability and immunity requires the courts to identify when someone acts on behalf of the state. In *West v. Atkins*, the Court found that part-time physicians contracting with public prisons to provide medical care "function within the state system" and, therefore, their actions "can fairly be attributed to the State" (487 U.S. 55–56, 1988). However, in *Richardson v. McKnight*, the court claimed that a private prison acting "without government supervision or direction" is not entitled to immunity for "the mere performance of a government function" (521 U.S. 408–409, 1997). In spite of this, the Ninth Circuit Court of Appeals found that a private "entity may engage in state action where it exercises 'powers traditionally exclusively reserved to the State'" (*Pollard v. GEO Group Inc.*, 629 F.3d 855, 2010).[21]

The second step in determining accountability and immunity requires the court to identify whether the actions taken constitute constitutional violations. In *Procunier v. Navarette*, the Court acknowledged that not all constitutional rights are clearly identifiable. Instead, the Court requires officials to have basic knowledge that "the action he took within his sphere of official responsibility would violate...constitutional rights" (434 U.S. 562,

1978). Although Justice Rehnquist argued for a situational test in *Wood v. Strickland*, where immunity for government employees includes a "varying scope . . . dependent upon the scope of discretion and responsibilities of the office" (420 U.S. 330, 1975), the Court created an objective reasonableness test. In *Harlow v. Fitzgerald*, the Court explained objective reasonableness as an examination of when "government officials performing discretionary functions, generally are shielded from liability for civil damages insofar as their conduct does not violate clearly established statutory or constitutional rights of which a reasonable person would have known" (457 U.S. 818, 1982).

The constitutional implications of private prison are the seemingly contradictory conclusions made by the courts regarding private prison accountability and liability. Often, courts call for congressional action to identify how private entities accept responsibility for the functions they provide.[22] Without congressional action, the Court, in *Richardson v. McKnight*, alluded to the contracts between public and private actors as the basis for determining accountability and liability. In his dissent, Justice Scalia chastises the majority for identifying the contractual relationship between the government and private prison as one that "separates the two categories—so that guards paid directly by the State are 'public' prison guards and immune" from liability for constitutional violations, "but those paid by a prison-management company 'private' prison guards and not immune" (521 U.S. 422, 1997). For Scalia and the other dissenters, the decision in *Richardson* treats "two sets of prison guards who are indistinguishable in the ultimate source of their authority over prisoners, indistinguishable in the powers that they possess over prisoners, and indistinguishable in the duties that they owe toward prisoners" differently in their accountability and liability for constitutional violations (521 U.S. 422, 1997).

Case Law

The Supreme Court case of *Hope v. Pelzer et al.* (536 U.S. 730, 2002) provides an interesting examination of constitutional implications as they relate to accountability and liability for prison officials. After being twice handcuffed to a hitching post, Larry Hope filed a claim of "cruel and unusual punishment" against three public prison guards at the Alabama facility where he was an inmate. The guards argued that Hope was handcuffed to the post to "sanction him for disruptive conduct" (536 U.S. 733, 2002) in accordance with prison policy and state law. The constitutional question before the Court was whether the guards qualified for qualified immunity[23] against suit.

To determine the applicability of immunity, the Court first addressed whether the actions taken against Hope established constitutional violations of his rights. Although the guards followed policies and regulations available to them, the Court agreed with a U.S. Department of Justice report in that "Alabama's systemic use of the hitching post [was] improper corporal punishment" and, thereby, "violated the Eighth Amendment" (536 U.S. 737, 2002). Furthermore, the court majority ruled that the circumstances surrounding Hope's punishment, which included physical restraint for seven hours, exposure to heat, refusal to provide hydration and allow bathroom breaks, and taunting by the guards, all added up to "'unnecessary and wanton' inflictions of pain . . . that [was] 'totally without penological justification'" (536 U.S. 737–738, 2002). As such, the Court found that Hope's rights had been constitutionally violated.

Turning to the question of immunity, the Court questioned whether the rights violated were, as required for qualified immunity, not "clearly established statutory or constitutional rights of which a reasonable person would have known" (536 U.S. 739, 2002). Relying on the knowledge that the Department of Justice "specifically advised the [Alabama Department of Corrections] of the unconstitutionality of its practices [using the hitching post] before the incidents in this case took place" (536 U.S. 744, 2002), the Court found that the guards should have reasonably known that the "obvious cruelty" in their actions "violated Hope's constitutional protection against cruel and unusual punishment" (536 U.S. 745, 2002). The *Hope* decision requires prison officials to not only know prison policies, state regulations, and federal law, but also case law dealing with prison issues and reports, such as that by the Department of Justice, about the daily practices used for prison administration. The decision expands constitutional protection for inmates at the same time it increases constitutional implications for private prisons by recognizing the accountability and liability of prison employees.

Concluding Remarks

As evidenced throughout this chapter, there are three main constitutional implications of private prisons: delegation of public functions to private actors, constitutional rights of inmates, and liability and accountability for private prison employee actions. By delegating public functions to private actors, prison privatization challenges the discrepancy between public and private spheres of action. This allows government regulation over private actors, if public managers choose to include regulatory measures in their contracts with private prisons. If not, private prisons provide government correctional functions without constitutional restraints placed on government-run prisons. Although the second scenario may benefit government and private actors monetarily, it is detrimental to democratic values and, ultimately, inmate constitutional rights.

When private prisons provide correctional functions, prison management includes a wide, comprehensive range of control over basic constitutional needs, in particular those protected by the Fifth, Eighth, and Fourteenth Amendments. To ensure that private prisons do not engage in unchecked constitutional violations, public managers should include government regulation and oversight in their contracts. Without guaranteeing the constitutional rights of inmates imprisoned in private prisons, government privatization of a fraction of its correctional facilities creates inequality among the incarcerated population as it allows different avenues for inmates' retribution for constitutional violations. Lacking a clear requirement for private prisons to accept responsibility for constitutional violations, the government consents to the failure by private prisons to accept liability and accountability for their actions.

The logic laid out by the Supreme Court in *Richardson v. McKnight* allows public managers to wash their hands of the actions taken by private prison management and employees. The Court's reasoning is that private prisons must accept full liability and accountability for their actions, especially when government does not monitor said actions. Although liability and accountability are important, the decision by the Court dismisses the very public function private prisons deliver. As such, the Court discards the constitutional implications of private prisons by failing to recognize that public and private delivery of correctional functions is indistinguishable. Unless, or until, the High Court rules on whether delegation by public entities to private prisons constitutes action under the state law doctrine, it will be left to public managers to create contracts with private prisons that will deal with these constitutional implications. If public managers do not include clear guidelines related to these constitutional implications in their contracts, congressional action, similar in fashion to Title 42 U.S.C. section 1983, will be necessary to ensure that actions taken by private and public prison officials are treated interchangeably by the law.

Notes

1. This number includes all persons on probation or parole and in jail or prison.
2. These numbers include inmates held in local, state, or federal correctional facilities only and do not include those on probation or parole. The data can be accessed on the Bureau of Justice Statistics website: http://bjs.ojp.usdoj.gov/index.cfm.
3. The object of this research—constitutional implications of private prisons—is examined through the case study of judicial decisions related to prisons. The individual case law used to examine judicial jurisprudence, identify precedent, and scrutinize judicial complexity with regard to private prisons as state actors provided the context of the case study (Creswell 1997).
4. Although Savas (2000) does argue that, by declaring some goods to be worthy goods, we do identify certain services as inherently public.
5. In *Bivens*, the United States Supreme Court ruled that although there is no provision in the United States Constitution for monetary damage for violations of constitutional rights, when a person's constitutional rights are violated by a state actor, that person deserves the right to sue said actor for "an award of money damages for the consequences of its violation" and, therefore, "where legal rights have been invaded, a federal statute provides for a general right to sue for such invasion" (403 U.S. 396, 1971).
6. Title 42 U.S.C. section 1983 of the Civil Rights Act of 1871 says that "[e]very person who, under color of any" state law, deprives a citizen of "rights, privileges, or immunities secured by the Constitution and laws" can be held liable to the injured party for damages. The only exception in the act against legal action is for judicial actors working within their judicial capacity. The Supreme Court has extended absolute and qualified immunity under section 1983 to various executive, legislative, and judicial actors when found acting

under the color of state law. The court is not, however, clear as to the application of section 1983 immunity when it comes to private actors who act on behalf of the government. I examine this area of accountability and liability for private actors in the last section of this chapter.

7. See chapter 4 for a more detailed discussion of *Richardson v. McKnight.*

8. The court relied on the public function theory as outlined in *Andrews v. Federal Home Loan Bank of Atlanta* (998 F.2d 214, 1993), which states that "exercise by a private entity of powers traditionally exclusively reserved to the State" does not mean that the state is "evading the Constitution by delegation" of government duties to private entities (998 F.2d 218, 1993).

9. In a unanimous decision, the Fifth Circuit ruled in *Rosborough v. Mgmt. & Training Corp.* (350 F.3d 459, 2003) that "confinement of wrongdoers—though sometimes delegated to private entities—is a fundamentally governmental function. These [private] corporations and their employees are therefore subject to limitations imposed by the Eighth Amendment" (350 F.3d 461, 2003). The Sixth and Eleventh Circuit Courts both held that private prisons "perform[ ] the 'traditional state function' of operating a prison" *Street v. Corr. Corp. of Am.* (102 F.3d 810, at 814, 6th Cir., 1996), *Skelton v. Pri-Cor, Inc.* (963 F.2d 100, at 102, 6th Cir., 1991), and *Ancata v. Prison Health Servs., Inc.* (769 F.2d 700, at 703, 11th Cir., 1985).

10. In fact, Metzger (2003, 1396) boldly states that "the powers exercised by private entities as a result of privatization often represent forms of government authority, and that a core dynamic of privatization is the way that it can delegate government power to private hands."

11. In the 1979 case *Bell v. Wolfish* (441 U.S. 520, 1979), the United States Supreme Court discussed some of the democratic values inherent even for incarcerated inmates. In the Court's own words, their "cases have held that sentenced prisoners enjoy freedom of speech and religion under the First and Fourteenth Amendments, *see Pell v. Procunier, supra; Cruz v. Beto,* 405 U.S. 319 (1972); *Cooper v. Pate,* 378 U.S. 546 (1964); that they are protected against invidious discrimination on the basis of race under the Equal Protection Clause of the Fourteenth Amendment, *see Lee v. Washington,* 390

U.S. 333 (1968); and that they may claim the protection of the Due Process Clause to prevent additional deprivation of life, liberty, or property without due process of law, *see Meachum v. Fano, supra; Wolff v. McDonnell, supra*" (441 U.S. 545, 1979). The court continued by stating that "convicted prisoners do not forfeit all constitutional protections by reason of their conviction and confinement in prison," but their rights can be subject to "restrictions and limitations" (441 U.S. 545, 1979).

12. In his book, Wiecek (1988) discusses six fundamental principles of American government, including fundamental law, separation of powers, checks and balances, the Supremacy Clause, federalism, and popular sovereignty.

13. An example of the import of prison management over basic needs is the issue of prison safety. Unlike private citizens, inmates confined within prison walls require prison management to provide safety on a number of different levels. Scott Camp, Gerald Gaes, and William Saylor (2001, 8–9), in their article "Quality of Prison Operations in the U.S. Federal Sector: A Comparison with a Private Prison," identified three aspects to prison safety. First, inmate safety requires management to ensure that individual inmates do not assault other inmates. Next, staff safety involves protection for prison employees against action by violent inmates. Finally, safety within the prison necessitates safe environmental conditions in communal areas, such as "housing units, the dining hall, and the place of work" (Camp, Gaes, and Saylor 2001, 9).

14. The Supreme Court supports this position as it stated in *Bell v. Wolfish*, "[p]rison administrators ... should be accorded wide-ranging deference in the adoption and execution of policies and practices that in their judgment are needed to preserve internal order and discipline and to maintain institutional security" (441 U.S. 547, 1979). The Court reiterated this point in 1981, stating that "a prison's internal security is peculiarly a matter normally left to the discretion of prison administrators" (*Rhodes v. Chapman*, 452 U.S. 349, 1981).

15. At the behest of President Clinton, Vice President Al Gore put together a task force to investigate the effectiveness of government bureaucracy (Gore 1993; Moe 1994; Thompson 2000). In 1993, Gore's *Creating a Government that Works Better and Costs Less*, a

Report of the National Performance Review, portrayed a broken bureaucracy that is costly to the American people and provides ineffective and deficient services. The layers of red tape, administrative failures, and needless rules and regulations had rendered the system of government inadequate (Gore 1993; Moe 1994; Thompson 2000). Pushing for a government to operate more like business, Gore's (1993) report outlined ways the government could become more entrepreneurial (results oriented) and less bureaucratic (rules oriented) (Freeman 2003; Moe 1994; Thompson 2000). The report supported development of partnerships between public and private institutions in the form of contracting out for delivery of government functions (Freeman 2003; Hill and Hupe 2002; Thompson 2000). These relationships, aimed at downsizing federal bureaucracy, were formed at national, state, and local levels.

16. Groundbreaking work on the overhaul of the public service sector came in 1993 with Al Gore's *Creating a Government that Works Better and Costs Less.* In this work, Gore claims that managing public entities like private companies means less bureaucracy and more forward thinking as well as less following rules and more goal achievement. Regrettably, Moe (1994) argues that this can never be because public and private organizations are inherently different. Aside from the rules and regulations Gore (1993) debunks, Moe (1994) finds the guiding principles of civil service are such that market-based incentives and competition-laden processes would not fare well. Freeman (2000, 2003) supports this viewpoint in her discussion of administrative law and private actors.

17. Grassroots Leadership is an organization against private, for-profit prisons. According to its website, Grassroots Leadership works to "put an end to abuses of justice and the public trust" by stopping prison privatization (Grassroots Leadership 2010). Their statement of principle states that "[f]or-profit private prisons, jails and detention centers have no place in a democratic society. Profiteering from the imprisonment of human beings compromises public safety and corrupts justice. In the spirit of democracy and accountability, we call for an end to all incarceration for profit" (Grassroots Leadership 2010). Organizations such as Grassroots Leadership work to inform the public about what they consider to be unconstitutional delegation

of government authority by paying private corporations to manage prisons.

18. These statistics are from December 30, 2005, and are accessible at the Bureau of Justice Statistics website: http://bjs.ojp.usdoj.gov/index.cfm?ty=tp&tid=13.

19. A recent Justice Department report found that although private prisons pledge savings of up to 20 percent, savings are closer to 1 percent (Austin and Coventry 2001). Although the report found a "positive effect on prison administration, making it more responsive to reform," the cost savings were "achieved through lower labor costs" (Austin and Coventry 2001, iii). Low labor costs often equate to less qualified employees, a practice that, in turn, leads to more constitutional violations (Austin and Coventry 2001; DiIulio 1990; Metzger 2003). In addition, Morris (2007) argues that prison privatization creates hybrid pathologies, which create a new problem while trying to fix another. Privatization gets rid of government monopolies, but long-term contracts (common in the prison business) create private monopolies.

20. See chapter 4 of this volume for a more comprehensive discussion of the Court's development of the doctrines of absolute and qualified immunity.

21. *Pollard* identifies four tests to determine whether someone engages in state action, including "the government nexus test, the joint action test, the public function test and the state compulsion test" (629 F.3d 855, 2010). This is consistent with Justice Scalia's dissenting opinion in *Richardson v. McKnight* where he asserts that "immunity is determined by function, not status," and "private status is not disqualifying" (521 U.S. 416, 1997).

22. *Richardson v. McKnight*, 521 U.S. 399, at 403, 1997; *Correctional Services Corporation v. Malesko*, 534 U.S. 61, throughout, 2001; *Holly v. Scott*, 434 F.3d 287, at 298, 2006; *Pollard v. GEO Group, Inc.*, 629 F.3d 855, at 864, 2010; to name a few.

23. Developed from Title 42 section 1983 claims against public officials for constitutional violations, the U.S. Supreme Court created the doctrine of qualified immunity to "strikes a balance between compensating those who have been injured by official conduct and protecting government's ability to perform its traditional functions" (*West v. Atkins*, 487 U. S. 167, 1988).

References

Austin, James, and Garry Coventry. 2001. *Emerging Issues on Privatized Prisons*. Washington, DC: National Council on Crime and Delinquency for the Office of Justice Programs, U.S. Department of Justice.

Beckett, Julia, and Heidi O. Koenig, eds. 2005. *Public Administration and Law*. ASPA Classics. Armonk, NY: M. E. Sharpe.

Brown, Trevor L., and Matthew Potoski. 2003. "Contract-Management Capacity in Municipal and County Governments." *Public Administration Review* 63 (2): 153–164.

Brown, Trevor L., Matthew Potoski, and David M. Van Slyke. 2006. "Managing Public Service Contracts: Aligning Values, Institutions, and Markets." *Public Administration Review* 66 (3): 323–331.

Camp, Scott D., Gerald G. Gaes, and William G. Saylor. 2001. "Quality of Prison Operations in the U.S. Federal Sector: A Comparison with a Private Prison." Federal Bureau of Prisons, Washington, DC.

Chang, Tracy, and Douglas Thompkins 2002. "Corporations Go to Prisons: The Expansion of Corporate Power in the Correctional Industry." *Labor Studies Journal* 27 (1): 45–69.

Civil Rights Act of 1964, Pub. L. 88-352, 78 Stat. 241 (1964).

Cohen, Steven. 2001. "A Strategic Framework for Developing Responsibility and Functions from Government to the Private Sector." *Public Administration Review* 61 (4): 432–440.

Cooper, Phillip J. 2006. *Governing by Contract: Challenges and Opportunities for Public Managers*. Washington, DC: CQ Press.

Cooper, Phillip J. 2007. *Public Law & Public Administration*. 4th ed. Belmont, CA: Thomson Wadsworth.

Cooper, Terry L. 1991. *An Ethic of Citizenship for Public Administration*. Englewood Cliffs, NJ: Prentice Hall.

Crawford, John W., Jr., and Steven L. Krahn. 1998. "The Demanding Customer and the Hollow Organization: Meeting Today's Contract Management Challenge." *Public Productivity & Management Review* 22 (1): 107–118.

Creswell, John W. 1997. *Qualitative Inquiry and Research Design: Choosing among Five Traditions*. Thousand Oaks, CA: Sage Publications.

DiIulio, John J., Jr. 1990. "Prisons that Work: Management Is the Key." *Federal Prisons Journal* 1 (4): 7–15. http://www.bop.gov/news/PDFs/sum90.pdf.

Dunham, Douglas. 1986. "Inmates' Rights and the Privatization of Prisons." *Columbia Law Review* 86 (7): 1475–1504.

Durant, Robert F. 1987. "Toward Assessing the Administrative Presidency: Public Lands, the BLM, and the Reagan Administration." *Public Administration Review* 47 (2): 180–189.

Ewoh, Andrew I. E. 1999. "An Inquiry into the Role of Public Employees and Managers in Privatization." *Review of Public Personnel Administration* 19 (Winter): 8–27.

Fernandez, Sergio, Hal G. Rainey, and Carol E. Lowman. 2006. "Privatization and Its Implications for Human Resource Management." In *Public Personnel Management: Current Concerns, Future Challenges,* edited by Norma M. Riccucci, 204–224. San Francisco, CA: Longman.

Fernandez, Sergio, and Craig R. Smith. 2006. "Looking for Evidence of Public Employee Opposition to Privatization: An Empirical Study with Implications for Practice." *Review of Public Personnel Administration* 26 (4): 356–381.

Freeman, Jody. 2000. "The Contracting State." *Florida State University Law Review* 28 (Fall): 155–214.

Freeman, Jody. 2003. "Extending Public Law Norms through Privatization." *Harvard Law Review* 116 (5): 1285–1352.

General Accounting Office. 1996. *Private and Public Prisons: Studies Comparing Operational Costs and/or Quality of Service.* Report to the Subcommittee on Crime, Committee on the Judiciary, House of Representatives. GAO/GGD-96-158. Washington, DC: General Accounting Office.

Glaze, Lauren, Todd Minton, and Heather West. 2009. Bureau of Justice Statistics Correctional Surveys.

Goodnow, Frank J. 2004. "Politics and Administration." In *Classics of Public Administration*, 5th ed., edited by Jay M. Shafritz, Albert Hyde, and Sandra Parkes, 35–37. Belmont, CA: Wadsworth.

Gore, Al. 1993. *Creating a Government that Works Better and Costs Less.* Accompanying Report of the National Performance Review. www.fas.org/irp/offdocs/npr.

Government Accountability Office. 2007. *Bureau of Prisons Needs Better Data to Assess Alternatives for Acquiring Low and Minimal Security Facilities.* Report to the Subcommittee on Commerce, Justice, and Science, Senate and House Appropriations Committees. GAO-08-6. Washington, DC: Government Accountability Office.

Grassroots Leadership. 2010. "Mission and Policy." http://grassrootslea dership.org/.

Hargis, H. Jessica. 2009. "Not to Be Overlooked: How the United States Supreme Court Shapes the Administrative State." PhD diss., University of Texas at Dallas.

Hart, Oliver, Andrei Shleifer, and Robert W. Vishny. 1997. "The Proper Scope of Government: Theory and an Application to Prisons." *Quarterly Journal of Economics* 112 (4): 1127–1161.

Henig, Jeffrey R. 1989–1990. "Privatization in the United State: Theory and Practice." *Political Science Quarterly* 104 (4): 649–670.

Hill, Michael, and Peter Hupe. 2002. *Implementing Public Policy.* Thousand Oaks, CA: Sage Publications.

Kelly, Alfred H., Winfred A. Harbison, and Herman Belz. 1991. *The American Constitution: Its Origin and Development*, 7th ed., vols. 1 and 2. New York: W.W. Norton.

Kettl, Donald F. 1993. *Sharing Power: Public Governance and Private Markets.* Washington, DC: Brookings Institute.

Kettl, Donald F. 2002. *The Transformation of Governance: Public Administration for Twenty-First Century America.* Baltimore, MD: John Hopkins University Press.

Levinson, Daryl. 2000. "Making Government Pay: Markets, Politics, and the Allocation of Constitutional Costs." *University of Chicago Law Review* 67 (2): 345–420.

Logan, Charles. 1992. "Well Kept: Comparing Quality of Confinement in Private and Public Prisons." *Journal of Criminal Law and Criminology* 83 (3): 577–613.

Lundmark, Thomas. 2008. *Power and Rights in U.S. Constitutional Law.* 2nd ed. New York: Oxford University Press.

Lynch, James, and William Sabol. 1997. "Did Getting Tough on Crime Pay?" Crime Policy Report no. 1. *Urban Institute.* http://www.urban.org.

McDonald, Douglas C. 1992. "Private Penal Institutions." *Crime and Justice* 16:361–419.

McDonald, Douglas C., and Kenneth Carlson. 2005. "Contracting for Imprisonment in the Federal Prison System: Cost and Performance of the Privately Operated Taft Correctional Institution." Federally funded grant final report, document no. 211990. http://www.ncjrs.gov/pdffiles1/nij/grants/211990.pdf.

McDonald, Douglas C., Elizabeth Fournier, Malcolm Russell-Einhourn, and Stephen Crawford. 1998. *Private Prisons in the United States: An Assessment of Current Practice*. Boston, MA: Abt Associates.

McFarland, Stephen, Chris McGowan, and Tom O'Toole. 2002. "Prisons, Privatization, and Public Values." Paper presented to Professor Mildred Warner, Privatization and Devolution CRP 612, Cornell University, Ithaca, NY, December. http://government.cce.cornell.edu/doc/pdf/PrisonsPrivatization.pdf.

Metzger, Gillian E. 2003. "Privatization as Delegation." *Columbia Law Review* 103 (6): 1367–1502.

Moe, Ronald C. 1987. "Exploring the Limits of Privatization." *Public Administration Review* 47 (6): 453–460.

Moe, Ronald C. 1994. "The 'Reinventing Government' Exercise: Misinterpreting the Problem, Misjudging the Consequences." *Public Administration Review* 54 (2): 111–122.

Morris, J. C. 2007. "Government and Market Pathologies of Privatization: The Case of Prison Privatization." *Politics & Policy* 35 (2): 318–341.

Ostrom, Vincent. 1974. *The Intellectual Crisis in American Public Administration*. Tuscaloosa: University of Alabama Press.

Poole, Robert W., Jr., and Philip E. Fixler Jr. 1987. "Privatization of Public-Sector Services in Practice: Experience and Potential." *Journal of Policy Analysis and Management* 6 (4): 612–625.

Rohr, John A. 1986. *To Run a Constitution: The Legitimacy of the Administrative State*. Lawrence: University Press of Kansas.

Rosen, Jeffrey. 2006. *The Supreme Court: The Personalities and Rivalries that Defined America*. New York: Times Books Henry Holt and Company.

Rosenbloom, David H., James D. Carroll, and Jonathan D. Carroll. 2004. *Constitutional Competence for Public Managers*. Belmont, CA: Wadsworth Group.

Salamon, Lester M. 2003. "The Resilient Sector: The State of Nonprofit America." In *The State of Nonprofit America*, edited by Lester M. Salamon, 3–61. Washington, DC: Brookings Institution Press.

Savas, E. S. 2000. *Privatization and Public-Private Partnerships*. New York: Chatham House Publishers.

Segal, Geoffrey. 2002. "Supreme Court Rules on Private Prison Liability: Inmates at Private and Government Run Prisons Should Have Same Rights." Reason Foundation. http://reason.org/news/show/supremecourt-rules-on-private.

Shichor, David. 1995. *Punishment for Profit*. Thousand Oaks, CA: Sage Publications.

Shichor, David. 1996. "Private Prisons." In *Encyclopedia of American Prisons*, edited by Marilyn D. McShane and Frank P. Williams III, 364–672. New York: Garland Publishing.

Singer, P. W. 2003. *Corporate Warriors: The Rise of the Privatized Military Industry*. Ithaca, NY: Cornell University Press.

Skowronek, Stephen. 1982. *Building a New American State: The Expansion of National Administrative Capacities, 1877–1920*. Cambridge: Cambridge University Press.

Terry, Larry D. 1998. "Administrative Leadership, Neo-Managerialism, and the Public Management Movement." *Public Administration Review* 58 (3): 194–200.

Terry, Larry D. 2005. "Reflections and Assessment: *Public Administration Review*, 2000–05." *Public Administration Review* 65 (6): 643–645.

Thompson, James R. 2000. "Reinvention as Reform: Assessing the National Performance Review." *Public Administration* 60 (6): 508–521.

Waldo, Dwight. 2007. *The Administrative State: A Study of the Political Theory of American Public Administration*. New Brunswick, NJ: Transaction Publishers.

Whittington, Keith E. 2007. *Political Foundations of Judicial Supremacy: The Presidency, the Supreme Court, and Constitutional Leadership in U.S. History*. Princeton, NJ: Princeton University Press.

Wiecek, William M. 1988. *Liberty under Law: The Supreme Court in American Life*. Baltimore, MD: John Hopkins University Press.

Case List

Ancata v. Prison Health Servs., Inc., 1985. 769 F.2d 700.

Andrews v. Federal Home Loan Bank of Atlanta. 1993. 998 F.2d 214.

Bell v. Wolfish. 1979. 441 U.S. 520.

Bivens v. Six Unknown Agents of Federal Bureau of Narcotics. 1971. 403 U.S. 388.

Civil Rights Cases of 1883. 1883. 109 U.S. 3.

Correctional Services Corporation v. Malesko. 2001. 534 U.S. 61.

Daniel v. Paul. 1969. 395 U.S. 298.

Estelle v. Gamble. 1976. 429 U.S. 97.

Harlow v. Fitzgerald. 1982. 457 U.S. 818.

Holly v. Scott. 2006. 434 F.3d 287.

Holt v. Sarver. 1969. 300 F. Supp. 825.

Hope v. Pelzer et al. 2002. 536 U.S. 730.

Hutto v. Finney. 1978. 437 U.S. 678.

Katzenbach v. McClung. 1964. 379 U.S. 294.

Louisiana ex rel. Francis v. Resweber. 1947. 329 U.S. 459.

Pollard v. GEO Group, Inc. 2010. 629 F.3d 843.

Procunier v. Martinez. 1974. 416 U.S. 396.

Procunier v. Navarette. 1978. 434 U.S. 555.

Rhodes v. Chapman. 1981. 452 U.S. 337.

Richardson v. McKnight. 1997. 521 U.S. 399.

Rosborough v. Mgmt. & Training Corp. 2003. 350 F.3d 459.

Skelton v. Pri-Cor, Inc. 1991. 963 F.2d 100.

Street v. Corr. Corp. of Am. 1996. 102 F.3d 810.

Tillman v. Wheaton-Haven Recreation Association. 1973. 410 U.S. 431.

West v. Atkins. 1988. 487 U.S. 42.

Whitley v. Alberts. 1986. 475 U.S. 312.

Wood v. Strickland. 1975. 420 U.S. 308.

9

A Comparative Analysis of Educational Realities in State and Private Prisons

Gwen Lee-Thomas and Rhonda L. Myers

Most people would agree that education is still the great equalizer that allows anyone from anywhere to have access to a better quality of life. Yet what about education as an equalizer among our U.S. prison population? Actually, the literature consistently indicates that those who are incarcerated tend to be less educated in terms of having a high school diploma, a general equivalency diploma (GED), or some form of college, and they tend to come from a lower socioeconomic status than their non-incarcerated peers (Erisman and Contardo 2005; Harlow 2003). Regardless of the amount of education incarcerated persons have at the time they are imprisoned, research also shows that 95 percent will be released at some point in their lives (American Council on Education 2008), and if they are educated at least with a GED at the time of their release (along with other coping life skills), they are 29 percent less likely to become a repeat offender (Harer 1995; Steurer, Smith, and Tracy 2001).

One concern that has become even more prevalent among proponents of educating inmates for successful reentry into society is the growth of private prisons. The privatization of prisons has been viewed by many as a cost-effective approach for states to maximize use of taxpayer dollars and simultaneously remain committed to public safety. Yet others believe the trade-off between proposed savings and the realities of accountability and quality of humane experiences are not always acceptable (Zito 2003). The arguments regarding whether or not the privatization of prisons is more effective than public (state and federal) prisons often refer to the reduced quality of programs and services, the lack of compliance and accountability to society at large, higher rates of recidivism, the hiring of less qualified (or at least non-union) staff, and private prison lobbying (Zito 2003). These issues of privatized prisons that are typically highlighted in the literature by opponents and proponents alike provide a somewhat balanced view of the pros and cons; however, very few studies deal specifically with the quality of educational services provided to inmates when comparing private and public prisons.

Because most prisoners will be released back into society at some point but will have a better chance of being more productive law-abiding citizens if educated while incarcerated, it is important to look at the likelihood of these opportunities occurring before they are released, regardless of whether the facilities are public or private. As Erisman and Contardo (2005, v) state:

> Higher education can improve conditions within correctional facilities, enhance prisoner self-esteem and prospects for employment after release, and function as a cost-effective approach to reducing recidivism. Educating prisoners also allows them access to the many economic and social benefits associated with higher education. Postsecondary correctional education offers a chance to break the cycle of inequality and benefit both the formerly incarcerated person and the society in which he or she lives.

Few states have provided empirical data on the comparisons between private and public educational systems for inmates, so what is provided here is an overview of the history and present-day purpose of correctional education, a brief conversation on the percentage of educational programs offered in public and private prisons, and a summary of what is still needed to look more empirically at comparisons between public and private correctional education.

Brief Overview: History of Correctional Education

The 19th Century ushered in an emphasis on increasing literacy in many prisons. The state of Pennsylvania served as the impetus behind this push because of the custodians of their prisons wanted prisoners to be able to read the bible.

Ultimately, "schooling" in prison gained prominence among practitioners as a means to rehabilitate the behaviors of criminals and an opportunity for "inmates to help maintain the correctional facility" (Steurer 2001, 49).

The periods of expansion for correctional education include pre-1930s, 1930–1964, and 1965 to the present (adapted from CEA 2008). The pre-1930s movement encompassed the framing of correctional education through practice and its expansion to include special education, the founding of the American Correctional Association (ACA) in 1870, and the formation of foundational research in educating inmates (ACA 2011).

From 1930 through 1964, there was much advancement in correctional education, including adult basic education and special education, and the creation of the Correctional Educational Association (CEA), which is the largest affiliate of the ACA. In addition, the end of this era was marked by the growth of social education programs that stemmed from World War II recovery efforts.

The shift in correctional education that began in 1965 involved the inclusion of postsecondary education in prisons, more integrated teacher preparation, larger efforts in correctional education research in the United States and abroad, and the growth and influence of the CEA (Steurer 2001). The U.S. Department of Education website says that the Office of Correctional Education (OCE) was established in 1991 as a result of the Perkins Vocational and Applied Technology Education Act. Currently, OCE is housed in the U.S. Department of Education's Office of Vocation and Adult Education. A review of the recent literature on correctional education shows expansion of the multifaceted aspects of correctional education, such as inmate tutoring, measures of effectiveness, and funding sources.

Present-Day Need for Correctional Education

The belief that education is a critical component to deter criminal activity and reduce recidivism continues to be supported time and again in the literature. In addition, the public's attitude toward the education of inmates has also changed over the past few decades; however, the commitment to accountability is still warranted on the policy and public fronts. Specifically, the literature demonstrates that correctional education proposes to reduce prisoner idleness, control prison populations (recidivism), and train inmates to perform work for the prison facility (Dirkx, Kielbaso, and Corley 1999; Dodla 2003;

Steurer 2001; Steurer, Smith, and Tracy 2001. To that end, according to Stephan (2008), more than 90 percent of all state and federal prisons and almost 60 percent of all private prisons offer some form of educational programs to inmates. With regard to postsecondary education, "postsecondary correctional education was still available only to about 5 percent of prisoners, and degree completion rates were low" (Erisman and Contardo 2005, vi).

When comparing the percentage of educational programs in public (state and federal) and private prisons, Harlow (2003) revealed that private prisons consistently provide fewer education programs than public prisons. For instance, in 2000, 61.6 percent of the 242 private prisons provided adult basic education, compared with 80.4 of state prisons and 97.4 percent of federal prisons. These comparisons are consistent across various types of correctional education programs, including, but not limited to, secondary education, vocational education, special education, and study release programs. Interestingly, whereas only 27.3 percent of private prisons and 26.7 percent of state prisons provided college courses, 80.5 percent of federal prisons provided college courses. These figures are important because Erisman and Contardo (2005) contend that offering correctional education programs is critical since most inmates need remediation before even considering any progress toward a certificate or degree program.

Another reality regarding educational comparisons between public and private prisons was posed by two psychologists who have worked in the Arkansas prison system for more than 40 years combined (public and private). Both agree that the privatization of prisons can cause more harm than good to inmate education. This is due to reasons that are not as clearly highlighted in studies because they relate more to the individual realities of those who provide the education. Specifically, both public and private prisons hire teachers for their educational programs; however, those teachers employed by public prisons must demonstrate credentials required by the state. It is not argued that the teachers at private prisons do not hold the same credentials as those hired in public prisons, but the requirements may be different. Another difference between public and private prison educational staff, based on the experiences of those who provide the one-on-one education for inmates, is the quality of benefits offered. It is believed by these veterans of the prison system that long-term benefits for health care and retirement for faculty who are state employees in the state of Arkansas are much better than those for non-state employee faculty in private prisons. These differences are believed to contribute to the longevity of employment (reduced employee turnover), quality of teaching (credentials required by the state that may not be required by private prisons), and benefits.

Although both psychologists agree that education is key to recidivism, both also agree that policy makers must be willing to ensure that policy is written with the type of language that will consistently promote correctional education, especially with regards to ensuring that the minimum qualifications and credentials of teachers and faculty meet those of the state. In addition, there should be a commitment to requiring standards in educational resources (tutoring, study skills, certifications, dual credit programs with local colleges and universities, etc.) at both public and private correctional institutions. Without these assurances, little to no change in recidivism rates should be expected. One final suggestion made by the psychologists is that prisons (private and public) should offer more entrepreneurial education for inmates since many of them have difficulty finding jobs once released, but they could become certified in a particular trade and start their own businesses. This approach opens up a new conversation on economic development and growth in addition to specifically enhancing the workforce.

Ultimately, the rapid increase in the U.S. prison population has led to an increased need for correctional education (Harlow 2003). According to the Pew Center on the States (2008), the U.S. prison population has nearly tripled from 585,084 to 1,596,127 between 1987 and 2007; currently, one out of every 100 U.S. adults is incarcerated in a local, state, or federal facility (quoted in Winterfield et al. 2009, 1). Lower literacy rates among incarcerated persons have also magnified the need for correctional educational programs. For example, Harlow (2003) reported that although 18 percent of the general U.S. population has less than a high school diploma, 40 percent of inmates in state prisons, 27 percent in federal prisons, and 47 percent in local jails do not have a high school diploma. As mentioned earlier, because 95 percent of incarcerated persons will be released at some point, and because education plays a key role in recidivism, it would benefit society greatly if policies, procedures, and standards of systematic accountability across levels of prisons (federal, state, and local) for both private and public institutions were developed, implemented, and required to ensure that those who are released have a greater chance of becoming productive citizens of society.

What Is Needed in the Correctional Education Literature?

The prison literature is limited in examining comparisons between public and private prisons in the area of correctional education, its effect on recidivism, and its contribution to productive reentry into society. The comparative prison literature primarily focuses on issues related to budgeting and finance, effectiveness of privatization, and quality of incarceration. Only a few studies have compared public and private prison educational programming (Perrone and Pratt 2003; Seiter 2008; Winterfield et al. 2009), so there is a great need to provide empirical comparisons given the criticality of education to reducing recidivism.

Programmatic Offerings

Secondary and adult basic education are the two predominant educational offerings of public and private prisons (Harlow 2003). In addition, a number of public and private prisons offer special education, vocational training, study release, and prerelease programs (Dodla 2003). The low literacy rates and low high school diploma achievement of inmates, compared with non-inmates, have contributed to the demand for these types of educational programs. Although the literature has documented the types of education programs provided by public and private prisons in the United States, there are no studies comparing the quality of education programs in both types of prisons.

Accreditation of Educational Programs

The closest form of accountability for quality educational programs in prisons is the accreditation of correctional education programs offered by the CEA (2008), which currently accredits the educational programs of 60 public and private prisons. Of the 60 accredited prisons listed by the CEA (2008), only one private prison company was identified, Management and Training Corporation. The Southern Association of Colleges and Schools (SACS) also offers accreditation, and the GEO Group reports that five of its private prison facilities are accredited by SACS to offer educational programs. Although the literature on correctional education program accreditation is limited, accreditation as a measure of accountability should become more of a requirement, rather than an option, to ensure the quality of educational programs and warrant their effectiveness.

Recidivism as a Measure of Success

The correctional education literature is consistent in reporting that recidivism rates are significantly reduced among participants in educational programs, particularly adult basic education, vocational training, and postsecondary education classes (Erisman and Contardo 2005; Flanagan 1994; Lochner and Moretti 2004; Page 2004; Seiter 2008; Steurer, Smith, and Tracy 2001; Winterfield et al. 2009). Only a few studies compare the recidivism rates of correctional education participants in public and private prisons (Seiter 2008). In general, Seiter (2008) reports mixed results regarding the differences between public and private prison recidivism rates, however, not necessarily with respect to correctional education. Cheung (2002, as cited in Seiter 2008) found no significant differences between the recidivism rates of inmates released from public versus private prisons, whereas Lanza-Kaduce, Parker, and Thomas (1999, as cited in Seiter 2008) report that private prisons have lower recidivism rates and less serious re-offenses. Among the reasons for the mixed and inconclusive results are influences of varying management styles rather than prison ownership type and poor matching of facilities in public/private comparisons (Perrone and Pratt 2003).

Herein lies the need for additional research with regard to recidivism rates as a measure of success. If education is a critical component to reducing recidivism, then it must also become a variable in the formula for measuring recidivism. Education is believed to be the equalizer in society at large. More importantly, it provides options for employment, caring for family, and enhancing self-esteem and self-efficacy, and it challenges people to create productive ways of contributing to their quality of life.

Conclusion

Regardless of whether a person is incarcerated or not, education makes a difference in how people view and respond to the choices they believe are available to them to create a quality of life. Therefore, education can be considered a public good, and if the state or federal government (public) takes responsibility for those who make decisions that result in their becoming an offender, then the state must ensure some form of a quality education of inmates regardless of whether they are housed in public or private prisons—and this includes any form of education from the GED to a bachelor of arts degree or an advanced graduate degree from an accredited college. State and federal governments should hold public and private prisons accountable not only for providing correctional education but also for the quality of education provided. In other words, are the teachers credentialed at a level that ensures quality education? Is the funding appropriately distributed? Are the educational programs accredited? Are the educational programs appropriate for the needs of the student inmates? Are the programs accessible? Does inmate education progress remain continuous when inmates are transferred to different facilities?

Furthermore, are private prisons accountable to their communities by providing education to the inmates who eventually leave their institutions? For the most part, most inmates housed in private prisons tend to be at medium- and low-risk security institutions and are more likely to leave at some point in their lives. The argument that we have a system that knowingly releases people unprepared to be productive citizens and who will more than likely recidivate can be considered a serious violation of public trust. Therefore, it is incumbent upon the private prisons to educate their populations as a commitment to the communities in which they work, live, and conduct business.

Finally, the public should hold the state and its legislatures accountable for the quality of life, services, and education inmates receive as potential and future neighbors and co-laborers. Society is not made up of just non-offenders. It consist of all of us, and it is only as strong as its weakest link.

References

American Correctional Association (ACA). 2011. "Public Correctional Policy on Offender Education and Training." In *Public Correctional Policies*. https://www.aca.org/government/policyresolution/PDFs/Public_Correctional_Policies.pdf.

American Council on Education. 2008. "Higher Education behind Bars: Postsecondary Prison Education Programs Make a Difference." http://www.acenet.edu/AM/Template.cfm?Section=Home&CONTENTID=29503&TEMPLATE=/CM/ContentDisplay.cfm.

Batiuk, M. E. 1997. "The State of Postsecondary Correctional Education in Ohio." *Journal of Correctional Education* 48 (2): 70–72.

Dirkx, J. M., G. Kielbaso, and C. Corley. 1999. *A Study of Vocational Education Programs in the Michigan Department of Corrections.* http://www.ippsr.msu.edu/Documents/AppliedPolicyGrants/dirkx.pdf.

Dodla, J-F. 2003. *A Pre-release Career and Pathways Transition Program for Low-Security Inmates in Maximum-Security Facilities within Queensland Corrections.* Workshop 22: International Forum for Education in Correctional Settings Australia, IFECSA Conference. http://www.acea.org.au/Content/2003%20papers/Paper%20Dodla.pdf.

Erisman, W., and J. B. Contardo. 2005. *Learning to Reduce Recidivism: A 50-State Analysis of Postsecondary Correctional Education Policy.* Washington, DC: Institute for Higher Education Policy.

Flanagan, T. J. 1994. *Prison Education Research Project: Final Report.* Huntsville, TX: Criminal Justice Center Education for Public Service. http://www.eric.ed.gov/PDFS/ED395209.pdf.

Harer, M. D. 1995. *Prison Education Program Participation and Recidivism: A Test of the Normalization Hypothesis.* Washington, DC: Office of Research, Federal Bureau of Prisons.

Harlow, C. W. 2003. *Education and Correctional Populations.* U.S. Department of Justice, Office of Justice Programs, Bureau of Justice Statistics. Special Report. http://www.ojp.usdoj.gov/bjs/abstract/ecp.htm.

"History of Correctional Education." U.S. Department of Education, Office of Vocational and Adult Education. http://www2.ed.gov/about/offices/list/ovae/pi/AdultEd/correctional-education.html.

Lochner, L., and E. Moretti. 2004. "The Effect of Education on Crime: Evidence from Prison Inmates, Arrests, and Self-Reports." *American Economic Review* 94 (1, March): 155–189.

Page, J. 2004. "Eliminating the Enemy: The Import of Denying Prisoners Access to Higher Education in Clinton's America." *Punishment and Society* 6 (4): 357–378. http://pun.sagepub.com/content/6/4/357.

Perrone, D., and T. C. Pratt. 2003. "Comparing the Quality of Confinement and Cost-Effectiveness of Public versus Private Prisons: What We Know, Why We Do Not Know More, and Where to Go from Here." *Prison Journal* 83 (3): 301–322.

Pew Center on the States. 2008. *One in 100: Behind Bars in America 2008.* Washington, DC: Pew Charitable Trusts. http://www.pewstates.org/uploadedFiles/PCS_Assets/2008/one%20in%20100.pdf.

Seiter, R. P. 2008. *Private Corrections: A Review of the Issues.* Washington, DC: Corrections Corporation of America.

Stephan, J. J. 2008. National Prisoner Statistics Program: Census of State and Federal Correctional Facilities, 2005. http://bjs.gov/content/pub/pdf/csfcf05.pdf.

Steurer, S. J. 2001. "Historical Development of a Model for Correctional Education and Literacy." *Journal of Correctional Education* 52 (2): 48–51.

Steurer, S. J., L. Smith, and A. Tracy. 2001. *The Three State Recidivism Study.* Lanham, MD: U.S. Department of Education, Office of Correctional Education.

Werner, D. R. 1997. "Fire and Ice: The Tumultuous Course of Post-Secondary Prison Education." *Journal of Correctional Education* 48 (2): 42–44.

Winterfield, L., M. Coggeshall, M. Burke-Storer, V. Correa, and S. Tidd. 2009. *The Effects of Postsecondary Correctional Education. Final Report.* Washington, DC: Urban Institute, Justice Policy Center.

Zito, M. 2003. "Prison Privatization: Past and Present." International Foundation for Protection Officers. http://www.ifpo.org/articlebank/prison_privatization.html.

10

Performance Measures and Private Prisons

Michael Montgomery

The primary purpose of this chapter is to discuss performance measurement of prisons, and more specifically, private prisons. As the reader will soon discover, performance measurement of a private prison is conducted for numerous purposes, but to a large extent, it appears to be an exercise in comparing the quality of operations and costs with those of public prisons. This chapter will examine the literature on this topic and reveal actual performance measures for prisons. Operational performance measures and financial measures will be explored, as will the specific method of conducting an audit, or inspection, of a prison to determine the rating of the performance measures.

The American Correctional Association (ACA), through its Commission on Accreditation of Corrections, has developed standards for the design and operation of prisons and for quality-of-life issues affecting inmates and their treatment. These standards have been in existence for many years and are perfectly good performance measures to determine if a prison may be operating in a safe, secure, and just manner. Interestingly, although the ACA standards dominate U.S. prison operations, as well as a number of other correctional endeavors, they are not the only standards by which public and private prisons are measured. Accreditation is a costly and often time-consuming exercise that is beyond the financial and/or management capabilities of some government entities. However, items of measurement other than the ACA standards can render a beneficial and usable inspection to make some determinations on how well a prison is operating toward its stated goals and mission.

Measuring the performance of any public service or program is an important element in good management. Legislators who allocate money and citizens whose taxes pay for services want to have some level of confidence that their money is being well spent. This is a simple concept in theory, that is, programs are evaluated as to their effectiveness according to established goals. If the goals are being met, then funding for the program should be continued; if goals are not being met, then adjustments must be made or the program should be curtailed so as not to waste taxpayer's money. Although the concept is sensical and fairly straightforward, there are complexities with some governmental services because goals may be conflicting, difficult to measure, lacking consensus from stakeholders, and/or simply too costly.

One such public service that is difficult to measure is corrections, especially institutional corrections. Although prisons and jails have been a standard public service in the United States since the late 1700s, the ability to measure their effectiveness has been problematic since their inception. Today, with legislation such as the Government Performance and Results Act of 1993, federal, and many state, agencies are mandated to measure their performance. If we are to assume that the ideological goals of corrections are deterrence, incapacitation, retribution, and rehabilitation, then we need to be capable of measuring these goals to determine our progress. Similarly, on a more practical level, if we determine that a primary goal of prison operations is to manage a safe, secure, and efficient prison, then we must establish some goals that are measurable to determine if our efforts are effective in producing positive outcomes and doing so in an economical manner.

A somewhat newer element of institutional corrections is the addition of private prison operations in a number of states and local jurisdictions that have incorporated these special correctional enterprises. Prisons and jails that are operated by private corporations or nonprofit organizations under contract with a government entity would seem to fall outside the realm of a public entity. However, the funding that pays for the operation of private prisons is the identical source of the funding for public prisons: tax money from the state or local government. Consequently, a state department of corrections having the authority to provide correctional services can delegate that authority to private firms if enabling legislation provides for this potential. Therefore, a private prison can operate only under the aegis of government authority and pursuant to a negotiated contract with government. Because government-operated prisons are assessed as to their performance, it only stands to reason that private prisons must also be evaluated as to their effectiveness and efficiency.

This chapter discusses the reasoning, the historical developments, the operational aspects, and the future of measuring the performance of our nation's private prisons as they exist in the Federal Bureau of Prisons and in states that have enabling legislation for the existence of private prisons. The purpose is not to discuss the propriety, espoused advantages or disadvantages, legality, or any other facets of private prisons other than performance measures, as these issues are adequately covered in other chapters.

Private Prisons

In order to discuss performance measures of private prisons, we must have an understanding of what a private prison is and how it might be different from a public prison. This section contains an abbreviated description of private prisons, as other chapters have covered this topic more in-depth.

Private prisons exist through the concept of *privatization*, which in general terms is the use of private agencies to perform services normally conducted by public agencies. These public services may include, for example, waste management, utilities, computer or information services, transportation, highway construction and repair, and other normal government functions. Historically, prisons have been operated predominantly by state governments in the name of departments of corrections. In these modern times, prisons are now a public service that is open to privatization. Cheung (2004, 1) reminds us that "[t]oday, the privatization of prisons refers both to the takeover of existing public facilities by private operators and to the building and operation of new and additional prisons by for-profit prison companies."

The method by which private prisons come into existence is varied, but the following typical description should provide a foundation of understanding. A private prison is usually initiated when a government entity decides a new prison should be built or when an existing prison has exceeded the financial ability of the entity, and the governing body wants private companies to bid on a formal request for proposals (RFP) to operate the existing prison.

Private prison companies develop elaborate proposals addressing all the provisions contained in the RFP. These proposals are quite comprehensive in addressing all the areas of a prison operation, which may include the construction and total operation of a new prison. Staffing, training, salaries, facility location, design, security, medical and food services, transportation, inmate treatment services, and all manner of operations are addressed in the RFP. The operational and service section in a proposal is usually followed by a cost section that details how much the private company will charge for the entire proposal, described in terms of inmate cost per day. All interested companies submit an RFP, and these are evaluated by a rigorous and, one hopes, objective method. Recommendations from the reviewing committee are forwarded to the government authority that must make a final decision. The company that is awarded a contract is often the lowest bidder or, in the eyes of the authorities, the bidder who has submitted the best proposal. The best bidder may be the one who offers innovative methods of performing correctional functions, the one that has a plan to integrate the private prison into the state's existing system, or the one that is the most experienced.

Once the private company is selected, the government entity and executives of the private company meet to negotiate a final contract, which shall be binding for a specific period, typically a three-year period with opportunities to extend the contract for several more years. If the contract is a design/build/operate contract, it will typically be for a 20-year period, after which the facility becomes the property of the government entity that signs the contract. After a contract is agreed upon, it is signed by all parties, which may include the governor of the state. Once the contract is signed, the private company will begin the process of taking over an existing facility or will commence site preparation and construction of a new prison.

Private companies are paid by the government entity, usually once a month, based on the number of inmates held in the prison. This per diem rate is established in the contract, but the actual pay per month will fluctuate as the exact number of inmate days will generally change month per month.

Blakely and Bumphus (2004, 27–31) describe a private prison as "a facility that incarcerates offenders for profit." Therefore, the amount that the company charges the government entity per inmate per day must include a profit margin. This simple factor is what separates a public prison from a private prison—the profit factor. This factor is also what appears to foment the greatest consternation with the concept of private prison operations. That is, private prisons, like all businesses are motivated by profit to remain operational. State-run, or public prisons, operate solely as a service to the public and have no profit incentive. Although most public prisons do have various methods by which revenues can be generated, these funds are not regarded as profit and are used to defray a portion of the cost of operating the prison or are forwarded to the state as part of the overall state budget.

For some, the idea that private prisons must operate in a manner to acquire profits is a legal and/or ethical issue that cannot go unchallenged. Since the inception of privately operated prisons, there have been legal challenges on many specific issues, and many are grounded on the ideology of the profit motive. Those opposed to the private prison concept have based a portion of their opposition on the belief that private companies will cut costs at every conceivable area to gain maximum profit, and these cost-cutting measures will come at the expense of good, sound correctional practice. The more cost cutting, the more a prison operation will suffer. Underfunded budget areas, such as staff salaries, staff training, inmate services, inmate treatment programming, and other operational aspects, are known to be causes of staff and inmate unrest and can result in serious and expensive consequences. The implications for comparing the quality of operations of public and private prisons can best be studied with this understanding.

Prison Performance Measures

Wright (2005, 371) describes performance measurement as a "label that has been used to describe a variety of efforts to document results of organizational activities." This is accurate but does not include a host of other items that can be measured to determine the quality of a prison's operations. For example, a category of measurable items in prisons, known as "conditions," includes such nonorganizational activities as "space in living areas" and "social density." Consequently, a definition of prison performance measurement needs to include items or dimensions beyond organizational activities and must attempt to capture all items that can actually be measured. There have been a good number of attempts to do exactly that, and each of these attempts has met with some degree of success.

A related issue to prison performance measurement is that of *benchmarking*. This involves the use of performance data from various prison agencies to permit and encourage comparison. For example, benchmarking can be used to compare two similar prisons, one public and one private. These comparison efforts can indicate where operational strengths lie and show the presence of potential best practices. Benchmarking has some real value, as Kopczynski and Lombardo (1999, 133) point out:

1. To recognize good performance and to identify areas for improvement
2. To use indicator values for higher-performing jurisdictions as improvement targets by jurisdictions that fall short of the top mark
3. To compare performance among a subset of jurisdictions believed to be similar in some way
4. To inform stakeholders outside the local government sector
5. To solicit joint cooperation in improving future outcomes in respective communities

Attaching measurable prison performance outcomes to mission statements and goals is an excellent management strategy and has come to be a normal activity of proper prison leadership. Comparing these outcomes with those of similarly operated prisons can indicate strengths and weaknesses of each participating prison. This practice is especially meaningful when comparable public and private prisons are audited using the same performance standards that may be contained in a private prison contract. If the performance measurements can genuinely measure outcomes, then a performance audit can be exceptionally valuable in determining which prison may be superior in the various categories of measurement. A typical performance audit may reveal that the public prison is superior in several service areas, while the private facility may have better security processes. Both prisons can then determine if some changes to operations may be in order to achieve the best possible operation.

There is value in conducting an examination of performance indicators on single prisons as well. This is especially true if one year's performance can be compared with performance in subsequent years. Again, this can reveal strengths and weaknesses in the prison operations and management. After strengths are identified, further examination may be warranted to determine the reason for the high performance so it may be duplicated with other areas of a prison operation.

History of Prison Performance Measurement

The history of prison performance measurement is difficult to establish as some sort of performance evaluation has been going on in prisons since the beginning of detention and incarceration. State commissions, blue ribbon committees, religious organizations, and even individuals (Elizabeth Fry, John Howard, Austin Wilkes, John Augustus, and others) took interest in sporadically examining prisons for quality of life and other performance measures. The beginning of a formal means of inspecting prisons on accepted performance measures seems to be Moos's Correctional Institutional Environmental Scale, used by the Federal Bureau of Prisons in the mid-1960s. This instrument was determined not to possess acceptable validity and was soon replaced in the Federal Bureau of Prisons by the Prison Social Climate Survey (PSCS) (Saylor 2006).

The PSCS was implemented in 1988 and contained performance measures in seven sections: sociodemographics, personal safety and security, quality of life, personal well-being, work environment, community environment and housing preferences, and a special interest section. This survey instrument was administered to staff and inmates at federal prisons to obtain the perceptions of both groups about how the prisons were being operated. Using survey data from inmates can be risky from a research design and statistical perspective, but Camp, Gaes, and Saylor (2001) assert that using inmate survey data is a viable method for determining the performance of prisons.

Another method used by the Federal Bureau of Prisons to monitor the performance of their prisons was the Key Indicator and Strategic Support System. Key indicators of performance were established to include items related to inmates, staff, finances, services, and security. These data were provided to central office personnel and facility administrators to gauge their performance. Several state correctional systems adopted this method to implement performance-based management (Wright 2005, 372).

In 1993, Congress passed the Government Performance and Results Act (GPRA). This act mandated that federal agencies submit strategic plans to include a mission statement, goals and objectives, and a plan on how the goals were to be measured and attained. Further, federal agency budgets were required to contain these measures to determine the output of each funded area. This was clearly an effort to instill a level of fiscal accountability for each program or service of all federal agencies (GPRA 1993). The act was a catalyst for a host of management theories promoting performance-based budgeting and implemented a movement in many states to adopt similar accountability and budgeting initiatives. The act also pushed many states to establish some sort of method, using objective instruments, to measure prison performance.

TABLE 10.1

Dimensions and Subdimensions of Quality of Confinement Measurements for Prisons

Security
Security procedures
Drug use
Significant incidents
Community exposure
Freedom of movement
Staffing adequacy

Activity
Involvement and evaluation
Work and industry
Education and training
Recreation
Religious services

Safety
Safety of inmates
Safety of staff
Dangerousness of inmates
Safety of the environment
Staffing adequacy

Justice
Staff fairness
Limited use of force
Grievances (number and type)
Grievance process
Discipline process
Legal resources and access
Justice delays

Order
Inmate misconduct
Staff use of force
Perceived control
Strictness of enforcement

Conditions
Space in living areas
Social density and privacy
Internal freedom of movement
Facilities and maintenance
Sanitation, noise, and food
Commissary and visitation
Community access

Care
Stress and illness
Health care delivered
Dental care
Counseling
Staffing for programs and services

Management
Job satisfaction
Stress and burnout
Staff turnover
Staff and management relations
Staff experience
Education and training
Salary and overtime
Staffing efficiency

One of the more prominent instruments to measure prison performance was designed by academician Charles Logan in 1992. This instrument was designed for the purpose of determining the performance of prisons and continues to be in use today in some jurisdictions. Table 10.1 shows the categories and items that are measured with this instrument. Keep in mind that this is not the complete instrument, as each item is broken down to very specific areas that are measurable with either available documentation or survey responses from staff and inmates. Logan's prison performance measurement instrument was later enhanced through a publication of the Bureau of Justice Statistics–Princeton Project (DiIulio et al. 1993).

In the design of an instrument to measure performance, Kravchuk and Schack (1996, 357) recommend that certain principles ought to be incorporated:

1. Formulate a clear, coherent mission, strategy, and objectives.

2. Develop an explicit measurement strategy.

3. Involve key users in the design and development phase.

4. Rationalize the programmatic structure as a prelude to measurement.

5. Develop multiple sets of measures for multiple users, as necessary.

6. Consider the customer(s) of programs and systems throughout the process.

7. Provide each user with sufficient detail for a clear picture of performance.

8. Periodically review and revise the measurement system.

9. Take account of upstream, downstream, and lateral complexities.

10. Avoid excessive aggregation of information.

Wright (2005) reported on efforts of the Association of State Correctional Administrators to establish a national performance measurement system for prisons, which began in 1999 with the establishment of a subcommittee to address the issue. The idea was to develop a standardized performance measurement device that correctional agencies could use to respond to the mandates of GPRA. The association used seven different prison performance indicator models, which included Logan's model, a Federal Bureau of Prisons model, two state instruments, and several others (Wright 2005, 375). This effort resulted in the committee's selecting ten performance categories, of which eight were directly related to performance and two were contextual measures (Wright 2005, 386):

Performance Measures

1. Public safety

2. Institutional safety

3. Programming

4. Substance abuse and mental health

5. Human resource management

6. Justice

7. Population management

8. Health

Contextual Measures

1. Offender Profile

2. Costs

The magnitude of this task required the committee to initially focus on just four of the ten categories. These included public safety, institutional safety, substance abuse and mental health, and offender profile. Each of these categories was composed of multiple key indicators; for example, institutional safety had nine items to measure. Since 2004, six states have been using the new instrument and submitting data from the four categories. Funding was continued through 2008, but progress has slowed for adoption of the instrument to all states.

The Management Training Corporation (MTC 2006, 3–4) has recommended four critical dimensions of prison performance to be achieved for a successful operation:

1. Safety and security

2. Quality of life

3. Reentry preparation

4. Management

Each of the four dimensions has multiple and measurable outcome standards for which the prison managers should be judged. Management should be held accountable for the outcomes and put emphasis on reducing recidivism by highlighting reentry efforts. Aptly stated, "Corrections organizations must be held accountable to a standard greater than the current practice. Simply releasing offenders and 'hoping for the best' is no longer viable given the financial burden on state and federal budgets" (MTC 2006, 8).

Private Prisons and Performance Measurement

Private prisons have existed since the early 1980s and began with a contract to operate a facility under administrative control of Hamilton County, Tennessee (Cheung 2004). Two of the primary arguments espoused by the proponents of private corrections are "that cost-savings and efficiency of operation place private prisons at an advantage over public prisons" (Cheung 2004, 1). Although many advantages and disadvantages are touted for privatizing a prison operation, the two primary advantages, as stated earlier, are directly related to quality of operations and costs. Consequently, these two facets of prison management need to be scrutinized carefully to determine if there really is a difference between the performance of public and private prisons. Operating a prison more efficiently than another can be accomplished fairly easily, but operating a prison more efficiently while simultaneously providing comparable quality operations is presumably no easy task. State departments of corrections are not on the high end of what legislators want to fund from taxpayers' money. Therefore, many correctional budgets are already meager and often do not permit much excessive spending. For a private prison to operate at a lower cost than a public prison, which is already operating on a tight budget, appears difficult but necessary. This is because it is doubtful that a government entity would contract with a private prison that would cost more on a daily basis than the public prison.

In a nutshell then, private prisons must be inspected and examined to be certain that contract provisions are being complied with, and to determine if payments to the private prison are within the parameters established in the contract. One other reason exists. One of the attractions of having a private prison in a state or federal prison system is the opportunity to copy creative management practices and innovative operational policies and procedures. In their RFPs, a number of states said that they are looking for private corporations that may offer some new methods of operating prisons, methods that are less costly, more effective, or both. Simply stated, governments may want to learn more effective and efficient management practices from the private sector. In essence, "private prisons may serve as a 'yardstick' or 'benchmark' that creates an empirically-based standard by which public prisons can compare themselves" (Blumstein, Cohen, and Seth 2007, 9). Government is not known for its efficiency, but private corporations must be on the forefront of best practices to remain profitable. For these reasons, private prisons and public prisons must be examined on performance items to determine comparability or superiority.

One state that requires a performance evaluation for all private prisons is Florida. This state is unique in that the monitoring services are conducted by an agency outside of the Department of Corrections. Performance evaluations, or audits, are conducted through the auspices of the Department of Management Services, Bureau of Private Prison Monitoring, which is under the guidance of DMS policy number 09-102, promulgated in December 2010. This policy outlines the procedures of how an audit may be conducted and how to deal with performance measures that are noncompliant. The agency employs a contract monitor who has an office at the prison to perform continuous on-site inspections, review documentation, and conduct interviews with staff and inmates. As external agencies conduct their agency's inspections, these reports are forwarded to the Bureau of Private Prison Monitoring for analysis. Typical external agencies would be the Department of Health, State Fire Marshal, Occupational Safety and Health Administration, Department of Corrections, and other government agencies related to the operation of a prison (Bureau of Private Prison Monitoring 2009, 3). Failure to comply with established performance measures can result in monetary sanctions and ultimately the cancelling of the contract.

The Florida Bureau of Private Prison Monitoring was created on July 1, 2004 (OPPAGA 2008), for the purpose of monitoring the compliance of the private prisons in the state. Reports critical of the monitoring services provided by the bureau have resulted in improvements in the service, including the construction of a 300-item checklist to be used for monitoring. Even with the new instrument, a report from the Office of Program Policy Analysis and Government Accountability (OPPAGA) recommended that more rigorous monitoring was needed because of various substantive weaknesses in the private prisons' operations (OPPAGA 2008, 3). Florida, as with other states, requires the private contractor(s) to pay for the services and salaries of personnel to monitor the prison.

Public versus Private Correctional Facilities: Quality

Many studies have been conducted since the 1980s regarding the comparison of quality issues in public and private prisons. Public and private prisons cover a wide range of security classifications, capacities, demographics of the inmate population, states, and specialization of facilities, and this makes comparison somewhat difficult. One simply cannot get any kind of accurate comparison unless the prisons being compared are as similar as possible. Further, the operation and management contract can make comparison complex. For example, if the contract does not require rehabilitation programs similar to what the public prison offers, then this aspect of comparison can be inappropriate or inaccurate. Even the issue of the prison's location can influence the results of a comparison. If a public prison is located near an urban area with a large workforce and where professional staff and services are readily available, then the staff turnover rate and delivery of services may be superior to those in a private prison located in a remote rural area. All of these issues, and more, relate to the necessity, but difficulty, in truly comparing any two prisons.

It is interesting to note that although many studies have been conducted on the quality of operations using a comparison of public and private prisons, a good number have found nearly opposite findings. This may be a result of not comparing truly similar prisons, but it may have to do with the motivations of the researchers or the funding of the study. It is certainly no secret that there are researchers whose personal philosophy opposes private prisons, which may slant their results to show that private prisons are not comparable to public prisons. Consider the political implications of a large government entity having to admit that a private company can operate a prison cheaper and still make a profit. Of course, the exact opposite is also true as researchers whose research is funded by the private corrections industry may concentrate on those factors that will make their results look superior for a private prison. One must be particularly careful in examining the results of data in this area of research.

Like other areas of research, conducting comparison studies on public and private prisons has been going on now for more than 25 years. Consequently, not only are there quite a few studies but enough information has been available to conduct multiple analyses of comparison studies. These quasi-meta-analysis kinds of research efforts are always helpful, if conducted correctly, to offer a summation of many studies. Fortunately, several exist in this specialized area of corrections.

One such study was conducted by the Reason Foundation in 2002. Segal (2005) examined 16 studies conducted from 1985 through 2000 by various states' departments, national organizations, and an academician and an additional study of 13 juvenile public and private facilities. In all, comparisons were made in 35 studies in the United States and 7 in the United Kingdom (Segal 2005, 1–8). According to Segal (2005, 6), 15 of the 17 studies showed that quality in private prisons was comparable or superior to those in public prisons, and he explained: "First, it is remarkable that such a wide variety of approaches spanning over a decade and half of research conducted in states across the nation repeatedly comes to the same conclusion—that privatization does not reduce quality.... Furthermore, there is clear and significant evidence that private prisons actually improve quality."

The U.S. General Accounting Office (GAO 1996) performed a similar examination of multiple prisons but came to different conclusions. The GAO selected what they considered the most robust research comparing public and private prisons at the time. The results were mixed as to the comparability of quality of operations and costs of private prisons to public prisons. In fact, the authors stated that the existing studies "offered little generalizable guidance for other jurisdictions about what to expect regarding comparative operational costs and quality of service if they were to move toward privatizing correctional facilities" (GAO 1996, 3).

Similar results were obtained in a study conducted by Abt Associates in 1997 (McDonald et al. 1998). That is, although certain areas of operation seemed to favor private prisons, other operational areas did not. The Abt study examined private prison operations in 28 states for a total of 91 contracts. The authors related that many of the studies conducted up to 1997 were flawed and resulted in erroneous findings. Their conclusion was that "they believe that it is not possible to make any general statements about the ability of private contractors to ensure quality correctional services in comparison to public prison management" (McDonald et al. 1998, 55).

In Logan's study (1992) of three women's prisons in which one was state operated, one privately operated, and one operated by the Federal Bureau of Prisons, several factors appeared to influence the findings of the high performance of the private prison. These factors are interesting as they, for the most part, seem to be outside the parameters of a monitoring instrument:

1. A well-designed facility

2. Greater operational and administrative flexibility

3. Decentralized authority

4. Higher morale, enthusiasm, and sense of ownership among the staff

5. Greater experience and leadership among the top administrators

6. Stricter, "by the book" governance of inmates (Logan 1992, 577–613)

These six factors are in agreement with the Abt study finding that "existing evaluations assume that any observed differences in performance may be created by a variety of other factors that often are not under the direct control of management" (McDonald et al. 1998, 55–56).

Logan (1996) did a follow-up study of the three women's prisons in New Mexico, and his conclusions yielded similar findings as the earlier study, specifically that the private prisons outperformed the public prisons. Also, as a separate analysis, Logan interviewed and surveyed staff that had previously worked at a public prison and were now employed by the private prison. This analysis "showed a pattern of superior achievement on management-related performance measures when the private operation of New Mexico's prison for women was compared to its previous operation by the state itself" (Logan 1996, 83). However, this type of survey analysis may be suspect as questioning employees who may have left the public prison in less than honorable circumstances may not be the best method to obtain credible results.

Camp, Gaes, and Saylor (2001) attempted to enhance the use of surveys to collect information about performance measures in comparison studies. Surveys are often viewed as having weak validity and being problematic because of inaccurate reporting, use of poorly constructed instruments, inadequate research designs, and negligent choice of subjects or settings (Nettler 1978, 107). However, these researchers contend that the proper survey instrument with appropriate questions can be valuable in assessing inmate and staff views of the performance of prisons. Camp, Gaes, and Saylor's (2001) study, using a survey, indicated mixed results in comparing operations of a private prison with three similar federal prisons. Some factors were better for the public prisons, while for others, the private facility had the higher performance.

One performance area of great importance is the recidivism rate. Although recidivism has been challenged as the premier performance indicator, it remains an important indicator that prisons are achieving their stated goals and mission. Comparing recidivism rates between public and private prisons can be difficult as the demographics of the inmate populations and the treatment programming must be very similar. Lanza-Kaduce, Parker, and Thomas (1999) conducted such a recidivism study in Florida comparing offenders released from two private prisons and two public prisons. Recidivism was measured for only one year, but the results were that the offenders released from the private prisons had a lower recidivism rate than the public prisons. Yet, this was only one study, and it was supported by the for-profit prison industry. Although the results may be accurate, they remain suspect as the objectivity of the researchers cannot be firmly established.

Public versus Private Prisons: Cost

Beyond operational issues when comparing public and private prisons is the item of cost. This is a somewhat contentious but highly important issue as the need or desire for a private prison in a state or federal system is somewhat negated if the costs are not lower than those for a public prison. Private prisons can provide more of a benefit than just costs as they can be up and running more quickly than a public prison in most instances. This is an attractive feature to governments that are under a legal mandate to hastily provide for more inmate bed space or face monetary sanctions. Nonetheless, a private prison is expected to operate less expensively than a comparable public prison, and costs are carefully monitoring to be certain this is the case. Some states have statutory requirements that any private prisons must operate at a certain percentage below the state department of corrections (Morris 2007).

This factor should ensure that the private prison is operating less expensively than a comparable public prison, but that is not necessarily so. Those states that provide monitoring services figure this expense as part of the overall costs of a private prison unless the private prison is already paying for these services in the contract. Central office personnel of state departments of corrections will spend some portion of their time on monitoring, visiting, communicating, meeting, planning, or otherwise performing tasks directly related to a private prison in their corrections system. These indirect costs are often factored into the overall costs of having a private prison in a corrections system. Another similar area is inmate lawsuits. State attorneys or department counsel will need to respond to lawsuits generated by inmates housed in a private prison even if just to file for a motion of summary judgment, and these hours must be considered in the states' expense for a private prison.

The determination of costs for private companies is also challenged by states that are unsure of the true expenses involved in operating a prison. For example, the cost of recruiting, interviewing, conducting background investigations, testing, hiring, administering promotional exams and activities, and overseeing issues related to employment termination are often outside the budget of the department of corrections and under a separately funded state department of personnel or human services. These costs must be figured into the private prison's budget, as must costs for legal services, hospital guard services, computer services, buildings and grounds maintenance, and other areas potentially outside a public prison's budget. Further, private prisons that are constructed and operated by a private company have to include the costs of land acquisition, excavation, architectural fees, construction costs, and debt service in their budgets.

Another very important issue to consider when comparing costs of public and private prisons is the concept of comparability itself. It is unfair and a poor method of comparison to examine two or more facilities that are not very similar in nearly every aspect. This is what makes comparisons difficult and potentially nonsensical. One should be able to easily determine that two dissimilar prisons cannot be compared; that is, a maximum-security prison and a medium-security prison, or a men's prison and a women's prison of similar sizes, or a 1,500-bed prison and a 500-bed prison. These present obvious dissimilarities, and even weighted cost factors may not provide a true cost comparison. But even a comparison of two 1,000-bed, medium-security, all-male prisons located in the same state presents challenges. Issues such as age of the facility, types of programming offered, prison industries offered, an urban or rural location, costs of utilities, and some other factors can render comparability unsound.

Lastly, it should be understood that a private prison company is not likely to disclose the actual cost of operation because a certain proportion of revenue earned must be for profit. This profit margin is an important element of any business venture and is generally regarded as proprietary information. To completely disclose the profit margin would expose this figure to competing private corrections companies that could use the information to their unfair advantage, especially with future contracts. Consequently, this profit percentage figure may be withheld from examination during a cost comparison. There is an argument to be made about what costs should be considered proprietary, especially when public funds are being consumed. Although it seems that the government entity would insist on requiring a specific percentage of profit that could be disclosed to the public or include that provision in the proposal, the actual profit margin vacillates month to month to account for expenses that fluctuate. Yet, in spite of these inherent difficulties, ample studies have been conducted to make some comparisons of costs between public and private prisons.

One such early comparison study was conducted by Sellers (1989), who examined three public adult prisons, three private adult prisons, and two juvenile facilities. Data collection was performed by the use of on-site visits to each facility and structured interviews. Many aspects of the operation of each facility were included in the comparison. Seller's (1989, 241) conclusions were "that the private prison facilities studied were run at lower cost than the public prison facilities. Moreover, the private facilities were often in better repair and seemed to offer a better living experience for inmates."

Archambeault and Deis (1997/1998) conducted a study comparing three identically constructed prisons in Louisiana. Two were operated by two different private companies and one was operated by the state. This was a study of three truly comparable prisons in design, capacity, classification of male inmates, and other inmate demographics. As would be expected, the public prisons were superior in some aspects and the private facilities in other aspects. The authors noted that the private facilities performed significantly better than the state-operated facility on most of the measures compared and that private prisons were appropriate for state correctional systems, but no system should privatize all of its prisons as the competitive advantage would be removed. In terms of cost comparisons, the two private prisons were more cost-effective to operate.

Pratt and Maahs (1999) conducted a meta-analysis of 24 cost-effectiveness studies encompassing 33 evaluations of public and private prisons for men. Their contention was that previous studies were not rigorous in their methodologies and had other flaws rendering the findings suspect. Pratt and Maahs focused on the independent variables of number of inmates, age of facility, and security level of the prison. It was their belief that these three variables had to be considered for an accurate comparison of a public and private prison. Number of inmates was critical in their analysis as they espoused that the more inmates housed in a facility the less expensive was the operation due to economies of scale (Pratt and Maahs 1999, 361). Age of facility was included because older facilities are not likely to take advantage of newer and less staff-intensive designs, and the maintenance costs of older facilities should generally be higher. The security level of the institution was also controlled in the comparison as it was presumed that maximum-security prisons are more costly than medium- or minimum-security prisons. The results of the analysis pointed to mixed findings of the comparison because economies of scale, age, and security level of the facility predominantly determined the cost (Pratt and Maahs 1999, 367). The conclusions were that privatizing a prison would not likely remedy the burdensome financial situation of a state correctional department.

In 2003, Perrone and Pratt did a follow-up study, once again examining all the studies on public and private prison comparisons up through 2000. The authors examined quality and cost issues and found that the measures of quality in the comparisons were inconclusive. With the cost comparisons, the researchers recognized that the studies examined revealed a clear finding that private prisons were less expensive than public prisons. However, the caveat is that the studies were flawed, and as a result, "there was no overall significant pattern of cost savings for private over public prisons" (Perrone and Pratt 2003, 316). Again, the authors claimed that by not controlling for the number of inmates, age of the prison, and the security classification of the prison, it would be difficult to determine whether a public or private prison was more or less expensive. Recommendations of the researchers included abandoning the case-study method of researching private prisons. Because all prisons have some differences, the study of one prison tells us little about all the others. Second, we should be studying management practices in our research efforts to the same degree as we study contracting and budgeting issues. This means we should be looking at the management practices private companies use for cost savings and at other efficiencies to see which ones could be incorporated into government correctional systems. Last, for the national correctional system, we should be establishing a centralized database to maintain up-to-date information that can be compared for all prisons, be they public or private (Perrone and Pratt 2003, 318).

Gaes (2008), in a report from the National Institute of Justice, believes lessons have been learned from comparison studies. In March 2007, the National Institute of Justice hosted a meeting of practitioners, academicians, researchers, and private prison company executives—both proponents and opponents of prison privatization—to discuss the best criteria to use when performing studies on cost and quality evaluations (Gaes 2008, 1). Lessons from this meeting included the following:

1. Cost comparisons are deceivingly complex, and great care should be taken when comparing the costs of privately and publicly operated prisons.

2. Special care should be given to an analysis of overhead costs.

3. A uniform method of comparing publicly and privately operated prisons on the basis of audits should be developed.

4. Qualitative measures of prison performance, such as serious misconduct and drug use, should be incorporated into any analysis.

5. Future analytical methods could allow simultaneous cost and quality comparisons. (1–2)

Further, Gaes restated the issue observed by Pratt and Maas that the inmate population size needs to be included and adjusted to account for economies of scale; that is, large prisons are less expensive on an inmate per day basis that smaller prisons (Gaes 2008, 2). This may be an important issue when comparing multiple prisons of different sizes, but it seems unnecessary when comparing prisons of the same size inmate population. Finally, Gaes pleads for a common and acceptable method to be developed to measure prison performance. Given the results of the many studies attempting to measure prison performance, this appears to be an excellent recommendation and a task that needs to receive serious attention.

Mears (2006) has conducted a study of supermax prisons that is of importance to this discussion, not for the purposes of comparing public and private operations of these controversial prisons, as no private supermax prison exists at the time of this writing, but because of the skepticism surrounding the human and fiscal costs of their existence. Using performance measurements to examine the efficacy of these special prisons seems to be an appropriate expenditure of time, effort, and funding. As a society, practitioners, legislators, and citizens ought to have a better understanding of these prisons to be certain they are worth the financial and social costs.

The Future of Measuring Performance for Public and Private Prisons

The future of privatization looks to be bright as government entities seek the least expensive manner to incarcerate offenders. With recent comparison studies of public and private prisons showing mixed results or opposing results, is it worth the time, effort, and funding to continue conducting these comparison studies? Note that several of the best researchers in our discipline claim that most of the past studies have been flawed to some degree. Is it likely that future studies may contain the same flaws or yet-to-be-discovered flaws? Should we be looking at associations of performance measures with statistics that can show statistically significant differences? Most importantly, with all the potential variables to measure, are any two facilities truly comparable?

From this writer's perspective, measuring the performance of prisons is a fundamental obligation of government. Taxpayers are recognizable stakeholders in the operation of any prison, public or private, as taxpayers are the ultimate funding source for both. Citizens deserve to know about the performance of our prisons and ought to know if a private company can operate a prison at least as inexpensively and professionally as the government. This concept is in the realm of public accountability and should extend into reentry efforts, because if offenders are returning for new charges or violations of parole, our efforts at correcting human beings may not be working. In order to be able to make these comparisons, private prisons cannot make proprietary claims about their operations when taking money from government. When they do not provide full disclosure, true and accurate comparisons cannot be made.

Many private companies and public corrections departments, including the Federal Bureau of Prisons, conduct interorganizational audits of their facilities. This may or may not be for the purpose of comparing facilities, but it is an excellent method to monitor the performance of prisons. Though some of the instruments used to perform these audits may not be sophisticated, they serve a useful purpose. Moreover, many individual prisons have staff for the express purpose of conducting performance audits. These self-audits are necessary as ACA reaccreditation approaches. Compliance officers or managers are becoming part of normal staffing patterns for public and private prisons. These interorganizational audits and self-audits should continue and should be expanded as a mandatory standard for ACA accreditation. It is out of this effort that a national, or standardized, performance measuring instrument could be devised.

When comparing public and private prisons, care must be taken to account for the particulars in the contract of a private prison. One common claim of private prison opponents is that private prisons do not offer enough rehabilitation programs, but these persons are not aware that this is because the governing agency that constructed the contract did not think rehabilitation efforts were worth the expense, so they were not included. In other words, it may not be that the private prison company doesn't see the worth in rehabilitative treatment but that the contract doesn't require it.

Another issue to be examined, according to Pratt and Maahs (1999), Gaes (2008), and others is the number of inmates housed in the prison. Some researchers contend that this is an important issue and should result in an adjustment factor when comparing prisons of different sizes. The thinking is that there is an inverse relationship between inmate population and cost per inmate per day. This deserves some careful thought, but a more appropriate measure in this writer's view is the average daily population and the percent of occupancy. The real economy of scale is established when a prison is housing inmates over its operational capacity, for example, at 105 percent, simply because additional staff may not be hired to deal with the additional inmates. The inmates just double up or triple up in cells, and this accounts for a dramatic decrease in costs as prison budgets are heavily weighted in staffing costs. Therefore, if comparing prisons of different sizes, then a figure for comparison may be average days of percent of occupancy.

Hatry (1999) reminds us that conducting comparative performance audits can actually be harmful. When measurements are based on erroneous data or are unfair, the lower performer will be chastised by the media and political opponents. Further, these poor quality performance comparisons take valuable time from busy practitioners and elected officials to address. However, even poor quality comparisons can have some value if they initiate examination to determine why some areas were rated poorly and action is taken to correct the deficiencies. Summing up the value of comparison performance studies, Hatry (1999, 104) gives the following advice:

> To the extent that (a) care is taken, (b) adequate caveats are inserted into reports, (c) public officials and the media are educated as to the

limitations of the information, and (d) operating agencies themselves take the data seriously, comparative performance measurement can be a useful way to achieve improved government services.

It should be clear that measuring the performance of prisons and comparing these measures between public and private prisons are worthwhile endeavors. However, to achieve accurate and useful results is a complex task. Since Logan's efforts (1992, 1996), a number of performance measuring instruments have been formulated to capture the best information to accomplish a true comparison. It should be evident that a final product has not yet been devised to appropriately measure prison performance, especially in comparing public and private prisons. Although there have been several attempts to develop the perfect instrument, these efforts are not complete. We must continue our efforts toward this lofty goal so we can finally make some determination if public prisons are genuinely superior in quality and cost than private prisons. The only alternative is to pronounce the task too complex and fraught with issues outside of measurement and to continue our present course.

References

Archambeault, William. G., and Donald R. Deis, Jr. 1997/1998. "Cost Effectiveness Comparisons of Private versus Public Prisons in Louisiana: A Comprehensive Analysis of Allen, Avoyelles, and Winn Correctional Centers." *Journal of the Oklahoma Criminal Justice Research Consortium* 4. http://www.doc.state.ok.us/offenders/ocjrc/97_98/Cost%20 Effectiveness%20Comparisons.PDF.

Blakely, Curtis R., and Victor W. Bumphus. 2004. "Private and Public Sector Prisons—A Comparison of Select Characteristics." *Federal Probation* 68 (1): 27–31.

Blumstein, James F., Mark A. Cohen, and Suman Seth. 2007. *Do Government Agencies Respond to Market Pressures? Evidence from Private Prisons*. Vanderbilt Law and Economics Research Paper No. 03-16; Vanderbilt Public Law Research Paper No. 03-05. http://ssrn.com/ abstract=441007.

Bureau of Private Prison Monitoring. 2009. "Response to Official Visits and Audits of Privately Operated Facilities." Policy No. 09-102. Tallahassee: Florida Department of Management Services.

Camp, Scott D., Gerry G. Gaes, and William G. Saylor. 2001. "Quality of Prison Operations in the US Federal Sector: A Comparison with a Private Prison." *Punishment and Society* 4 (1): 27–53.

Cheung, Amy. 2004. *Prison Privatization and the Use of Incarceration.* Washington, DC: Sentencing Project.

DiIulio, John J., Jr., Geoffrey P. Alpert, Mark H. Moore, George F. Cole, Joan Petersilia, Charles H. Logan, and James Q. Wilson. 1993. *Performance Measures for the Criminal Justice System.* NCJ-143505. Washington, DC: U.S. Department of Justice, Office of Justice Programs, Bureau of Justice Statistics.

Gaes, Gerry. 2008. "Cost, Performance Studies Look at Prison Privatization." *NIJ Journal* 259. http://www.nij.gov/journals/259/prison-privatization.htm.

GAO (U.S. General Accounting Office). 1996. *Private and Public Prisons: Studies Comparing Operational Costs and/or Quality of Service.* Washington, DC: GAO.

GPRA (Government Performance and Results Act). 1993. Office of Management and Budget. http://www.whitehouse.gov/omb/rewrite/mgmt gpra/gplaw2m.html#h2.

Hatry, Harry. 1999. "Mini-Symposium on Intergovernmental Comparative Performance Data." *Public Administration Review* 59 (2): 101–104.

Kopczynski, Mary, and Michael Lombardo. 1999. "Comparative Performance Measurement: Insights and Lessons Learned from a Consortium Effort." *Public Administration Review* 59:124–134.

Kravchuk, Robert S., and Ronald W. Schack. 1996. "Designing Effective Performance-Measurement Systems under the Government Performance and Results Act of 1993." *Public Administration Review* 56 (4): 348–358.

Lanza-Kaduce, Lonn, Karen F. Parker, and Charles W. Thomas. 1999. "A Comparative Recidivism Analysis of Releasees from Private and Public Prisons." *Crime & Delinquency* 45 (1): 28–47.

Logan, Charles H. 1992. "Well Kept: Comparing Quality of Confinement in Private and Public Prisons." *Journal of Criminal Law and Criminology* 83 (3): 577–613.

Logan, Charles H. 1996. "Public vs. Private Management: A Case Comparison." *Criminal Justice Review* 21 (1): 62–85.

McDonald, Douglas, Elizabeth Fourier, Malcolm Russell-Einhorn, and Stephen Crawford. 1998. *Private Prisons in the United States: An Assessment of Current Practice.* Cambridge, MA: Abt Associates.

Mears, Daniel P. 2006. *Evaluating the Effectiveness of Supermax Prisons*. Project No. 2002-IJ-CX-0019. Washington, DC: Urban Institute, Justice Policy Center.

Morris, John C. 2007. "Government and Market Pathologies of Privatization: The Case of Prison Privatization." *Politics and Policy* 35 (3): 318–341.

MTC (Management Training Corporation). 2006. *Measuring Success: Improving the Effectiveness of Correctional Facilities*. Centerville, UT: MTC Institute.

Nettler, Gwynn. 1978. *Explaining Crime*. 2nd ed. New York: McGraw-Hill.

OPPAGA (Office of Program Policy Analysis and Government Accountability). 2008. *While DMS Has Improved Monitoring, It Needs to Strengthen Private Prison Oversight and Contracts*. Report No. 08-71. Tallahassee, FL: OPPAGA.

Perrone, D., and Travis C. Pratt. 2003. "Comparing the Quality of Confinement and Cost-effectiveness of Public versus Private Prisons: What We Know, Why We Do Not Know More, and Where to Go from Here." *Prison Journal* 83 (3): 301–322.

Pratt, Travis, and Jeff Maahs. 1999. "Are Private Prisons More Cost-effective than Public Prisons? A Meta-analysis of Evaluation Research Studies." *Crime & Delinquency* 45 (3): 358–371.

Saylor, William G. 2006. "Comments on the Design of the Prison Social Climate Survey." Federal Bureau of Prisons. http://www.bop.gov/news/research_projects/published_reports/cond_envir/oresaylor_comments.pdf.

Segal, Geoffrey F. 2005. *Comparing Public and Private Prisons on Quality*. Los Angeles: Reason Foundation.

Sellers, Martin P. 1989. "Private and Public Prisons: A Comparison of Costs, Programs and Facilities. *International Journal of Offender Therapy and Comparative Criminology* 10 (1): 241–256.

Wright, Kevin N. 2005. "Designing a National Performance Measurement System." *Prison Journal* 85 (3): 368–393.

11

Private Prisons and Contracts

Amy M. McDowell and John C. Morris

The privatization of prison facilities and services is a growing business sector. As governments seek cost-effective solutions to address growing inmate populations, policy makers often view privatization as an attractive alternative. Coupled with a growing sentiment that the private sector is a more efficient allocation mechanism for traditionally public goods and services, governments at all levels are increasingly entering into contractual relationships with corporations to design, build, and/or operate prison facilities.

The recent movement toward prison privatization began in the 1980s. The Reagan era ushered in a new focus on market solutions to public problems (Conlan 1988; see also Johnson and Heilman 1987). Driven by a core belief in the primacy of the private sector, advocates for privatization sought new opportunities to increase market activity and simultaneously reduce the size, scope, and cost of government. The net result of this activity was an increase in public–private contracting at the national, state, and local levels (Savas 2000). More governments engaged in privatization, and the range of services considered for privatization increased as well.

Any discussion of the privatization of corrections services in the United States will inevitably involve a discussion of contracting. Although many forms of privatization are possible (see Morris 1999; Savas 2000), contracting remains the most common form of privatization in the United States. Moreover, a contractual document is often the basis for other forms of privatization as well. A franchise agreement, for example, is a common arrangement used by local governments to ensure the availability of infra-structure-intensive services such as cable television programming. It is a privatization arrangement in that it involves an agreement between a unit of government and a private company, and its status as a franchise arrangement delineates specific roles for government, its private franchisee, and citizens. However, all of the relationships are governed by a set of contractual arrangements (between government and the private company to ensure both exclusive rights and payment of franchise fees, and between the company and citizens to ensure delivery of services and payment for those services).

A contract is fundamentally a legal document that enumerates roles and responsibilities for the people or organizations that are parties to the contract. Although some contracts are simple, straightforward, and perhaps limited to a single point in time, other contracts may involve complex duties and responsibilities over an extended period. Contracts are enforceable through the court system, which provides not only an avenue to ensure fidelity with the agreement but also an important accountability mechanism for each of the parties to a contract. Because the courts can compel contract performance, the interests of all parties can thus be protected.

The issue of accountability is especially important when the good or service under contract involves the coercive power of the state, and prisons represent the direct application of that coercive power (Moe 1987; Robbins 1988). By law, only governments are given the power to hold a person against his or her will. Moreover, governments may only exercise this power within carefully prescribed limits, and only by following closely monitored processes. Indeed, any party other than the government who attempted to detain a person against his or her will would soon be the subject of the state's coercive power.

For a government to specifically assign its coercive power to a private sector actor is a process not to be undertaken lightly. Citizens expect that a government that does assign its coercive power to a private company will hold that company accountable to the legal and ethical expectations of citizens, just as citizens would hold the government accountable for its exercise of coercive powers (Donahue 1989). When coercive powers are assigned to the private sector, as is the case with prison privatization, the contractual arrangements between government and its private sector partners are thus brought sharply into focus.

The purpose of this chapter is to discuss the fundamental issues of contracting for prison services. We begin with a discussion of the legal principles of contracts and the role that contracts play in public accountability. We then illustrate these principles through an examination of a series of contracts executed by the State of Mississippi in the 1990s to help alleviate severe prison overcrowding in state prison facilities. We conclude with some comments and observations about the most critical elements of contracting arrangements in prison services.

A Primer on Contracts and Contract Law

General principles of contract law are an important consideration in drafting contracts for the private provision of prison services. In addition to generalized principles of contract law, there are also more specific contract considerations that parties should carefully consider within the context of drafting contracts for private prison service arrangements. This section of the discussion will focus on some of the general contracting principles, beginning with a brief discussion of reasons underlying the creation of a written contract to memorialize the parties' mutual understanding of the services to be provided.

When parties draft a written contract, they often approach the task with the idea of memorializing the agreement that is reached by the parties (Barnett 1995). In the case of a written contract, a formal record of the agreement and its terms is created that the parties can rely on in the future to clarify concerns that may arise during the course of the contract's period of enforcement (Barnett 1995). Although this is the primary reason many parties use a written contract, there are other advantages as well. A written contract permits nonparties to review the memorialized agreement to gain an understanding of the terms of the service(s) to which the parties agreed (Restatement [Second] of Contracts, §209). Examples of nonparties who may have reason to cite or rely on a written contract include third parties involved in the provision of services, such as subcontractors (Barnett 1995), or courts that are charged with interpreting or enforcing portions of the contract. In this latter example, contract clauses that provide for suggested or more specific remedies in the event of a breach of contract may prove particularly useful (Barnett 1995).

These proposed uses for a written contract suggest four considerations that the parties should take into account when undertaking to draft a contract that will govern the provision of prison services. First, the parties will be concerned with the underlying bargain that is struck between the parties and the creation of the contract itself (Barnett 1995). Second, the parties will want to consider any potential issues involving nonparties as well as the degree to which it is desirable to identify such relationships and the principles that will govern them in the contract (Barnett 1995). Third, the parties should consider any contract terms necessary to ease the task of interpreting the contract should a review of the contract in a court of law become necessary in the future (Restatement [Second] of Contracts, §202). Similarly, the parties should weigh considerations involving any potential future enforcement of the contract terms. Fourth, the parties may wish to consider including clauses to address breach of contract and desired remedies (Restatement [Second] of Contracts, §236 and Chapter 16).

Creation of a contract requires three elements: mutual assent between the parties, consideration, and the lack of defenses to contract formation (Barnett 1995; Restatement [Second] of Contracts, Chapters 2 and 4). Mutual assent represents that an understanding or agreement has been reached by the parties, that is, one party has made an offer to contract with a second party, and the second party has accepted the offer (Barnett 1995). The offer should clearly identify the parties to the agreement and the subject matter of the agreement (Restatement [Second] of Contracts, §§24 and 33). The party accepting the offer must have the authority to accept the offer, must do so unequivocally, and must communicate his or her acceptance to the party making the offer (Restatement [Second] of Contracts, §§50 and 52).

The second step of contract creation requires that the parties exchange consideration (Barnett 1995). Consideration has two requirements: first, the parties must exchange promises, such as a promise to provide prison services in return for a specified monetary figure; and second, the parties must exchange promises involving something of legal value (Restatement [Second] of Contracts, §71). In the case of prison services, for example, the value may be represented by the monetary value of the services or the monetary amount to be exchanged for the provision of such services.

The third element for creation of a contract requires that there be no defenses to the formation of the contract between the parties (Barnett 1995). Examples of common defenses that may be raised by a party to negate contract formation include a mistake with regard to the terms of the agreement, misrepresentation or fraud, no exchange of consideration, lack of legal capacity to contract, or unconscionability such that the terms of the agreement are substantially one-sided (Barnett 1995).

Although the three elements of mutual assent, consideration, and lack of defenses to contract formation must be met to create a valid contract, the parties will often want to include other clauses in the written agreement to memorialize their understanding. As a result, the contracting parties may wish to consider the remaining three types of general contracting principles when finalizing their written agreement. These include nonparty clauses, contract interpretation/enforcement clauses, and breach-of-contract and/or remedy clauses.

The first of these remaining general principles addresses the relationship of nonparties to the agreement. For example, the parties may wish to consider if the contract is intended to create a benefit for a third party (Restatement [Second] of Contracts, §302). In the case of contracts for private provision of prison services, a public–private partnership contract with a private provider may need to consider any benefit intended on behalf of the government, such as the state or local government that created the public–private authority. Another example is future assignees, such as a private provider who assumes responsibility for provision of prison services from the original provider under the terms of the agreement. The parties should consider what the relationship of these nonparties will be to the agreement and whether such nonparty relationships will be permitted. In the case of assignees, for example, the parties may choose to include a contract clause that prohibits any future assignment of rights or delegation of responsibilities (Restatement [Second] of Contracts, Chapter 15).

With respect to the second remaining consideration, the parties should take into account any contract clauses that may assist with the interpretation and/or enforcement of the terms of the parties' agreement. In essence, the parties should include enough specificity in the contract that a third party, such as a court of law, would be able to ascertain the essential points of the parties' understanding. As a general rule, courts will not look to information outside the written contract to ascertain the terms of the parties' agreement (Restatement [Second] of Contracts, §§214 and 216). As a result, the parties will want to strive for clarity and comprehensiveness in the contract.

Lastly, the parties may wish to consider including contract clauses that address breach of contract and desired remedies. The parties may specify, for example, the jurisdiction in which any potential lawsuits pertaining to the agreement must be filed. A provision to arbitrate any dispute arising from the contract in lieu of filing a lawsuit is another potential clause that the parties may wish to include, if legally permissible within the state. With regard to remedies, the parties may wish to specify desirable or preferred remedies, such as monetary damages for nonperformance, specific performance, or liquidated damages (Restatement [Second] of Contracts, Chapter 16). The parties may also wish to consider including a contract clause requiring the non-breaching party to mitigate damages to the extent possible.

An Analysis of Prison Privatization Contracts

Although the general principles of contract law are common across most states, specific contract details can differ substantially from contract to contract. Because a comprehensive review of all potential contractual arrangements would be well beyond the scope of this chapter, we will focus our attention on the contractual arrangements developed by Mississippi in the mid-1990s to help alleviate substantial overcrowding in its state prisons. As is the case with many policy decisions, the decision to privatize prison services in Mississippi was the result of a particular set of problems, political trends, and opportunities present at the moment. We begin with a discussion of the circumstances that led to the decision to pursue prison privatization. We then analyze the three different arrangements, and the contracts that created and governed those arrangements, through the lenses provided by our earlier discussion of contract law.

A Pressing Problem

By the mid-1980s, Mississippi had begun to experience a significant growth in its state corrections spending. In the 20 years between FY 1986 and FY 2006, state spending on corrections rose some 300 percent and was accompanied by a nearly fivefold increase in the number of incarcerated inmates (MDOC 2007). As early as 1972, the state was placed under a court order resulting from *Gates v. Collier*, which required the state to undertake measures to alleviate overcrowding and substandard conditions in state prisons.

The state's inmate population had grown significantly as a result of mandatory minimum sentence and truth-in-sentencing laws enacted in the

1980s and 1990s (Wiseman et al. 1997). A product of a get-tough-on-crime stance on the part of the state legislature, these laws were designed to provide negative incentives to would-be criminals and to make citizens feel safer. In addition, eligibility for federal funding under the Federal Crime Bill of 1994 required the state to demonstrate its commitment to tougher sentencing; a requirement in the state's truth-in-sentencing law that applied truth in sentencing to all felonies (both violent and nonviolent) was intended to be evidence of this commitment (Wiseman et al. 1997, 47). As detailed elsewhere in these volumes, these laws often required jail time for minor, nonviolent offenses. Even though crime rates were generally decreasing in this period, these laws significantly increased the number of inmates in state prison facilities.

Several sources of pressure were building on the state's correctional system. In addition to the requirements of *Gates v. Collier* and the growing inmate population, there was growing dissatisfaction with the operation of the state's parole board, creating calls to decrease the number of inmates eligible for parole and thus marginalizing the actions of the parole board (Morris 2007). In addition, the state's main correctional facility at Parchman was old, overcrowded, and in very poor repair. Although the state had recently built a new facility just outside of Jackson, the new facility did little to alleviate the growing pressures on the system.

These pressures were exacerbated by the state's difficult financial conditions. Typically in the bottom 10 percent of states in terms of per capita income and tax capacity, Mississippi simply did not have the resources to invest heavily in new prison construction. Operational budgets for the Mississippi Department of Corrections (MDOC) were already growing alarmingly, and many legislators openly resented the spending requirements imposed by the court in *Gates v. Collier*. The general financial condition of the state also affected the state's bond rating, and state policy makers were not keen to commit their limited bonding authority to prison construction (Puckett 1997).

It was not until the summer of 1994 that the state legislature moved to address the problems of prison space and the requirements of the *Gates v. Collier* decision. After failing to reach agreement in the regular legislative session, the governor convened a special session of the legislature to consider alternatives to the problem at hand. The legislators considered a number of proposals, including the construction of prison camps, in which inmates would be housed in tents. Other proposals included shipping inmates to prisons (either public or private) in other states, charging inmates a fee for their incarceration, repealing mandatory sentencing laws, and decriminalizing nonviolent drug offenses. Although a number of alternative solutions were discussed, the consensus that emerged was to house state prisoners in private facilities within the state. A significant number of legislators preferred this option over the transport of inmates to other states, as this would place an undue hardship on the families of the inmates (Puckett 1997).

The result of the legislative activity was the passage of Senate Bill (S.B.) 2005, which was quickly signed into law by the governor. The main provision of S.B. 2005 was the creation of the State Prison Emergency Construction and Management (SPECAM) board. Consisting of the attorney general, the state treasurer, and the lieutenant governor, the legislation gave SPECAM several specific powers:

- Construct new state facilities, or expand existing facilities;
- House state inmates in private facilities in other states;
- Contract with private companies to house inmates in private facilities within Mississippi;
- House state inmates in tents;
- Adjust the reimbursement rates (and terms of contracts) for state inmates held in county jail facilities;
- Allow for the early release of certain classes of offenders; and
- Allow the exemption from some state procurement laws, construction standards, and bidding requirements. (Mississippi Code Annotated § 47-5-1211 *et seq.*)

In short, rather than decide a specific course of action from the several options under consideration by the legislature, S.B. 2005 moved to defer the decision to SPECAM to choose from a range of policy choices in lieu of a firm legislative policy decision.

Although S.B. 2005 offered several alternatives, an analysis of the legislation reveals a clear legislative intent for privatization arrangements within the state. Sections 4 through 15 of the bill are almost exclusively dedicated to the allowable provisions of these contractual arrangements, even going so far as to specify the allowable locations for private prisons in the state, the requirement for the contracted price to be at least 10 percent less than the state's calculated per-inmate-per-day cost, a requirement for adequate insurance to be held by the contractor, and a provision that sovereign immunity would not apply to the contractor.

Fully aware of the legislative opposition to some of its allowable options and preference for privatization, SPECAM focused immediately on its options to involve the private sector in the delivery of prison services (Puckett 1997). Although private prisons existed in many states and were both willing and able to accept inmates from Mississippi, the members of SPECAM rejected this option for two reasons. First, the long-standing policy of MDOC (and thus of the state) was to house state inmates as close to their families as was feasible. Such proximity reduced the burden on families wishing to visit their incarcerated family members and provided important ongoing ties to the inmate's community. To house inmates out of state would not only provide undue hardship on the families, but it would also remove the community influence thought to be an important element of rehabilitation. Second, anecdotal evidence from other states convinced the board that the potential costs of transportation, coupled with the potential for accountability issues, outweighed any potential cost savings (Puckett 1997). The board's attention was thus focused on the development of an in-state private prison capacity.

One Problem, Three Distinct Arrangements

Having decided on a course of action, SPECAM moved quickly to create the arrangements to entice private companies to do business with the state. Given the limitations of the state's operating budget and bonding authority, SPECAM chose to follow several different arrangements (Morris 2007). The board issued a request for proposals (RFP) for the construction of a 1,000-bed, medium-security facility to be built in Marshall County, in the northwestern region of the state. Six firms responded to the RFP, and a design/build/operate contract was subsequently awarded to Wackenhut Corporation. SPECAM[1] simultaneously approved a contract for a second facility in LeFlore County in the Mississippi Delta and, 18 months later, for a third facility in Wilkinson County, in the extreme southwest corner of the state. In addition, the board moved to restructure existing contracts with

TABLE 11.1

Summary of Privatization Arrangements in Mississippi

	Marshall County Model*	LeFlore County Model*	Regional Jail Model*
Ownership	Private company; ownership reverts to the state upon retirement of the debt	County development authority	County government
Management	Private company, under contract to state	Private company, under contract to development authority	County sheriff; state contract for minimum number of beds; counties may choose to contract for private management
Size (number of beds)	1,000	1,000	250 (size of prison varies; state contracts for a minimum of 250 beds at each county facility)
Monitoring	Contract monitor; ACA accreditation	Contract monitor; ACA accreditation	ACA accreditation
Risk protection	Indemnification	Indemnification	Sovereign immunity

*These names refer to the three models discussed in the text. The Delta Correctional Facility in LeFlore County is operated by CCA, the Marshall County Correctional Facility is operated by Wackenhut (now known as the GEO Group), and the regional prisons are currently operated by county sheriffs. The arrangement for the facility located in Wilkinson County is identical to the LeFlore County model.

Source: Adapted from Morris (2007).

county sheriffs and approved a series of new regional county jails. Although all but the contracts with the counties were limited to medium-security inmates and facilities, each of these arrangements was unique in its approach, and thus in the contractual terms created for each arrangement. Table 11.1 summarizes the basic elements of each arrangement.

The Marshall County Model

The contract between SPECAM and Wackenhut (now known as the GEO Group) was executed on June 1, 1995, roughly a year after the passage of S.B. 2005. The RFP issued by SPECAM called for the design, construction, and operation of a 1,000-bed, medium-security facility to be built in Marshall County. The agreement called for Wackenhut to design, build, and operate the facility and to arrange for private financing of the facility. The facility was completed in about a year and started accepting inmates in 1996.

The contract term was five years, renewable in two-year increments. The contract designates a per-inmate management fee of $25.13 per day, with a built-in annual fee increase of 3 percent. Because S.B. 2005 requires the costs to be at least 10 percent less than the state costs, the compensation to Wackenhut decreases if the state's per-inmate costs decline during the contract period. In other words, the cost to the state can only increase by 3 percent per year, but the state recoups any savings if its own costs decline during the contract period.

The contract also requires the state to make separate payments for debt service to Wackenhut. Although Wackenhut bears the initial risk of the loan, the state is obligated to pay the principal and interest on that loan. Under this model, the state is not obligated to seek its own financing or to issue state bonds to cover the costs of construction; the debt burden is initially carried by Wackenhut. The costs to be paid by the state include about $20.43 million in construction costs, a 0.75 percent underwriter's discount, 49.5 basis points, and $100,000 in issuance costs to the lender. The state is ultimately paying the construction costs but is spreading those costs over 20 years. The net effect is that the construction costs appear more like operational costs than infrastructure costs. The funds used to satisfy the contract payments were allocated to MDOC as part of the annual appropriations process; the state thus avoids obligating its own bonding authority. All payments to Wackenhut are subject to an annual appropriation by the legislature. Ownership of the facility reverts to the state when the debt is retired.

The major advantage of this arrangement to Wackenhut is that the facility itself ultimately costs it nothing. Although Wackenhut bears the risk of a contract that may not be renewed by the state (or a legislature that refuses to appropriate funds to pay the contract), the full costs of construction are borne by the state. However, because Wackenhut owns the debt, it is able to depreciate the facility for tax purposes, and thus receive a substantial federal tax subsidy. Coupled with profit margins generated through the management portion of the contract, the arrangement is a lucrative one for the private company.

The LeFlore County Model

A second model used by the state was to employ an intermediary between the state and the private contractor. In this case, the state created a public authority, the Delta Correctional Facility Authority, and gave that authority the power to issue bonds, which were backed by the state government. The authority was also given the power to enter into a contract with a private company to design, build, and operate a 1,000-bed, medium-security facility in Greenwood. Construction began in late 1995, and the facility opened in late 1996.

There are thus two separate contracts: a five-year contract (renewable in two-year increments) between MDOC and the public authority, and a second contract between the public authority and the Corrections Corporation of America (CCA).[2] The contract between the state and the public authority is very similar in structure and specificity to the contract between SPECAM and Wackenhut, and it requires the same performance by the parties. The major exception is that the compensation in this model does not include payment by the state for debt service—these costs are borne by the public authority; the state only compensates the public authority for the management/operations costs. The public authority in turn contracts with CCA, which provides the management services to the public authority. In short, the public authority becomes a go-between for MDOC, thus releasing MDOC of direct responsibility for debt service and management/operations services. As with the Marshall County model, the state's contract with the public authority is contingent on legislative appropriations to MDOC to pay those costs.

Some 18 months after the execution of the contract with the Delta Correctional Facility Authority, MDOC executed another contract with the newly formed Wilkinson County Industrial Development Authority. Located in the far southwestern corner of the state, the Wilkinson County facility was also designed to be a 1,000-bed, medium-security facility. The public authority issued industrial development bonds to raise the necessary capital to build the facility, and subsequently contracted with CCA to manage and operate the facility. As with the LeFlore County model, two contracts are in place: one between MDOC and the public authority, and the other between the public authority and CCA. In all respects, the contract between MDOC and the Wilkinson County authority is identical to the contract between MDOC and the Delta authority.

The Regional Jail Model

A third contractual arrangement was also developed by the state. For many years, MDOC had paid county sheriffs to house state inmates in county jails. This was initially a short-term arrangement to expedite court appearances by inmates, but as the state began to face more severe overcrowding, an increasing number of state inmates were housed in county facilities for the duration of their sentences. County sheriffs complained for many years that the state's reimbursement rates were unfairly low and that the counties thus bore a substantial portion of the costs of housing state inmates.

These concerns were addressed by S.B. 2005, allowing SPECAM (and later MDOC) to approve a series of regional county jails and requiring MDOC to guarantee a minimum of 250 state inmates to be housed in these facilities; they thus became known as "250 prisons." These facilities, owned by a single county or (more often) a group of counties, were spread geographically around the state. The counties were responsible for the construction and operation of these facilities but were free to enter into management and operations contracts with private companies. The state required these facilities to meet the same standards as those imposed on the state's private sector partners, and they were subject to similar reimbursement rates (although at a rate still somewhat less than the rates offered to Wackenhut or the two public authorities). The state did not assume responsibility for any construction costs or debt service for these facilities. In most other respects, the contracts executed under this model are essentially identical to those executed under the LeFlore County model discussed in the preceding section.

Although questions of prison siting in Mississippi had for many years been subject to the NIMBY syndrome, many counties began to see these 250 prisons as a vehicle for economic development and job creation. With the success of the first two or three facilities, more counties began petitioning MDOC and the state legislature for similar contracts.[3] MDOC quickly determined that it did not have enough inmates in custody to meet the demands made by county officials for new contracted facilities, but they did subsequently adjust the rates paid to county sheriffs for state inmates held in traditional county jails.

Important Contract Considerations for Privatization of Prison Services

Although the Mississippi experience indicates that the need for prison services may be satisfied by selecting among three different models of privatization, it would be shortsighted to overemphasize the differences among the three arrangements. In fact, the number of similarities between the models is strikingly similar, suggesting that there are several important considerations to be addressed when contracting for these services. Although the four considerations of contracting remain equally important within the context of prison privatization, two areas appear to be particularly relevant to prison services: nonparty and enforcement clauses.

In the Mississippi experience, three categories of clauses are used to address nonparty issues in the agreements: contract monitors, inmates, and employees. The inclusion of a contract monitor clause, for example, may be particularly desirable within a privatized prison setting for the simple reason that it provides an opportunity for a neutral contract monitor to be assigned, on a dedicated basis, to monitor ongoing performance to the contract's specifications. This is a useful arrangement because the contract monitor may provide an early warning that specific aspects of the contract are in potential violation. In turn, this provides the parties with an opportunity to take corrective action, allowing the avoidance of potentially costly violation of federal or state standards and prevention of a breach of contract. Examples of duties that a contract monitor may undertake within the prison context include review of incident reports; record-keeping practices; facilities operations; and compliance with fire, health, safety, and sanitation codes (Wackenhut § 4.37; Delta § 4.37). Thus, the addition of a contract monitor to the agreement has some clear advantages. On the other hand, the parties may find it an unnecessary requirement in the case of a regional prison model.

The second type of nonparty clause that has significance within the privatized prison setting are the inmate clauses. This is the portion of the agreement that the parties will use to document their understanding with regard to common issues involving inmate housing and care, such as circumstances under which an inmate may receive credit for good behavior toward early release from prison; when an inmate may be transferred to or from higher security; provisions for on-site and off-site medical and dental care for inmates, including which party will bear the associated costs; and procedures for inmate work release. These provisions may constitute a substantial portion of the contract, as the parties strive to provide adequate detail to memorialize the specifics of their agreement.

Detailed clauses documenting the parties' agreements with regard to inmates may generally fall under the categories of procedural activities or services provided to inmates. Examples of procedural activity clauses may include assignment to and within a facility; admitting and booking, safety and emergency procedures, including riot response; record keeping; grievance procedures to address inmate complaints; disciplinary procedures; use of force regulations; security and control procedures; access to courts; and inmate delivery to or release from a facility. Examples of inmate service clauses may include specifics regarding inmate housing; maintenance of inmate funds; inmate care, including food, laundry, health, and transportation services; programs for recreation, law library access, counseling and mental health services; telephone and mail service privileges; religious observances; visitation; and educational and vocational programs.

The third type of nonparty clause that may be of use in a contract for private prison services concerns the employees of the agencies providing the services. Each of the Mississippi models incorporated provisions to address issues regarding training, testing for contagious diseases, and background checks. These considerations are important elements to ensure compliance with various federal and state standards that regulate corrections. For example, Mississippi's approach to training required that employees of the agencies receive training to "meet or exceed" the training provided by the state department of corrections, and in full compliance with the ACA standards (Issaquena County §§ 5.3 and 6.3). Similarly, the requirement for employees to be tested for contagious diseases is meant to maintain compliance with the mandates of the State Bureau of Preventive Health (Issaquena County §§ 5.4 and 6.4). Lastly, the background check provision provides a necessary mechanism by which to authorize preemployment criminal checks for prospective employees (Issaquena County § 6.5).

The second area of contract provisions that has a great impact upon the private provision of prison services is in the area of contract enforcement. The Mississippi models included contractual clauses that operate to limit the parties' mutual risk and to guide an impartial tribunal in the event that one party seeks to enforce the terms of the agreement against a co-party. Examples of the types of clauses that address such concerns include, among others, indemnification and immunity, inmate escape, and lack of funding for services. To protect the parties' respective interests and to offset some of the potential contractual risks inherent in an arrangement for private prison services, the Mississippi models relied on two methods. For the Marshall and LeFlore County models, both involving services by private providers, indemnification clauses were used; the regional jail models incorporated the provisions of sovereign immunity to address similar issues (Wackenhut §§ 7.1 and 7.2; Delta §§ 7.1 and 7.2; Issaquena County §§ 7.1 and 7.6).

In addition to indemnification and immunity provisions, the Mississippi agreements also included a variety of other provisions to address specific factors involving risk. With regard to inmate escape, for instance, the regional jail model agreement included specific provisions to address notification procedures; expenses of inmate recapture; extradition responsibilities; and costs associated with escape and recapture, including overtime wages, out-of-pocket expenses, and reimbursement costs (Issaquena County § 5.34). In another example, the Mississippi models also included a clause addressing the nonappropriation of funds, as all three models were for contract terms that extended beyond a one-year period (Wackenhut § 8.6; Delta § 8.6; Issaquena County § 8.2). These procedures make it clear that the parties to the services contracts understand that funding is contingent on the continued availability of funds appropriated by the state legislature and addresses the consequences in the event insufficient funds are available.

Conclusion

Any discussion of prison contracts is potentially a complicated discussion as laws, legal conventions, and historical practices can vary widely from state to state. Our purpose in this chapter is to provide insight into many of the issues and provisions that can arise in public–private contracts for prison services. Mississippi's use of three different contractual models for prison services provides the ability to compare and contrast these different arrangements in a single setting. Although the specific circumstances are unique to Mississippi, the general principles illustrated in these models are applicable to other states and provide an opportunity to compare the arrangements and contract provisions to those in other states. For example, although some states choose to allow private facilities to house inmates from other states, Mississippi specifically chose not to do so. Likewise, although some states contract directly with a private partner, Mississippi relied more heavily on intermediary organizations as a buffer between the state and the private sector. And, although some states sought maximum efficiency by requiring private companies to bid as low as possible, Mississippi effectively capped its savings at 10 percent.

Like any other contract, an important element of prison contracts is the assignment of risk among the parties to the contract. The assignment of risk, the conditions under which the risk is borne, and the sanctions or rewards associated with that risk are particularly important when the service involves the coercive power of the state. The stakes are high: the state may choose to assign a portion of its coercive power to the private sector, but government is still accountable to its citizens (Donahue 1989). If that coercive power is assigned to, and subsequently abused by, a private company, citizens will first turn to government for redress. As experiences in Ohio, Texas, and elsewhere have illustrated, governments that are not attentive to these issues may find that the long-term interests of both the government and its citizens are threatened by weak contracts. Moreover, given the differences in values, goals, and incentives of the two sectors (see Heilman and Johnson 1992; Kettl 1993), well-written contracts can ensure that the goals and incentives of both parties are incorporated into the arrangement in a clear and open manner.

Notes

1. Although SPECAM was heavily involved in the development of these models, SPECAM formally ceded its authority to MDOC in mid-1996. The participants interviewed affirmed that the members of SPECAM were "kept in the loop" concerning the decisions made by MDOC, but formal authority rested with MDOC.

2. Copies of the contract between the Delta Correctional Facility Authority and CCA were not made available to the authors; the parties cited the proprietary nature of the contract. However, interviewees confirmed that the contract was "very similar" to the contract between MDOC and the public authority.
3. See Hoyman, Weaver, and Weinberg (2008) for an analysis of similar pressures in North Carolina.

References

Barnett, R. E. 1995. *Contracts: Cases and Doctrine*. Boston, MA: Little, Brown and Company.

Conlan, Timothy. 1988. *New Federalism: Intergovernmental Reform from Nixon to Reagan*. Washington, DC: Brookings.

Donahue, John D. 1989. *The Privatization Decision: Public Ends, Private Means*. New York: Basic Books.

Gates v. Collier. 1972. 501 F.2d 1291 (5th cir.).

Heilman, John G., and Gerald W. Johnson. 1992. *The Politics and Economics of Privatization: The Case of Wastewater Treatment*. Tuscaloosa: University of Alabama Press.

Hoyman, Michelle, Jennifer Weaver, and Micah Weinberg. 2008. "Rural Prison Sitings in North Carolina: Competition and Community Leaders' Attitudes." In *Building the Local Economy: Cases in Economic Development*, edited by Douglas J. Watson and John C. Morris. Athens, GA: Carl Vinson Institute of Government, 233–248.

Inmate Housing Agreement among Mississippi Department of Corrections Issaquena County, Mississippi, Regional Correctional Facility and Sheriff of Issaquena County, Mississippi ("Issaquena"). 1995.

Johnson, Gerald W., and John G. Heilman. 1987. "Metapolicy Transition and Policy Implementation: New Federalism and Privatization." *Public Administration Review* 47 (3): 468–478.

Kettl, Donald F. 1993. *Sharing Power: Public Governance and Private Markets*. Washington, DC: Brookings.

Mississippi Code Annotated, § 47-5-1201 *et seq.* 1972.

Mississippi Department of Corrections (MDOC). 2007. Schedule of Costs by Category (All Programs) FY 1992–2006. http://www.mdoc.state.ms.us/.

Moe, Ronald C. 1987. "Exploring the Limits of Privatization." *Public Administration Review* 47 (6): 453–460.

Morris, John C. 1999. "Defining Privatization: A Response to Dominey." *Public Works Management & Policy* 4 (2): 152–155.

Morris, John C. 2007. "Government and Market Pathologies of Privatization: The Case of Prison Privatization." *Politics and Policy* 35 (2): 318–341.

Puckett, Steve. 1997. Interview conducted with Steve Puckett, Commissioner, Mississippi Department of Corrections, August, Jackson, MS.

Residential Services Agreement between Mississippi Department of Corrections (by and on behalf of the State of Mississippi) and Delta Correctional Facility Authority ("Delta"). 1995.

Restatement (Second) of Contracts. 1981.

Robbins, Ira P. 1988. "The Impact of the Delegation Doctrine on Prison Privatization." *UCLA Law Review* 35 (5): 911–952.

Savas, E. S. 2000. *Privatization and Public-Private Partnerships*. Chatham, NJ: Chatham House.

Wiseman, W. Martin, James B. Kaatz, John C. Morris, Kristine Kaatz, Elizabeth Morris, David Lee, Charles A. Campbell, Paul W. Grimes, Kevin Rogers, R. Gregory Dunaway, Peter B. Wood, and Gregory D. Morris. 1997. *Impact, Economic, Financial, and Management Analysis: Final Report Prepared for the Mississippi Department of Corrections*. Mississippi State: John C. Stennis Institute of Government, Mississippi State University.

12

Projecting the Future of Private Prisons

Byron E. Price

Private prisons in many respects can be described as "Teflon dons"—meaning they are always written off, but they always survive. Many of the problems that gave rise to private prisons in the 1980s, 1990s, and 2000s still exist, such as prison overcrowding, state fiscal woes, and the general direction of the country to be more punitive. The United States incarcerates about 50 percent more people than China, although China has 1.5 billion people. Thus, the term "Incarceration Nation" (Price 2006a) is very appropriate for describing the U.S. penal state. Another persistent belief that drives this discussion is the idea that governments are inefficient operators of prisons because they are not subject to the market mechanism. Moreover, it is opined that governments should not be in the business of prisons because of their unionized workforces, which are blamed for the inefficiency that exists within the system. Lack (2011) believes that "growing prison populations combined with budget pressures and further prison overcrowding is going to increase the use of private sector solutions."

According to the "Prisoners in 2008" report (Sabol, West, and Cooper 2009) for the years 2000–2008, federal privatization increased by 16.5 percent and state privatization increased by 6.8 percent. A close review of the data comparing federal growth versus state growth reveals an opportunity for private prison corporations to expand in the federal sector. On the other hand, states have been looking for ways to reduce correctional spending. States such as Indiana are considering parole and sentencing reform to mitigate the effects of correctional spending on its budget. Former governor Arnold Schwarzenegger of California proposed a constitutional amendment requiring the state to spend more money on education than corrections. Implicit in these reform efforts is a move away from incarceration to treatment and a shift in philosophy regarding the incarceration of nonviolent offenders. This change in philosophy may adversely affect private prison operators; however, other factors bode well for future growth possibilities in the private correctional industry. For instance, Shambora (2011) found that from 2000 to 2008 the number of inmates held in private facilities nationwide grew by 40 percent. As suggested, the market for increasing prison privatization can go either way, but presently, the news is good for the corrections business.

Indiana and California are microcosms of the macrocosm of problems states are having in their efforts to control correctional spending. Correctional spending is crowding out and competing with such budget items as early childhood programs. The Pew Center on the States (Warren 2008, 16) underscores this point with the following figures:

- Five states spend as much or more on corrections than they do on higher education.
- For every dollar spent on higher education, Alaska spends 77 cents on corrections.
- For every dollar spent on higher education, Georgia spends 50 cents on corrections.
- The 50-state average is that for every dollar spent on higher education, 60 cents is spent on corrections.

Furthermore, Scott-Hayward (2009) and the Pew Center on the States posits: "Second only to Medicaid, corrections has become the fastest growing general fund expenditure in the United States" (Warren 2008, 3).

As mentioned earlier, many of the problems of the past are still with states, such as prison overcrowding and increased spending on corrections at the expense of other budget items. These two issues are the crux of what ails states. During the "get tough on crime" and "war on drugs" campaigns, corrections populations skyrocketed. As a response to the overcrowding, states began to redirect expenditures to corrections, and national spending on corrections exceeded $200 billion. Just as it was in the 1980s when courts mandated states to reduce overcrowding in prisons, the 2000s have ushered in the same problems. Shambora (2011) cites the recently heard appeal before the U.S. Supreme Court mandating that California cut its prison population by 40,000. Instead of waiting on this decision, California has been shipping inmates to private prisons out of state since 2006 (Shambora 2011).

Finally, between the Corrections Corporation of America (CCA) and the GEO Group (which recently merged with Cornell Companies, the third-largest private corrections firm), the combined annual revenues of these companies is $3.2 billion. Shambora (2011) projected that from January 2011 to the middle of 2012, 31,500 beds would be outsourced to these agencies (Shambora 2011). Coupled with the perception that private prisons are recession proof (Lack 2011), as is the money that is being made from them, many observers of for-profit prisons believe they are "well positioned to benefit from the pressure on many states to cut costs" (Lack 2011). Thus, do private prisons have a future in corrections given that they are still controversial? The debate regarding their future has not abated. Besides the standard arguments provided for the necessity of private prisons and the much discussed issues such as state fiscal problems, several other issues may ensure private prisons have a future in the coming years: immigration reform, collateral consequences of a felony conviction, private prisons used as economic development, the persistent unemployment problems plaguing the country, and the shifting of economic sanctions to the formerly incarcerated. On the other hand, many states are beginning to reform their systems, and they are considering such actions as instituting medical parole; releasing nonviolent offenders; offering diversion programs to nonviolent offenders instead of incarceration; and reforming the probation and parole system—establishing a graduated system of punishment for parole and probation violators in respect to when to send them back to prison. These reforms have the potential to diminish the need for prison beds, but states could choose to provide those beds through the private sector rather than the public sector.

This chapter examines potential factors that will shape the future landscape of private corrections. The viability of private prisons in the future will be contingent upon many factors not yet determined, but the aforementioned issues will be important for years to come in this contentious debate regarding the need for private corrections.

Immigration Reform

The economic meltdown has uncovered weaknesses in the employment and housing sectors and has drawn attention to the weakness of the dollar (Baker 2009a, 2009b; Baker, Pelletiere, and Rho 2009; Miller 2010). Each separate activity has contributed to the call for immigration reform. Americans who have lost jobs have projected their blame on immigrants and have ascribed the weak economy and deficit to the government's allowing illegal immigrants to receive services designated for American citizens. Furthermore, they believe immigrants have suppressed wages, and thus are taking jobs from Americans, and have wrested leverage with corporations away from American workers because of their willingness to work for low wages.

The Immigration Reform Act of 1996 served as the impetus in the federal government's willingness to contract with for-profit prison corporations. By-products of this act were changes to sentencing laws governing undocumented immigrants. The act vested in prosecutors the authority to "plead former and current misdemeanor charges against undocumented immigrants as aggravated felony cases" (Miller 2010, 2). An obvious result of this policy, according to Cheung (2004), was a doubling of the number of noncitizens serving time in federal prison within two years of the implementation of this policy.

Federal privatization has been fueled by many of the same drivers of state prison privatization, such as overcrowding; punitiveness of the justice system; ideologues promoting neoliberal policies; and the standard arguments of efficiency, effectiveness, and quality. Furthermore, in the 1980s, 1990s, and early 2000s, private prison providers partnered with the American Legislative Exchange Council (ALEC) to pass truth-in-sentencing laws, habitual offender laws, mandatory sentencing laws, and other laws that shifted incarceration from a demand-driven good to a supply-driven good—they supplied prisons, which drove demand for prisons. As a result of their efforts, prison populations increased across the United States.

Today's debate regarding the viability of private prisons features ALEC prominently in this discussion on immigration reform, and the current fervor surrounding immigration reform has provided for-profit prisons with an opportunity to expand their market in the federal arena. They have managed to accomplish this task by enlisting an old partner to help grow their market. With ALEC, CCA and the GEO Group are strategically positioned to take advantage of the next wave of incarceration, which is occurring at the federal level as state privatization has been waning over the past few years.

The state of Arizona has been enlisted by ALEC and for-profit prison corporations to reform immigration, and it serves as the test case in respect to what immigration reform will look like in the future. Specifically, S.B. 1070, an immigration bill crafted by CCA and the GEO Group, in partnership with ALEC and Arizona legislators who hold membership in ALEC, will allow law enforcement officials in Arizona "to arrest anyone whom they believe may have committed a crime—such as being in Arizona without proper documentation" (Hodai 2010a, 3). Immigration reform is shaping up to be a call for mass incarceration of immigrants. For African Americans, it evokes images of the war on drugs and the "driving while black" campaigns. Those campaigns incarcerated so many black men that it has created a crisis in the African American community.

Hodai (2010a, 1) asserts that this piece of legislation, with its concomitant offences, will "effectively convert every state, county and municipal police officer into an enforcer of federal immigration law"; and he claims that many states are standing by to see if the law passes. Given the potential implications of this policy, the legislation should increase the number of undocumented people who get ensnared in federal detention centers. The legislation should also be a financial boon to the for-profit prison corporations such as CCA and the GEO Group.

Collateral Consequences of a Felony Conviction

Many states are serious about exploring ways to address their prison capacity issues and fiscal concerns as well as finding ways to become less dependent on private prisons to help alleviate their overcrowding problems. For many ex-felons, however, a prison sentence means overcoming difficulties in reestablishing a life in civil society in the face of barriers erected specifically to prevent their access to benefits and services available to other citizens. The fact of the matter is that once convicted of a felony, the likelihood of successful reintegration back into society is a long shot. Most ex-felons are not as fortunate as Michael Vick, the NFL quarterback who has resuscitated his career. Most ex-felons recidivate within three years of being released from prison because of the barriers concomitant with a felony conviction and the subsequent difficulties the conviction creates for them.

Vennochi (2010, 26) points out that "[j]ob-seekers, generally, must disclose felony convictions, and, in a majority of states, employers can even ask applicants to disclose arrests that did not lead to conviction." Research has shown that once the formerly incarcerated check the box on the employment application that they have been convicted of a felony, they are automatically disqualified for employment. Many do not disclose that they have a felony because of the discriminatory nature of this question on the application, and their prior experiences have shown them that checking the box always leads to their not securing an interview or job offer.

The formerly incarcerated are also subjected to a host of other restrictions that states place on former felons. There are restrictions on occupational licenses for felons; for instance, a felony conviction renders one ineligible for a barber's or cosmetologist's license. A felony drug conviction can prevent one from receiving welfare or food stamps. Citizens are also excluded from living in public housing if they have a felony drug conviction. Presently, with the nation experiencing the highest unemployment rate since the Great Depression (Samuels 2010), this is more likely to exacerbate the employment search for ex-offenders. Many ex-felons come out of prison unprepared to reintegrate because they lack education, soft skills, and social capital. The unfortunate aspect of being a felon is that the jury may sentence someone for 10 years, but the felony gives that person a life sentence in the employment arena.

Moreover, the denial of basic social services as a result of drug use and a felony conviction strikes the poor the hardest because they are "likely to require the assistance of a large number of public services" (Levi and Appel 2003, 1). According to the Drug Policy Alliance (Levi and Appel 2003), the following barriers associated with a drug conviction increase the likelihood that an ex-offender will return to prison:

- An amendment to the Higher Education Act of 1998 suspends eligibility for grant, loan, or work assistance for students convicted of drug-related offenses.

- The Personal Responsibility and Work Opportunity Reconciliation Act of 1996 permanently bars those with drug-related felony convictions from receiving federal cash assistance and food stamps during their lifetime, unless their state opts out.

- State foster care systems act aggressively to terminate parental rights of incarcerated women and parents who test positive for drugs.

A felony conviction also affects one's ability to vote, get licensing (e.g., a barber's license), and a business loan. As a result of these barriers, the likelihood of not returning to prison is grim for ex-offenders. The laws in many respects undermine states efforts to reform their prison system as well as reduce correctional expenditures and overcrowding concerns. Based on the impact the laws have on ex-offenders, especially poor ex-offenders, the likelihood of states reducing the amount spent on corrections appears to be a challenge they will not achieve, and this should ensure that private prisons remain a viable option when states seeks ways to reduce costs and prison populations.

Private Prisons as Economic Development

Huling (2002) ascribes the predilection for incarceration in the United States to the nation's inability to solve social problems brought about by globalization. However, this problem has been a boon to rural America because it has created a situation in which prisons have become a growth industry in rural America (Huling 2002). Prison construction advocacy (Dorlovich 2005) is an interesting phenomenon when one considers the moral implications of advocating for prisons, but the economy has forced many communities to vie for prisons.

Globalization and deindustrialization have forced communities who once shunned prisons to actively lobby for prisons to be built in their backyards. Rural communities have been hit the hardest by the economic restructuring brought about by globalization and deindustrialization, and Huling (2002, 1) contends that "[t]he acquisition of prisons as a conscious economic development strategy for depressed rural communities and small towns in the United States has become widespread." Furthermore, desperation has set in, and communities that compete for these prisons offer perks such as donated land, housing and infrastructure subsidies, and property and tax abatements to lure public or private prisons to their communities.

Observers of the practice of states siting prisons in communities as an economic development strategy find that little research has been conducted to determine if prisons bring about the purported economic growth they assert will occur. In the March 2004 *Social Science Quarterly* article "The Prison Industry: Carceral Expansion and Employment in U.S. Counties, 1969–1994," Hooks and colleagues (quoted in Deitch 2004) found that prisons do not spur economic growth in metropolitan or rural counties. Indeed, research finds that prisons have the opposite effect on economic growth in rural counties (Deitch 2004). Furthermore, Hooks and colleagues (quoted in Deitch 2004, 1) "[attribute] the counter-intuitive finding about prisons impending growth in rural counties to the fact that prison construction often limits alternative economic activity." To illustrate this point, Hooks and colleagues (quoted in Deitch 2004, 54) offer the following explanation:

> With communities competing to attract prisons, corrections bureaucracies are shifting infrastructure costs to local governments. Communities are being forced to supply prisons with "electrical services, roads, and other things to construct and operate a facility." ... Under these pressures, rural counties desperate for jobs are diverting large portions of limited infrastructure budgets to support a correctional facility and adapting a limited infrastructure to the needs of a (new or existing) prison. As a result, the infrastructure may be ill suited for other potential employers, and local governments have few funds left for other investments in the local infrastructure.

Despite these findings, private prisons have been successful in extracting subsidies from communities to sit prisons in those communities as an economic development strategy. Mattera et al. (2001, v) examined 60 private prisons that were constructed under the guise of being engines of economic development and found that:

- At least 44, or 73 percent of the 60 facilities received a development subsidy from local, state, and/or federal government sources.

- A total of $628 million in tax-free bonds and other government-issued securities were issued to finance the private prisons studied.

- Thirty-seven percent of the facilities received low-cost construction financing through tax-free bonds or other government-issued debt securities.

- Thirty-eight percent of the facilities received property tax abatements or other tax deductions.

- Twenty-three percent of the facilities received infrastructure subsidies, such as water, sewer, or utility hook-ups, access roads, and/or other publicly financed improvements.

- Subsidies were found in 17 of the 19 states in which the 60 facilities are located.

- Facilities operated by the two largest private prison companies, CCA and the GEO Group, are frequently subsidized.

- Among the facilities studied, 78 percent of CCA and 69 percent of GEO Group prisons were subsidized, suggesting that these companies had been aggressive in seeking development subsidies.

In 2010, Valdosta, Georgia, was one of the latest communities to seek prison construction as economic development. Ramos (2010) reports that CCA and the Valdosta-Lowndes County Industrial Authority (VLCIA) announced an economic development venture to construct a prison for a yet-to-be future need. When the time arrives, the prison will be built. According to Hodai (2010c), Hardin, Montana, and other rural communities are being fleeced by private prisons in respect to their entering into agreements to build prisons as an economic development strategy. Thus, recent developments suggest that the jobs pitch and economic development promises are enticing for rural communities devastated by large job losses. For-profit prison officials are shrewd businesspeople, and given the vulnerability of these communities to their sales pitch and the bleak future economic outlook, I suspect, *ceteris paribus* (i.e., all things being equal), prisons will continue to be used as tools to stimulate economic growth.

Unemployment

Immigration reform, the collateral consequences of a felony conviction, and prisons being built as economic development tools are issues connected to the unemployment epidemic. Given that economists believe high unemployment is here to stay, the likelihood of states abandoning immigration reform is highly unlikely. As iterated earlier, many Americans blame the loss of jobs and the general malaise in the economy on illegal immigrants. Underlying this call for immigration reform is the belief that once undocumented immigrants are deported, the job market will improve.

The formerly incarcerated would more than likely benefit from immigration reform as well. Many of the jobs held by illegal immigrants could be starter jobs for the formerly incarcerated because most ex-felons have educational and professional experience similar to that of immigrants. At present, ex-felons are uncompetitive in the employment arena because they are competing in the market with college-educated and credentialed professionals who are free of a felony conviction. As mentioned previously, illegal immigrants work for a pittance and are not likely to protest the wages they are paid or to know that it is an option to protest. Moreover, protesting is against illegal immigrants' interests and would more than likely subject them to deportation.

Incarceration actually masks the real unemployment rate (because prisoners are not counted in the Bureau of Labor Statistics on unemployment), which is currently reported to be 9.8 percent (Schuman 2010), and it contributes significantly to the unemployment rate, thereby also affecting the economic mobility of the incarcerated. Western and Pettit (2010, 4) contend that "[i]ncarceration negatively affects former inmates' economic prospects" in the following ways:

- Serving time reduces hourly wages for men by approximately 11 percent, annual employment by nine weeks, and annual earnings by 40 percent.

- By age 48, the typical former inmate will have earned $179,000 less than if he had never been incarcerated.

Given that most people recidivate within three years (Langan and Levin 2002), the idea that an ex-felon who has served time reduces his or her annual employment prospects by nine weeks in an already discriminatory labor market is, in many respects, a recipe for returning to jail. Coupled with the fact that ex-felons are subjected to various penalties, such as a lifetime ban on welfare and financial assistance and a protracted job search, prison will be a revolving door for many of them and will mitigate any reform states attempt to implement unless the reform is legislative in nature; legislation is needed to remove the barriers ex-felons encounter upon release.

Failure to reform laws will guarantee a seat at the table for private prisons in the future.

Shifting Economic Sanctions to the Formerly Incarcerated

As states reform their prison systems and look for ways to cut correctional expenditures, in their work *Changing Fortunes or Changing Attitudes? Sentencing and Corrections Reforms in 2003*, Wool and Stemen (quoted in Levingston 2007, 64) contend that "federal and state criminal justice officials are becoming more aggressive in shifting a range of criminal justice system costs onto defendants." The motive of this cost shifting is to ensure that the corrections systems operate profitably (Levingston 2007). This is not the only goal of this recent practice, however; there is also a vested interest in incarceration (Levingston 2007; Price 2006b). Beneficiaries of incarceration are the private prisons, CCA and the GEO Group investors, telephone companies, prison commissaries, and a host of other peripheral businesses.

The practice of shifting costs to the defendant affects the formerly incarcerated the most. Defendants are saddled with booking fees, photocopying fees, escort fees, medical fees, notary services, and anything they can be charged for. An even more egregious practice, according to Levingston (2007, 67), is that "they take 35 percent of every cent that a prison inmate's spouse sends to the inmate." At every phase of the process, state and jail officials are looking to ensure that they are not operating in the red, and any costs they can charge to accomplish that goal are extracted from the inmate. Given the barriers associated with a felony conviction and the inability to find gainful employment, the likelihood of defendants, probationers, or parolees paying the fines are remote. Bergstrom and Ruback (2006, 242) found that "more than $4.5 billion in economic sanctions are unpaid at the federal level and at the state level; New Jersey had more than $166 million in unpaid sanctions." Studies have found that those who are unable to pay probation fees have negative probation outcomes—their probation is violated and they return to prison.

The inability to pay the sanctions for those on deferred adjudication results, in some instances, in a felony conviction, which subjects the ex-offender to the various barriers associated with a felony conviction. Given these facts, the commercialization of prisoners is obvious and suggests that an iron triangle of incarceration has formed to profit from incarceration. Shifting economic sanctions to the poor bodes well for private prisons in the future. Taken together with unemployment, the barriers associated with a felony conviction, and the lack of legislative reform to remove those barriers, the future of private prisons looks good.

Reform: Potential Obstacles to Growth for Private Prisons

The recession has caused states across the country to face the worst fiscal crisis in decades. California is considering issuing IOUs to creditors because of the poor state of its fiscal health. Many states are suffering from declining revenues, which is forcing them to consider reforming their corrections systems (in which expenditures have grown increasingly since the 1980s). Coupled with the high rates of failure of probationers and parolees, which in many cases is the impetus for the growth of the prison population, states are rethinking incarceration and focusing on recidivism reduction strategies (Scott-Hayward 2009). A reform idea gaining attention is to strengthen community corrections, which is concerned with helping the formerly incarcerated reintegrate into society. States and municipalities are starting reentry programs and community supervision initiatives to improve outcomes of people on supervision (Scott-Hayward 2009).

As noted, many people return to prison because of probation violations or failure to comply with conditions of their release. Considering that more than five million people are on probation, parole, or post-prison supervision (Scott-Hayward 2009), this is a ripe area in which to consider ways to reduce expenditures associated with returning them to prison. States are relying on "evidenced-based policies and practices, which have been shown by research to reduce recidivism among individuals on community supervision" (Scott-Hayward 2009, 7). According to Scott-Hayward (2009), the following are examples of evidence-based policies and practices:

- Using graduated responses to violations
- Eliminating or minimizing supervision requirements for lower-risk people

- Using positive reinforcements as a means by which people can reduce their supervision time they need to be on probation
- Adopting incentive funding to redeploy state funds toward local efforts at rehabilitation

These reforms look very promising with respect to helping states lower the failure rates of those under community supervision. If states can implement the aforementioned reforms effectively, then they can reduce the overall corrections population, which should translate into monetary savings for states.

The economic crisis has caused states to rethink how they punish nonviolent offenders. Strategies such as revising criminal codes, downgrading certain offenses, reclassifying specific crimes (e.g., changing dollar amounts for property crime), and reducing penalties associated with drug possession (Austin 2010; McGarry 2010) hold promise for reducing the prison population and reducing the amount of money spent on incarceration. Unless the economy improves and states find ways to bring down their deficits, reforming corrections will continue to be center stage.

Finally, a reform movement focused on bringing down the costs of incarceration and lowering the prison population is gaining currency because of the idea of justice reinvestment. Tucker and Cadora (2003, 2) assert that "[t]he goal of justice reinvestment is to redirect some portion of the $54 billion America now spends on prisons to rebuilding the human resources and physical infrastructure—the schools, healthcare facilities, parks, and public spaces—of neighborhoods devastated by high levels of incarceration." Justice reinvestment is changing the dialogue from one of punitiveness to restoration. This shifting of the dialogue to focus on building human capital and away from the belief that prisoners are incorrigible miscreants may render the use of private prisons obsolete. The idea has yet to fully take hold, but taken together with the states' needs to lower corrections expenditures, it may prove to be detrimental to the future of private prisons.

Conclusion

Private prisons have been around since the 1800s, and the likelihood of their disappearing, as they did in the mid-1800s, is highly unlikely. In the 1800s, only the sheriff and a few businesses benefited from private prisons. Today, entire communities depend on the prison economy for their livelihood.

Although states speak of reform and reducing how much they spend on corrections, their efforts to reform are hampered by citizens whose jobs are at stake if the prison is closed or leaves the community. For-profit prison firms pump millions of dollars into campaigns and hire highly paid lobbyists to influence legislation and policies governing their industry.

The Arizona case is an example of how intertwined the private prisons are with politicians, which may provide a view into future dealings. Arizona governor Brewer's current deputy chief of staff and campaign chairman has ties to CCA. Both formerly lobbied for CCA directly and indirectly. The wife of her deputy chief of staff is still employed as a registered lobbyist for CCA, and her reelection campaign chairman is president of High Ground Public Affairs Consultants, which is an active lobbyist for CCA. CCA helped craft S.B. 1070 with ALEC and the assistance of its sponsor, state senator Russell Pearce.

Since the 1980s, private prisons have managed to blur the conflict-of-interest lines to ensure that they have direct access to those who make policy favorable to their industry. Even President Obama's 2010 U.S. marshal appointee, Stacia M. Hylton, formerly consulted for the GEO Group. This is problematic because the GEO Group has had tens of millions of dollars in contracts with the U.S. Marshals Service over the years.

One thing is certain in the future in regards to private prisons: they will definitely find a way to secure a seat at the table. Whether this translates into success, as it has in the past, remains to be seen, but these questions will remain important to both scholars and practitioners for many years.

References

Austin, Adrienne. 2010. *Criminal Justice Trends: Key Legislative Changes in Sentencing Policy, 2001–2010*. New York: Vera Institute of Justice.

Baker, Dean. 2009a. *CBO Projects More Severe Downturn*. Washington, DC: Center for Economic and Policy Research. http://www.cepr.net/index.php/publications/reports/cbo-projects-more-severe-downturn/.

Baker, Dean. 2009b. *The Housing Bubble and the Financial Crisis*. Washington, DC: Center for Economic and Policy Research. http://www.paecon.net/PAEReview/issue46/Baker46.pdf.

Baker, Dean, Danilo Pelletiere, and Jin Hye Rho. 2009. *Hitting Bottom? An Updated Analysis of Rents and the Price of Housing in 100 Metropolitan*

Areas. Washington, DC: Center for Economic and Policy Research. http://www.cepr.net/documents/publications/100city-2009-08.pdf.

Bergstrom, Marc H., and R. Barry Ruback. 2006. "Economic Sanctions in Criminal Justice: Purposes, Effects and Implications." *Criminal Justice & Behavior* 33:242–273.

Cheung, Amy. 2004. *Prison Privatization and the Use of Incarceration.* Washington, DC: Sentencing Project. http://www.sentencingproject.org/doc/File/Incarceration/inc_prisonprivatization.pdf.

Deitch, Michele Y. 2004. "Prison and Economic Development." *Correctional Law Reporter* (August/September):1–54.

Dolovich, Sharon. 2005. "State Punishment and Private Prisons." *Duke Law Journal* 55 (3): 437–546.

Hodai, Beau. 2010a. "Corporate Con Game: How the Private Prison Industry Helped Shape Arizona's Anti-Immigrant Law." *Axis of Logic*, June 22. http://axisoflogic.com/artman/publisher/printer_60421.shtml.

Hodai, Beau. 2010b. "Ties That Bind: Arizona Politicians and the Private Prison Industry: A Revolving Cast of Legislators Blur the Line between Public Service and Corporate Profits." *In These Times*, June 21. http://www.inthesetimes.com/main/print/6085.

Hodai, Beau. 2010c. "The Rainmakers: Banking on Private Prisons in the Fleecing of Small-Town America." *In These Times*, March 5. http://www.inthesetimes.com/main/print/5578.

Huling, Tracy. 2002. "Building a Prison Economy in Rural America." In *From Invisible Punishment: The Collateral Consequences of Mass Imprisonment*, edited by M. Mauer and M. Chesney-Lind, 1–10. New York: New Press.

Lack, Simon. 2011. "Three New Stock Positions: Corrections Corp., Coeur d'Alene, Borders." January 10. http://seekingalpha.com/article/245630-3-new-stock-positions-corrections-corp-coeur-d-alene-borders?source=yahoo.

Langan, Patrick A., and David J. Levin. 2002. *Recidivism of Prisoners Released in 1994.* Bureau of Justice Statistics Special Report. NCJ 193427. Washington, DC: U.S. Department of Justice, Office of Justice Programs. http://bjs.ojp.usdoj.gov/content/pub/pdf/rpr94.pdf.

Levi, Robin, and Judith Appel. 2003. *Collateral Consequences: Denial of Basic Social Services Based upon Drug Use.* New York: New York Drug Policy Alliance.

Levingston, Kirsten D. 2007. "Making the Bad Guy Pay: Growing Use of Costs Shifting as an Economic Sanction." In *Prison Profiteers: Who Makes Money from Mass Incarceration*, edited by T. Herivel and P. Wright, 52–79. New York: New Press.

Mattera, Phillip, Mafruza Khan, Greg Leroy, and Kate Davis for Good Jobs First. 2001. *Jail Breaks: Economic Development Subsidies Given to Private Prisons*. Washington, DC: Institute on Taxation and Economic Policy. http://www.goodjobsfirst.org/sites/default/files/docs/pdf/jailbreaks .pdf.

McGarry, Peggy. 2010. *The Continuing Fiscal Crisis in Corrections: Setting a New Course*. New York: Vera Institute of Justice.

Miller, David W. 2010. "The Drain of Public Prison Systems and the Role of Privatization: A Case Study of State Correctional Systems." *Discovery Guide*. http://www.csa.com/discoveryguides/prisons/review.php.

Price, Byron E. 2006a. "Incarceration Nation: For-Profit Prison Companies' Success Comes at a Huge Social Cost." *Worth* (August):40.

Price, Byron Eugene. 2006b. *Merchandizing Prisoners: Who Really Pays for Prison Privatization?* Westport, CT: Praeger.

Ramos, Kara. 2010. "Private Prison Company Picks Valdosta as Potential Site." *Valdosta (GA) Daily Times*, August 18. http://valdostadailytimes .com/local/x107495925/Private-prison-company-picks-Valdosta-as -potential-site.

Sabol, William, Heather C. West, and Matthew Cooper. 2009. "Prisoners in 2008." Bureau of Justice Statistics Bulletin. December. http://bjs.ojp .usdoj.gov/content/pub/pdf/p08.pdf.

Samuels, Alana. 2010. "It's a Bad Time for Job Seekers with Criminal Records." *Los Angeles Times*, November 30.

Schuman, Joseph. 2010. "Unemployment Epidemic May Be Here to Stay." *AOL News*, December 3. http://www.aolnews.com/2010/12/03/ us-unemployment-epidemic-may-be-here-to-stay/.

Scott-Hayward, Christine S. 2009. *The Fiscal Crisis in Corrections: Rethinking Policies and Practices*. New York: Vera Institute of Justice.

Shambora, Jessica. 2011. "When Crime Does Pay." *Fortune*, January 11. http://features.blogs.fortune.cnn.com/2011/01/11/when-crime-does-pay/ ?source=yahoo_quote.

Tucker, Susan B., and Eric Cadora. 2003. *Justice Reinvestment*. New York: Open Society Institute.

Vennochi, Joan. 2010. "A Felon's Forward Pass." *Boston Globe*, December 12, 26.

Warren, Jenifer. 2008. *One in 100: Behind Bars in America 2008*. Washington, DC: Pew Center on the States.

Western, Bruce, and Becky Pettit. 2010. *Collateral Costs: Incarceration's Effect on Economic Mobility*. Washington, DC: Pew Center on the States.

Conclusion

John C. Morris and Byron E. Price

Privatization questions often revolve around arguments of efficiency and quality of service. Proponents of private sector production and delivery of goods and services (Johnson and Watson 1991) cite market competition, innovation, and flexibility as the keys to better-quality service at a lower price (see Savas 1987), while opponents make arguments about the limitations of the market (differentiated products, asymmetric information, and underdeveloped markets). Others focus attention on the monetary cost of a good or service, debating whether privatization actually results in cost savings. Still others offer ideological and political arguments about the proper role and scope of government.

The chapters in this volume touch on a set of arguments not often considered in debates about prison privatization, yet the bases of these arguments lie at the heart of the process through which we arrive at our decisions. At its heart, the decision to privatize any good or service is necessarily a question of public policy, and it is thus a product of politics. If politics is truly the "authoritative allocation of values" (Easton 1953), then it follows that decisions about privatization represent decisions about values. As the chapters in this volume demonstrate, powerful interests have coalesced around the issue of prison privatization, and the pro-privatization interests have developed a comprehensive strategy to not only ensure access to provide incarceration services but also to ensure that demand for prison space continues to increase. While these interests are completely rational when viewed in the context of the groups advocating these positions, decisions based on these interests may have deleterious effects on the polity. In short, the clash of interests becomes a clash of values.

However, the value sets held by the opposing groups are rarely scrutinized in the course of policy debates. To the extent that values are discussed, they tend to be the most obvious values (such as efficiency), with no thought or time given to the underlying issues that often form the foundation of the arguments. Even when values are discussed more directly, Stone (1997) points out that the meanings ascribed to the values are rarely discussed (and less rarely agreed upon). While both sides may suggest that their position on the issue maximizes security for society, they likely have two different ideas about security. The net result is that the two sides talk past each other, without really considering the deeper value questions inherent in the debate.

Opponents of prison privatization face two significant hurdles in these political arguments. First, an argument against more stringent penalties for criminal offenses is often portrayed (or interpreted) as a "soft on crime" position. Elected officials at all levels of government and in both major political parties have been elected to office on the basis of "tough on crime" positions, and citizens have responded to the intrinsic messages within these positions. Second, the segments of the population most directly affected by incarceration policies are often the most disenfranchised groups in society already. American prisons are full of low-income, poorly educated members of minority groups; not only are citizens from these categories historically the most disenfranchised in our society, but they also bear the most direct burden of the consequences of these policies. Disenfranchisement equates directly to a lack of political participation and a lowered ability to organize effective interests, which means that policy debates in this arena are often very one-sided.

These debates are not simply clashes over interests or values; they touch on the heart of the unique American love-hate relationship with basic human rights and liberties. While the Founding Fathers expressed their thoughts, in part, through statements of human dignity in the Declaration of Independence and through the Bill of Rights, the Constitution also (at least implicitly) condoned the practice of slavery. While human rights and liberties are important, they were not truly universal in the 18th century, nor are they in the early 21st century. Indeed, women were not considered citizens in the United States until the 20th century, and the debate continues today as to whether convicted criminals should be stripped of their political rights. As the chapters in this volume demonstrate, not only does the United States incarcerate a greater percentage of its population than any other nation in the world, but the bulk of that incarceration falls heavily on specific subsets of the population.

This state of affairs also has serious consequences for issues of democratic theory. It is a long-held presumption that only a sovereign authority can wield coercive powers (the ability to withhold freedom, deprive another citizen of life, or to levy taxes, for example). The great contribution of democracy to the human experience is that coercive power is not held by a single sovereign, but rather, it is vested in a government representative of all citizens. The American Revolution was, in large part, the implementation of this principle—rather than submit to the arbitrary will of a sovereign who was not accountable to the citizens, Americans sought the right of self-determination through active participation in a government that was accountable to its citizens. Decisions made by government could thus be evaluated by citizens; if the citizens decided the government's actions (including the exercise of its coercive powers) were not consistent with the collective will of the citizenry, then the government could be held accountable.

Accountability thus becomes one of the central issues of prison privatization, yet it is almost never raised directly in policy debates. When the government contracts for private prisons, it necessarily cedes its coercive power to the private sector; the prison operator is effectively granted the right to incarcerate citizens. The government attempts to maintain some accountability from the private prison operator through contract provisions, but as the chapters in this volume show, this is, at best, an imperfect accountability mechanism. Issues of qualified immunity and indemnification are not easily solved, and they are often complicated when inmates from one jurisdiction are incarcerated in a different jurisdiction. The robustness of the contract as an accountability mechanism relies heavily on the quality and completeness of the original contract and on the government's ability and willingness to monitor the activities of the private prison operator to ensure that the government's interests (and thus the interests of citizens) are met. The net effect of prison contracting is that the accountability links between citizens and the services they receive become more tenuous (see Breaux et al. 2002; Morris 2007; see also Donahue 1989), and citizens are further removed from the entities providing goods and services on their behalf.

The political climate of prison privatization is thus one of powerful, wealthy, well-organized interests arrayed against disenfranchised, disorganized interests. When coupled with the broader political environment in this country, it is no surprise that private prisons have been the policy choice of many governments across the nation. While many policy trends tend to be cyclical in nature, there is little reason to believe that the use of private prisons will decline substantially in the near term. The potential for profits in this market, coupled with the powerful interests pursuing those profits, is likely to ensure that policy makers will continue to support market-based solutions for their incarceration needs.

Assessing the Landscape of Prison Privatization

The three volumes in this series have examined the breadth and depth of prison privatization in the United States. Prison privatization is not a new idea, nor is its use limited to the United States. Likewise, local, state, and national governments all make use of private prisons. The growth of the private prison industry has spawned the creation of ancillary industries to provide services to those prisons, and agreements between the private prison companies and these ancillary service providers have meant increased profits for all, often at the expense of the partner government and individual inmates. While these practices are clearly good for business, it is less clear that these practices are consistent with the broader goals of the polity. Indeed, an ideological shift toward conservatism, coupled with a pro-business, antigovernment attitude among citizens and policy makers, has produced a political environment that is not only amenable to prison privatization but also actively seeks market-based solutions to public problems.

While there is nothing inherently good or bad about market-based policy choices, it is important for students of policy and policy makers to understand the strengths and limitations of the choices available. Market-based solutions have the potential to offer real benefits, but to select this option necessarily makes choices about trade-offs. Government-based solutions are not perfect solutions, but they offer certain benefits that are lost when market-based solutions are chosen. In short, the real questions to consider are these: What do we want to accomplish, and what are we willing to forgo to get those things?

Ultimately, the key to good policy is a careful, thorough, and frank discussion of the desired goals and the alternative ways to meet those goals. If Dahl (1989) is correct in his observation that American democracy is less democratic than it can (or should) be, such discussions will be challenging.

In the end, however, the stakes in privatization decisions, and in prison privatization decisions specifically, touch on the very heart of democratic ideals. These decisions deserve nothing less than careful, informed, and considered debate to preserve the fundamental values inherent in the American democratic experiment.

References

Breaux, David A., Christopher M. Duncan, John C. Morris, and C. Denise Keller. 2002. "Welfare Reform, Mississippi Style: Temporary Assistance for Needy Families and the Search for Accountability." *Public Administration Review* 62 (1): 92–103.

Dahl, Robert A. 1989. *Democracy and Its Critics.* New Haven, CT: Yale University Press.

Donahue, John D. 1989. *The Privatization Decision: Public Ends, Private Means.* New York: Basic Books.

Easton, David. 1953. *The Political System: An Inquiry into the State of Political Science.* New York: Knopf.

Johnson, Gerald W., and Douglas J. Watson. 1991. "Privatization: Provision or Production of Services?" *State and Local Government Review* 23 (1): 82–89.

Morris, John C. 2007. "Government and Market Pathologies of Privatization: The Case of Prison Privatization." *Politics and Policy* 35 (2): 318–341.

Savas, E. S. 1987. *Privatization: The Key to Better Government.* Chatham, NJ: Chatham House.

Stone, Deborah. 1997. *Policy Paradox: The Art of Political Decision Making.* New York: W. W. Norton.

About the Contributors

Carol F. Black is an assistant professor of sociology at Newberry College, South Carolina, where she teaches social theory, stratification, sociology of gender, and social problems. Dr. Black received her PhD from Purdue University in 2008. In her dissertation, published as *Working for Justice: Families and Prison Reform* (Lambert Academic Publishing, 2010), she analyzed the work of six prison reform groups in five different states. Her article "Doing Gender from Prison: Male Inmates and Their Supportive Wives and Girlfriends" appeared in the journal *Race, Gender & Class* in 2010. Her research interests include intersectional work in criminal justice and racial and gender identity.

Brandi Blessett, PhD, is an assistant professor at the University of Central Florida. Her research interests include administrative discretion, social equity, housing, and community development. She has published in *Administrative Theory & Praxis* and the *Journal of Health and Human Services Administration*. She received her PhD from Old Dominion University in 2011.

Trina M. Gordon is an assistant professor and the director of the Counseling Psychology Program at the University of Houston–Victoria. She has worked as a staff psychologist for the Federal Bureau of Prisons. She has published articles and conducted presentations regarding forensic assessment/evaluation issues, mentally ill and female criminal offenders, dual diagnosis in offender populations, and prison reentry issues.

H. Jessica Hargis, PhD is a recent graduate of the School of Economic, Political and Policy Science at the University of Texas at Dallas. Jessica currently works as a professor of political science at Collin County College.

In both her master's and doctoral studies, Jessica's focus has been on the U.S. Supreme Court's role in public affairs, administrative law, and constitutional law. Along with examining how the U.S. Supreme Court influences public administration, Dr. Hargis enjoys studying the legal implications of government outsourcing. She presented two papers, one on prison privatization and the other on the U.S. Supreme Court's influence on public administration, at the 2010 American Society for Public Administration conference in San Jose, California.

Nancy A. Heitzeg is a professor of sociology and the co-director of the interdisciplinary Critical Studies of Race/Ethnicity program. Nancy received her BA and PhD in sociology from the University of Minnesota. She has written and presented widely on the subjects of race, class, gender and social control, color-blind racism, and social movements/social change. She was a presenter at the Oxford 20th Anniversary Round Table in 2008 and again in 2009. Dr. Heitzeg is the author of *Deviance: Rule-makers and Rule-breakers* and several articles exploring issues of race, class, gender, and social control, including "Differentials in Deviance: Race, Class, Gender, and Age" (*The Routledge Handbook of Deviant Behavior*, 2011); "Education Not Incarceration: Interrupting the School to Prison Pipeline" (*Forum on Public Policy*, Winter 2010); "The Racialization of Crime and Punishment: Criminal Justice, Color-Blind Racism and the Political Economy of the Prison Industrial Complex" (coauthored with Dr. Rose Brewer, which appeared in a special volume of *American Behavioral Scientist*, co-edited by Dr. Heitzeg and Dr. Rodney Coates, entitled *Micro-Level Social Justice Projects, Pedagogy, and Democratic Movements*, Winter 2008); and "Race, Class and Legal Risk in the United States: Youth of Color and Colluding Systems of Social Control" (*Forum on Public Policy*, Winter 2009).

Benjamin R. Inman is a PhD student in public administration and urban policy at Old Dominion University. A special agent with the Federal Bureau of Investigation in San Diego, California, he has conducted research into privatization issues related to homeland security and the privatization of military forces. He is planning dissertation research on privatization, accountability, and the coercive power of the state.

Amy M. McDowell is the manager of the ICM Fellows Program for the Institute of Court Management at the National Center for State Courts in

Williamsburg, Virginia, and serves as an adjunct instructor for the Department of Urban Studies and Public Administration, Old Dominion University, Norfolk, Virginia. She previously served as a staff attorney for the city of Hampton, Virginia, and the city of Virginia Beach, Virginia. She holds a JD from the University of Richmond and an MPA from Old Dominion University and serves as the editor of *Future Trends in State Courts*. She has published in *Public Personnel Management*.

Michael Montgomery was a correctional practitioner for more than 30 years in various management and executive positions in the public and private sectors. He worked in institutional corrections in Kentucky, Michigan, Ohio, and Tennessee and has taught criminal justice courses at six universities. He has a bachelor's and a master's degree from Eastern Kentucky University and a PhD in public administration from Tennessee State University. He currently teaches in the Department of Criminal Justice at Tennessee State University. His interests are in correctional leadership, training, and offender reentry.

John C. Morris is a professor of public policy and serves as the director of the PhD graduate program in the Department of Urban Studies and Public Administration at Old Dominion University in Norfolk, Virginia. He is a noted scholar in the field of public–private partnerships and privatization. He is the coeditor of *Building the Local Economy: Cases in Economic Development* (University of Georgia, 2008) and *Speaking Green with a Southern Accent: Environmental Management and Innovation in the South* (Lexington Books, 2010), and he has published more than 50 scholarly papers in such journals as *Public Administration Review*, *Journal of Politics*, *Policy Studies Journal*, *American Review of Politics*, *Review of Public Personnel Administration*, *State and Local Government Review*, *Politics and Policy*, and *Public Works Management & Policy*. He teaches courses in public policy theory, governance, policy evaluation, public–private partnerships, and intergovernmental relations, among others. He received his PhD from Auburn University and served as an associate professor at Mississippi State University before his arrival at Old Dominion University. He has also served as an evaluator and research coordinator for Policy Studies Associates, Inc.; the city of Auburn, Alabama; the Center for Governmental Services, Auburn University; and the John C. Stennis Institute of Government, Mississippi State University.

Rhonda L. Myers is a higher education practitioner who is passionate about helping students achieve their educational goals through academic achievement, leadership, and professional development. She has researched public administration in the areas of governance, effectiveness, organizational leadership, and for-profit organizations, primarily related to higher education. While serving in diverse capacities at various colleges and universities, she has grown in her knowledge of postsecondary education in the United States. Her current research interests include higher education governance and regulation of for-profit higher education institutions. After she completes her PhD in public administration at Old Dominion University, she looks forward to teaching and engaging students as they accomplish their higher education aspirations.

Byron E. Price is the dean of the School of Business at Medgar Evers College, The City University of New York, in Brooklyn. A leading scholar in the field of prison privatization, he is the author of the book *Merchandizing Prisoners: Who Really Pays for Prison Privatization*, published by Praeger Publishers in March 2006. Dr. Price has also published in the *American Review of Public Administration, Administration & Society, International Review of Public Administration, Public Productivity and Management Review, Personnel Mix Journal* (which was translated into Russian), and *PA Times.*

Anitra D. Shelton-Quinn is an assistant professor and the director of the School Psychology Program at the University of Houston–Victoria. Dr. Shelton-Quinn is a school psychologist with more than 13 years of experience working with children, families, and the schools who serve them. Her research interests include community mental health outreach, bullying, and youth resiliency. Dr. Shelton-Quinn's clinical interests include psychological assessment, school consultation, and child psychopathology.

Gwen Lee-Thomas is currently an assistant professor of higher education graduate programs at Old Dominion University. She received her PhD in education administration and her master's degree in curriculum and instruction, both from Indiana State University, in 1999 and 1996, respectively. Currently, she teaches multicultural university, organizational culture and administration, contemporary issues in higher education, and today's college students and diversity. Her research interests include cultural competence in leadership and organizational development and learning in higher education institutions as they relate to student outcomes and accreditation. In addition, her areas of interest extend into the larger societal community in preparing students for the interrelatedness of higher education and public-servicing entities that challenge the underlying assumptions of higher education as a public good or a private benefit crossing political, economical, and social boundaries.

Alexander "Sasha" Volokh is an associate professor of law at Emory University. Professor Volokh earned his BS from UCLA and his JD and his PhD in economics from Harvard University. He clerked for Judge Alex Kozinski of the Ninth Circuit and for Supreme Court justices Sandra Day O'Connor and Samuel Alito. Before coming to Emory, he was a visiting associate professor at Georgetown University Law Center and a visiting assistant professor at the University of Houston Law Center. He teaches torts, administrative law, law and economics, privatization, and legal history. His recent articles on prisons and privatization include "Privatization and the Law and Economics of Political Advocacy" (*Stanford Law Review*), "Privatization, Free-Riding, and Industry-Expanding Lobbying" (*International Review of Law and Economics*), "Prison Vouchers" (*University of Pennsylvania Law Review*), "The Constitutional Possibilities of Prison Vouchers" (*Ohio State Law Journal*), "Do Faith-Based Prisons Work?" (*Alabama Law Review*), and "Privatization and the Elusive Employee-Contractor Distinction" (forthcoming in the *UC Davis Law Review*).

Index